# Computer Systems
# and Networks

FASTTRACK

# Computer Systems and Networks

**Barry G Blundell**

with

Nawaz Khan

Aboubaker Lasebae

Muthana Jabbar

**THOMSON**™

Australia · Canada · Mexico · Singapore · Spain · United Kingdom · United States

**THOMSON**

## Computer Systems and Networks

Barry G Blundell

with Nawaz Khan, Aboubaker Lasebae and Muthana Jabbar

**Series Editor**
Walaa Bakry, Middlesex University

Middlesex University PRESS

**Publishing Partner**
Middlesex University Press

**Publishing Director**
John Yates

**Commissioning Editor**
Gaynor Redvers-Mutton

**Managing Editor**
Celia Cozens

**Production Editor**
Amy Blackburn

**Manufacturing Manager**
Helen Mason

**Marketing Manager**
Mark Lord

**Production Controller**
Maeve Healy

**Text Design**
Design Deluxe, Bath

**Cover Design**
Matthew Ollive

**Typesetter**
Keyline Consultancy, Newark

**Printer**
C&C Offset Printing Co., Ltd, China

ISBN : 978-1-84480-639-3

***British Library Cataloguing-in-Publication Data***
A catalogue record for this book is available from the British Library

# Contents

## The FastTrack Series

Thomson Learning and Middlesex University Press have collaborated to produce a unique collection of textbooks which cover core, mainstream topics in an undergraduate computing curriculum. FastTrack titles are instructional, syllabus-driven books of high quality and utility. They are:

- **For students**: concise and relevant and written so that you should be able to get 100% value out of 100% of the book at an affordable price
- **For instructors**: classroom tested, written to a tried and trusted pedagogy and market-assessed for mainstream and global syllabus offerings so as to provide you with confidence in the applicability of these books. The resources associated with each title are designed to make delivery of courses straightforward and linked to the text.

**FastTrack** books can be used for self-study or as directed reading by a tutor. They contain the essential reading necessary to complete a full understanding of the topic. They are augmented by resources and activities, some of which will be delivered online as indicated in the text.

## How the series evolved

Rapid growth in communications technology means that learning can become a global activity. In collaboration, Global Campus, Middlesex University and Thomson Learning have produced materials to suit a diverse and innovating discipline and student cohort.

*Global Campus* at the School of Computing Science, Middlesex University, combines local support and tutors with CD-ROM-based materials and the Internet to enable students and lecturers to work together across the world.

*Middlesex University Press* is a publishing house committed to providing high-quality, innovative, learning solutions to organisations and individuals. The Press aims to provide leading-edge 'blended learning' solutions to meet the needs of its clients and customers. Partnership working is a major feature of the Press's activities.

Together with Middlesex University Press and Middlesex University's Centre for Learning Development, Global Campus developed FastTrack books using a sound and consistent pedagogic approach. The SCATE pedagogy is a learning framework that builds up as follows:

- **Scope:** Context and the learning outcomes
- **Content:** The bulk of the course: text, illustrations and examples
- **Activity:** Elements which will help students further understand the facts and concepts presented to them in the previous section. This promotes students' active participation in their learning and in creating their understanding of the unit content
- **Thinking:** These elements give students the opportunity to reflect and share with their peers their experience of studying each unit. There are *review questions* so that the students can assess their own understanding and progress
- **Extra:** Further online study material and hyperlinks which may be supplemental, remedial or advanced.

## *Computer systems and networks*

This book provides an introduction to the basic operation of computer systems and basic material relating to the networking of computers. The reader is introduced to the basic elements that form the modern computer, such as the processor, memory devices, secondary storage devices and input/output devices. We describe how these devices are interconnected and explain the passage of signals between them.

The reader is introduced to the operation of simple logic gates – and examples are given, showing how these gates can be connected together to perform simple, but useful functions. The computer is discussed in the context of a general purpose programmable machine, and we describe how the operation of hardware can be determined by a series of instructions (software).

We also introduce fundamental concepts in relation to operating systems but no prior knowledge of computer systems is assumed. As such, this is an introductory-level book which lays the foundations for more advanced courses.

## Using this book

There are several devices which will help you in your studies and use of this book. **Activities** usually require you to try out aspects of the material which have just been explained, or invite you to consider something which is about to be discussed. In some cases, a response is provided as part of the text that follows – so it is important to work on the activity before you proceed! Usually, however, a formal answer will be provided in the final section of each chapter.

The **time bar** indicates *approximately* how long each activity will take:

short   < 10 minutes

medium 10-45 minutes

long   > 45 minutes

 **Review questions** are (usually) short questions at the end of each chapter to check you have remembered the main points of a chapter. They are a useful practical summary of the content, and can be used as a form of revision aid to ensure that you remain competent in each of the areas covered. Answers are provided at the end of the book.

## About the authors

### Barry Blundell

Barry Blundell is a physicist with many years of experience in teaching computer and IT-related courses and in developing digital systems. His research interests are multidisciplinary, and he is a leading researcher in the area of emerging 3D display and interaction systems for the advancement of human/computer communication. He is actively involved in forums promoting the ethical usage of computer technologies. Dr Blundell is the author of three research textbooks, several technical and undergraduate teaching books, and he is currently working on an introductory undergraduate computer graphics book.

**Nawaz Khan** is a lecturer at the School of Computing Science, Middlesex University, UK. He lectures on the topic of online database, web-based data transaction technologies, data warehousing and data strategies. His present associations include professional membership of IEEE and ACM, distance learning programme of Middlesex University and University of Liverpool, UK.

**Aboubaker Lasebae** is a senior lecturer in the School of Computing Science at Middlesex University. He previously worked for the Research and Development Centre in Tripoli, Libya, as a design engineer. Aboubaker is the co-author of several books on computer systems and networks and also on mobile and wireless networks.

**Muthana Jabbar** is a member of the Computer Communications Academic Group in the School of Computing Science at Middlesex University. He previously worked in industry and as a consultant to international and United Nations organisations in Europe and the Middle East. Muthana's teaching is diverse and includes computer architecture, network communications, network management and computer and network security management.

## Acknowledgements

Figures 9.9, 9.10 and Table 9.3 have been adapted from

*Computer Communications and Networking Topologies*, Gallo M & Hancock W

Published 2002 by Thomson Learning, ISBN 0-534-37780-7

Visit the accompanying website at **www.thomsonlearning.co.uk/fasttrack** and click through to the appropriate booksite to find further teaching and learning material including:

**For Students**

- Activities
- Multiple choice questions for each chapter.

**For Lecturers**

- Downloadable PowerPoint slides.

# CHAPTER 1

# Setting the scene

## OVERVIEW

Here we introduce various aspects of the modern computer. A computer comprises hardware and software, and the power of the computer is derived from the ability of software to control the functionality of hardware. In this way, a computer can be used for a wide range of tasks – indeed, the computer is a general-purpose, programmable, machine.

**Learning outcomes** On completion of this chapter you should be able to:

- Distinguish between hardware and software and understand the concept of a 'general purpose programmable machine'

- Identify the key characteristics associated with the 'stored program' computer model and name different forms of memory and storage devices employed in the modern computer

- Describe the computer in terms of a mathematical machine operating in the binary (base 2) number system

- Manually perform basic arithmetic in the binary number base and verify your results by means of a calculator

- Distinguish between different traditional categories of computer.

## 1.1 Introduction

In this introductory chapter we present various background material and key concepts that will be developed further in other parts of this book. In the next section we distinguish between the software and hardware components that comprise a computer and introduce the concept of a 'general purpose programmable machine'. Here, we identify the three ways in which a computer can execute a set of instructions: in sequence, by selection, and by iteration. This leads on in Section 1.3 to consideration of the 'stored program architecture' that was developed in the mid-1940s and enabled instructions to be represented as numerical codes stored within a computer's memory. At the time, this represented a major shift in thinking, and is a technique that underpins the modern computer architecture.

In Section 1.4 we discuss traditional categories of computer, specifically: the mainframe, the minicomputer, and the desktop machine. The mainframe gained considerable popularity in the 1960s, and ever larger computer installations evolved. Ultimately, systems of this sort became outdated not only because of the rapid advances that were being made in computer hardware, but also because of the complexity of the software needed to impose security and equitably share computing resources between users. The minicomputer provided a lower-cost computing solution and was particularly favoured by medium-sized businesses who were able to increase efficiency by, for example, employing automated inventory and payroll management systems. Furthermore, companies were able to employ affordable computer systems for activities such as computer aided design (CAD) and simulation. However, in the case of both the mainframe machine and minicomputer, the computer's resources are shared between a number of users. As a result, the performance offered to each user by these types of machine varies according to the number of people using the system and the types of computer program in execution. Such a lack of predictability is frustrating and was one of the factors that led to the development of the desktop personal computer (PC). As the name implies, the PC does not constitute a shared resource but is (traditionally) a single user machine. This form of computer was researched throughout the 1970s, and rapidly gained popularity from the early 1980s onwards.

All material stored and processed by computer technologies is represented numerically, and in Section 1.5 we briefly consider the computer as a mathematical machine in which computations are carried out using the binary number base (base 2). Here, we also refer to the computer as a digital machine whereby all signals may take on only certain (two) discrete values. In Section 1.6 we discuss the conversion of base 10 numbers to binary and binary number to base 10. Finally, in Section 1.7 we consider the range of values that may be represented by a certain number of binary digits. In this section, we introduce the terms 'bits' and 'bytes'. The former is used when referring to one or more binary digits, and the latter when considering a number represented by eight bits (or groups of eight bits).

## 1.2 What is a computer?

A computer consists of a set of electronic and electromechanical components able to accept some form of input, process this input in a way that can be specified by means of a set of instructions, and produce some type of output (see Figure 1.1). All computers follow the same fundamental sequence:

1  They accept instructions and data. This represents the 'input'.
2  They 'process' the data according to a set of instructions (by performing calculations and by making decisions – we will discuss this shortly).
3  They produce results in the form of information or actions. This represents the 'output'.

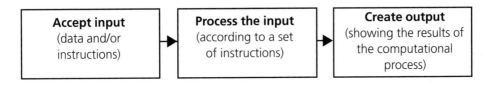

**Figure 1.1:** A computer accepts some form of input, processes this in accordance with a set of instructions and generates some type of output.

A computer comprises both 'hardware' and 'software' systems. These are briefly introduced below:

## *Hardware*

This represents the electronic circuits and/or electromechanical components from which the computer is constructed. As summarised in Figure 1.2, a basic computer system includes the following types of hardware:

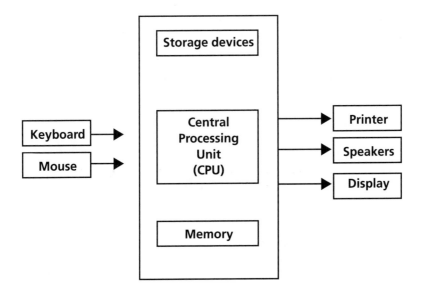

**Figure 1.2:** The computer is able to take input from various sources and provide output to devices such as the display screen and printer(s).

The basic computer consists of:

- Devices such as a keyboard, mouse and display through which we interact with the computer. In this respect we provide input to the machine via the keyboard and mouse and observe the results of the computational process by means of the display screen
- A central processing unit (CPU), which is able to follow ('execute') a series of instructions and controls most of the activities that take place within the machine
- A collection of memory devices able to store instructions and data during the operation of the computer
- Various storage devices able to store instructions and data even when the computer is turned off.

The most common form of computer in use today is the PC (Personal Computer). This was the name given to a computer configuration that evolved during the 1970s and which is a desktop machine (we will discuss computer configurations in a little more detail in Section 1.4). Figure 1.3 provides an illustration of some of the key components within a PC.

## Software

Computer hardware is in itself unable to perform any useful tasks – it must be provided with detailed and unambiguous instructions indicating exactly what actions are to be taken. Consequently, it is necessary to provide the hardware with a set of instructions that define the tasks that the hardware is to perform. These instructions (and any necessary data) are contained within 'computer programs'. Software is a term that is used when referring to programs in a general way, and encompasses instructions that are to be acted upon by a computer and the data that may be needed by these instructions. As we will discuss later in the book, software is 'permanently' stored by means of secondary storage devices (e.g. hard disks, floppy disks, or CD-ROM). Such media does not lose its contents when the computer is turned off (hence these devices are said to provide long-term storage capability). During the execution of a program, software is temporarily stored in main memory. However, the contents of main memory are usually lost when the computer is turned off or reset.

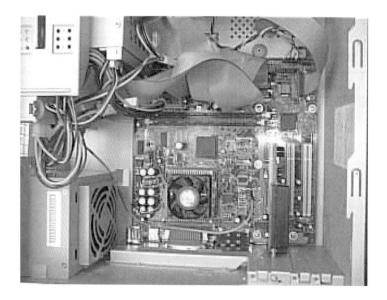

**Figure 1.3:** A photograph of the inside of a PC. This shows some major components located on the main circuit board (motherboard).

Modifying the instructions and/or data supplied to a computer can change the actions performed by the computer hardware. In this respect the hardware is said to represent a 'general purpose programmable machine' and this enables computer technologies to be used in many diverse areas of human endeavour.

**Activity 1.1**

### PC subsystems

Gain access to a PC (preferably an old machine), ensure that the computer is not plugged in, and remove the cover. By reference to Figure 1.3 or otherwise, identify the following components/ subsystems:

(a) The power supply      (b) The central processing unit (CPU)

(c) The main memory      (d) The hard disk

In the case that you have access to a machine that is no longer required (i.e. a broken computer), remove the CPU from the motherboard. Note the large number of pins (connections) that link between the chip and the motherboard. As with all connectors within the computer, these pins are gold plated (this helps to maintain good electrical connectivity). You are strongly advised not to remove the CPU from a working computer – the pins can be easily bent and it may prove quite difficult to re-seat the CPU in its socket!

Computers can perform calculations at a very high speed and have the ability to support the storage and rapid retrieval of enormous volumes of data. Furthermore, a computer is able to make 'decisions' during the execution of instructions. In fact, a computer can handle instructions in three general ways:

- **It can execute a sequence of instructions.** By way of analogy, consider baking a cake. Here you would follow a recipe, i.e. you would follow one instruction after another. A computer has the ability to execute a 'list' of instructions

- **It can execute instructions by iteration.** By this we mean that it can execute a series of instructions repeatedly. By way of analogy, and using the cake example, you could imagine somebody making ten cakes, each one after the other. Here they would execute the same instructions repeatedly as they produced each cake – this is a process of repeated 'iteration'

- **It can execute instructions by selection.** This is something we do continuously in our everyday lives. For example, when we get up in a morning, we may look out of the window to see what the weather is like. Subsequently we might make the following decision:

    "If the weather is good, wear light clothing, or else wear warmer clothing."

A computer is also able to select the next instruction that it should execute according to some condition. For example, a computer is able to execute instructions of the form:

    "If the value stored in a certain memory location is less than 10 do this...or else do this..."

The ability of a computer to execute instructions in sequence, by selection, and by iteration (see Figure 1.4) provides the basis for a machine that offers tremendous flexibility. These concepts are by no means new, and some 150 years ago a remarkable visionary called Charles Babbage identified with great foresight the potential of programmable hardware, and the three modes of instruction execution referred to above. However, many years were to pass before practical computing machines were constructed.

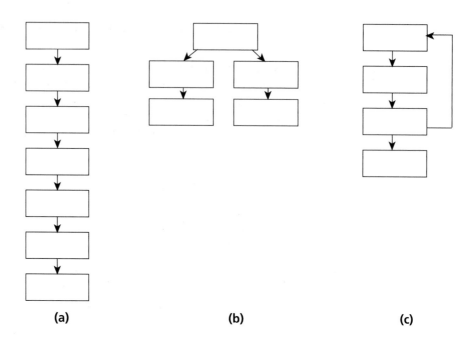

**Figure 1.4:** A computer is able to execute instructions (a) in sequence, (b) by selection and (c) by iteration. Here, we assume that each rectangle represents a program instruction.

**The essence of a computer**

Distinguish between the essential functionality of a computer and a conventional calculator.

## 1.3 The stored program model

Early electrical computers were programmed by means of cables and switches. These were used to interconnect the subsystems within the computer in such a manner that they would act in a certain (and desired) way on the input data. This was a time-consuming occupation – each time the 'program' was to be changed, the computer required wiring modifications! In the mid-1940s researchers realised that major benefits could be derived by representing instructions as numerical codes loaded into the computer's memory. In retrospect, this is an obvious solution but at that time it represented a major breakthrough and resulted in the development of the truly programmable computing machine.

This general technique is referred to as the 'stored program' computer model. Some books adopt the title of the 'von Neumann computer' or 'von Neumann architecture', and in fact while John von Neumann was one of the researchers working on this concept, he was certainly not the sole instigator of the approach (equal if not greater credit should be attributed to J. Presper Eckert and John Mauchly) – but the true history is frequently overlooked.

In this book we will adopt the title 'stored program architecture', and avoid the debate as to the correct origins of this technique.

In Figure 1.5 the general approach used in the stored program architecture is illustrated. As may be seen, we assume that the computer comprises a central processing unit and memory. Instructions and data are passed to the computer and stored within the memory. The central processing unit (usually abbreviated to the 'processor') is able to access the instructions and data from memory and perform the appropriate computations. The results of the computation are then returned to memory or are output in a form that can be understood by the operator.

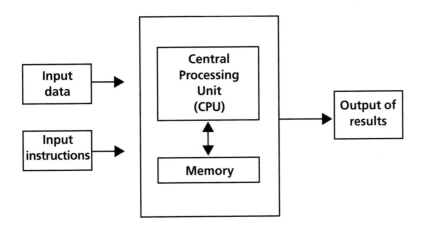

**Figure 1.5:** The stored program architecture. Here, instructions are represented by numerical codes and stored within the computer's memory.

As we will discuss in later chapters, the modern computer makes use of various forms of memory and storage devices. The main memory (normally referred to as random access memory (RAM)) contains the instructions and data associated with programs that are currently being run ('executed') by the processor. Additionally, within the processor itself there are a number of registers. These are locations where temporary numerical values can be stored during calculations, and which also perform other tasks for the processor (we will examine their purpose in some detail in Chapter 3). For the moment it is sufficient to note that registers can be accessed at very high speeds because they are located within the processor. On the other hand, main memory (RAM) operates at a lower speed but offers a far greater storage capacity.

The contents of registers and main memory are lost when a computer is turned off or reset. Naturally, we also require storage devices that can retain their contents even when the computer is no longer in operation, and for this purpose we make use of devices such as the hard disk, floppy disk, and optical disk (such as the CD-ROM and DVD).

The hard disk can store vast amounts of material but is usually fixed in place within the computer, and allows us to store and retrieve data and information within the computer itself. On the other hand, the floppy disk and optical disks represent forms of 'portable media', enabling material to be transferred between computers or stored in a secure repository.

Activity 1.3

**Memory and storage**

Suggest additional reasons for using different types of memory and storage media within a computer.

## 1.4 Forms of computer hardware

Before the late 1930s, computing machines had taken the form of mechanical and electromechanical systems. This was soon to change and the quest for the 'all-electronic' computer became the subject of intensive research (the first machine of this sort was the ENIAC – the Electronic Numerical Integrator and Calculator – which was developed during WWII and was primarily used for solving ballistics problems. The machine was some 33m long, 2.8m high and a metre or so wide – and employed 18,000 vacuum tubes.

Two of the most important breakthroughs that have occurred, and which made possible the modern computer, were the invention of both the *transistor* and the *integrated circuit*. These technologies enabled the development of more powerful and more reliable computer systems. A major driving force behind the development of the integrated circuit was the Apollo space programme that led to the voyages to the Moon in the late 1960s and early 1970s. Rockets making such journeys had to be equipped with computer technologies that could perform a multitude of tasks, including navigation (although it is amazing how rudimentary the computer systems used actually were). In parallel, from the late 1950s through the 1960s, the nuclear missile programme – which centred upon the development of intercontinental ballistic missiles – necessitated the use of computers for the detection of missiles in flight and for missile management and navigation.

The 1960s was the period in which large computers evolved. These computers were known as **mainframes** and such machines became bigger and bigger. Computers of this type take the form of large installations, and can support many users who share the computational capacity of the machine. It was at this time that the philosophy of 'economy of scale' came into being. Put simply: if you spend twice as much on a new mainframe, you get more than four times the processing power. Given this idea, it was natural for mainframes to become ever bigger. Unfortunately, bigger also meant more complicated and it became increasingly difficult to equitably share the processing power between users. The result was that operating systems became ever-more complex and used up more of the processing power of the machine – leaving less available to the users.

Mainframes developed during the 1960s and 1970s took the form of large computers located within large, clinical, air-conditioned facilities. Unfortunately, the very size of such machines ultimately impacted on their performance. Here, it is important to note that electrical signals do not travel instantaneously along wires – they propagate at a finite speed. Consequently, as connections become longer, it takes more time for signals to pass along the wires and this reduces computer performance. In order to increase performance, we endeavour to minimise the lengths of the interconnections between critical components – which leads to the design of compact computers. As mainframes grew in size, electrical signals had further to travel (propagate) and so performance was compromised.

**Minicomputers** are much smaller, and were intended to support the computing requirements of smaller organisations, rather than the large institutions serviced by mainframe machines. As with the mainframe, the processing power of the minicomputer is shared between a number of users. Within a business, typical tasks that would have been carried out in the 1970s by minicomputers included staff payroll calculation and stock inventories. As with any centralised machine, reliability is paramount. Should the minicomputer develop a technical problem, then all users are stopped in their work. Furthermore, when a computer is shared between users, one can never guarantee performance – this being determined by the number of programs running on the machine at any one time.

In the early 1970s, Xerox undertook pioneering work in an effort to develop the **personal computer**. Essential to the vision was the development of a desktop machine where each user has access to their own computer, and its resources are not shared. Consequently, performance is controlled by the user and not by others using the machine. Xerox also pioneered new interaction techniques, particularly the incorporation of the mouse (invented in the mid-1960s), and the graphical user interface that we use today. They also pioneered the development of the **WYSIWYG** wordprocessor ('What You See Is What You Get' – i.e. the document that appears on the computer screen is identical to the form of the document when printed).

The development work at Xerox took some time, and it was not until the early 1980s that the personal computer (PC) that we know today became readily available. Soon a variety of personal computers were produced by vendors such as Xerox, IBM, Commodore and Macintosh. Other companies appeared on the scene, and a wide range of products became available.

The 1980s denoted a period of rapid advancement in computer development and performance. It was also a period of the survival of the fittest, and intense corporate warfare broke out within the computer industry; excellent products seemed to disappear almost overnight. Occasionally, companies were taken over simply in order to suppress products. This was also a period when standards began to evolve and the issue of backward compatibility became paramount. In this context, support for backward compatibility means that when a new computer architecture is developed, it must still be able to execute older software products. The availability of DOS within current versions of Windows provides an example of adherence to backward compatibility.

Since the mid-1980s there has been a reduction in the diversity of computer architectures and operating systems. The main advances that have taken place are in the areas of computer performance, the increased capacity of storage media such as hard disks, and networking technologies (particularly the Internet). In later chapters we will be considering these issues in some depth.

## 1.5 Basic computer operation

Computers are digital machines that employ binary (number base 2) arithmetic. It is important to remember that whatever task you perform on a computer (including, for example, playing a CD or video, undertaking a word-processing activity or accessing Internet sites), the computer is operating on numbers: it is a mathematical machine.

The diversity and nature of the applications that can be supported by the modern computer often makes it difficult to imagine that the operation of the machine is underpinned by mathematics. For example, consider a word-processing activity. Within a document we may insert text (comprising alphabetic characters), diagrams and photographs. However, within the computer each of these forms of material is represented by sets of numbers. Each word-processing operation that we carry out results in the computer performing mathematical calculations on these numbers – in fact, the computer knows only about numbers.

Even when we create words and sentences in a document, these are not stored and manipulated by the computer as a series of characters, but as a set of numerical values – the operation of the computer is indeed based on mathematics.

A computer is said to be a 'digital' machine because all the components, wires, etc, operate only on discrete signals. This is rather like a conventional light switch. The light can only be turned on or off – it cannot be a half on, a quarter on, or a quarter off; the bulb has one of two states: illuminated or otherwise. This analogy with a light bulb serves us quite well, because not only is a computer a digital machine, but all computation is performed not in our conventional base 10 system (in which we represent numbers by means of ten symbols, 0 to 9), but in base 2 (for which we have only two symbols '0' and '1'). In the next section we briefly consider the base two number system.

# 1.6 Binary (number base 2)

In our everyday lives, we employ the decimal number system (base 10). Here, we make use of ten symbols ('0' through to '9'). The modern computer, however, operates in base 2 (binary), and in this number system we have only two symbols ('0' and '1'). In this section we provide a brief review of the binary system. It is important that you have a clear understanding of this number base, because it is critical to the operation of modern computer technologies.

Let us begin by considering how we represent numbers in base 10. As indicated above, we have at our disposal ten symbols (0,1,2,3,4,5,6,7,8,9). Consequently, if we want to represent a number (integer) up to the number nine, we simply make use of one of these symbols. But what happens if we wish to represent a number greater than nine? Suppose that we want to represent the number thirteen. We now allow our symbols to take on different meanings according to their position (placement). For example, when we write 13, we actually assign to the digit '1' a new meaning. Here it represents the number of tens. Thus, 13 really means one 10, and three units (1s).

Consider another example. Suppose we want to represent numerically three thousand four hundred and sixty-seven – we do so as follows:

| Thousands | Hundreds | Tens | Units |
|:---:|:---:|:---:|:---:|
| 3 | 4 | 6 | 7 |

As you can see in the above, the digit '3' indicates the number of thousands, the digit '4' the number of hundreds, the digit '6' the number of tens, and the digit '7' the number of units.

Each digit in the number has a different significance depending on the column in which it is located. Now look at the values ascribed to the columns. We have the number of ones (units), the number of tens, the number of hundreds, and the number of thousands. The next column would be the number of ten thousands, etc. From this pattern it should be clear that the columns can actually be represented in terms of 'powers' of ten:

Units = $10^0$ (remember that $10^0$ is defined as equalling 1)

Tens = $10^1$

Hundreds = $10^2$

Thousands = $10^3$

Because we are working in base 10, the values ascribed to each column in our numeric representation increase by a factor of 10 as we move along the number.

In base 2 (binary), the values of the columns increase by a factor of 2. Let us take an example: but in order to understand this you need to remember that, just as in base 10 we have ten symbols at our disposal, in base 2 we only have two symbols (represented as 0 and 1). Suppose we write the binary number 1100. What does this represent in our base 10 number system? Examine the following table:

| Eights ($2^3$) | Fours ($2^2$) | Twos ($2^1$) | Units ($2^0$) |
| --- | --- | --- | --- |
| 1 | 1 | 0 | 0 |

The binary number 1100 represents one 8, one 4, zero 2s, and zero units. Adding 8 and 4 together gives us 12. In short, the binary number 1100 corresponds to the base 10 number of twelve.

Consider a further example – the binary number 1111.

| Eights ($2^3$) | Fours ($2^2$) | Twos ($2^1$) | Units ($2^0$) |
| --- | --- | --- | --- |
| 1 | 1 | 1 | 1 |

As you can see, this corresponds to one 8, one 4, one 2, and one unit (1). Adding these together gives us 15. Thus the binary number 1111 corresponds to the base 10 number of fifteen. You can now convert binary numbers to base 10.

Activity 1.4

**Converting from binary to base 10**

Convert the following binary numbers to base 10.

(a) 1101          (b) 11111          (c) 1010101

The next step is to convert base 10 numbers into binary. As long as you remember the values assigned to the columns in both base 10 and base 2, you should encounter no problems with this.

Let us begin with a simple example. Consider the base 10 number 'five'. In order to convert this into binary, we write down the values of a few binary columns:

| 8s | 4s | 2s | 1s |
| --- | --- | --- | --- |
|  |  |  |  |

Now we remember that a binary number can only be expressed using 0s and 1s. Therefore, all we have to do is to insert 0s and 1s in the appropriate columns:

| 8s | 4s | 2s | 1s |
| --- | --- | --- | --- |
|  | 1 | 0 | 1 |

Thus the binary representation of the base 10 number five is 101. When expressing a number in binary we are simply looking at what 'column values' we need to use so as to form the base 10 number (five can be expressed as a 'four' plus a 'one'). Consider another example – the base 10 number twenty-seven. As this is a larger number, extra columns are needed:

| 64s | 32s | 16s | 8s | 4s | 2s | 1s |
|-----|-----|-----|-----|-----|-----|-----|
|     |     |     |     |     |     |     |

Here we have provided more columns than are necessary: naturally the 32 and 64 columns cannot assist us in representing twenty-seven as placing a '1' in either of these columns would give rise to a binary number larger than 27! However, if we place a '1' in the 16 column, a '1' in the 8 column (this would add to 24), then we have 3 left to represent. This can be achieved by placing a '1' in the 2 column and a '1' in the 1 column – as follows:

| 16s | 8s | 4s | 2s | 1s |
|-----|-----|-----|-----|-----|
| 1 | 1 | 0 | 1 | 1 |

Thus the binary representation of the decimal number twenty-seven is 11011.

**Activity 1.5**

### Converting from base 10 to binary

Convert the following base 10 numbers to binary:

(a) 9

(b) 36

(c) 73

### Binary arithmetic

Most scientific calculators support binary arithmetic ~~~~~~ ,node' key is usually provided to enable the calculator to operate in d' ~~~~~ .umber bases. This facility is also available in the calculator program supp' ~~~~~ . Windows. The calculator can be accessed by selecting 'programs', 'acc ~~~~~ , and then 'calculator' under the 'start' menu icon (at the bottom left-h ~~~~~ . of the screen). Once you have accessed the calculator, you need + ~~~~~ scientific' mode (this is available under the 'view' icon). To enable the ~~~~~ or to operate in base 2, check the 'bin' (binary) option. You will now ~~~~~ .iat only the '0' and '1' numbers on the keypad operate (as we have seen ~~~~~ ary we only have these two numerical symbols). Use this calculator to perfor' ~~~~~ following binary arithmetic. You should check the results that you obta' ~~~~~ manually converting each of the binary numbers to base 10, performing th ~~~~~ .thmetic in base 10 and converting the result back to base 2.

(a) 11 + 1 ~~~ =

(b) 11 ~~~ -11 =

(c) 100101 * 11 =

Note that * represents the multiplication operation.

## 1.7 Bits and bytes

Each binary digit ('0' and '1') is referred to as a 'bit', and a group of eight bits is called a 'byte'. Thus 16 bits constitutes two bytes, 64 bits are eight bytes, etc. It is important that we have a clear understanding of the number of values that can be represented by a certain number of bits. This can be readily determined by examining some simple cases. For example, consider two bits – they may take on the following values: 00, 01,10 and 11 Here we are simply counting – in binary and the binary numbers given here represent 0, 1, 2 and 3 in base 10. Thus two bits can represent four different values. Consider now the case of three bits. These may take on the following binary values: 000, 001, 010, 011, 100, 101, 110 and 111 Again we are simply counting in base 2 and you should confirm that these numbers represent 0, 1, 2, 3, 4, 5, 6 and 7. Thus three binary digits can represent eight different values.

### Counting in binary

Consider the case of four binary digits. List all possible values that may be represented by four bits, and state the number of values that they may be used to represent. As we have seen, two bits can be used to represent four different values ($=2^2$); three bits, eight different values ($=2^3$); and four bits, 16 values ($=2^4$). From this pattern it is readily apparent that an arbitrary number of n bits can be used to represent $2^n$ different values.

### Binary representation

Determine the number of binary values that may be represented by:

(a) 16 bits     (b) 32 bits     (c) 3 bytes

## 1.8 Summary

In this first introductory chapter we have introduced a number of key ideas that will be used as the basis for discussion in the coming chapters. As we have seen, although the computer is able to process different forms of media (such as graphics, video, audio and text), within the computer itself these are all represented by sets of numbers and processed by means of mathematical calculations. Additionally, although in our everyday lives we generally employ the decimal number base, computers operate in base 2 (binary). This is not an essential characteristic of the computing machine but greatly facilitates aspects of their implementation. Since operations are performed by the computer in base 2, a clear knowledge of base 2 arithmetic is an essential precursor to gaining a sound understanding the internal operation of computer-based technologies.

Despite the flexibility and power of modern computer systems, computer hardware is based on the interconnection of large numbers of very simple circuits ('logic gates'). In the next chapter we introduce a number of these 'gates' and show how they can be used to construct more complicated devices.

## 1.9 Review questions

**Question 1.1** State four essential characteristics of a computer.

**Question 1.2** A computer is said to be a 'digital machine'. What do you understand by the term 'digital' when used in this context?

**Question 1.3** Convert the base 10 number 21 to binary, and the binary number 1001 to base 10.

**Question 1.4** State two key features of the 'stored program' computer architecture.

**Question 1.5** How many different values may be represented by (a) 4 bits and (b) by 2 bytes?

**Question 1.6** What does the abbreviation 'CPU' stand for?

**Question 1.7** Multiply the binary numbers 101 and 110.

**Question 1.8** What do you understand by the phrase 'a general purpose programmable machine'?

# 1.10 Feedback on activities

### Activity 1.2: The essence of a computer

A conventional calculator is able to implement a number of predefined functions (we exclude from our discussion programmable calculators). On the other hand, a computer is a far more powerful tool as it is able to execute a series of instructions by sequence (one after the other), by selection (decision-making during the execution of the instructions) and by iteration (repeatedly executing a series of instructions until some form of condition occurs).

Consequently, the order of execution of instructions is not necessarily predefined, but is generally determined by the results obtained during the computational process.

### Activity 1.3: Memory and storage

One main reason for providing different forms of memory/storage device within a computer concerns the balance we seek to obtain between speed, storage capacity, and price. Higher-speed memory devices are more expensive in terms of their cost-per-unit of storage capacity. Therefore storage devices able to store larger volumes of data tend to be less expensive, but operate at a lower speed. Main memory (RAM) is more expensive (in terms of cost-per-unit of storage) than, for example, the hard disk drive. On the other hand, main memory operates at a higher speed.

### Activity 1.4: Converting from binary to base 10

(a) The binary number 1101 corresponds to 13 in base 10, i.e. one unit, zero 2s, one 4, and one 8.

(b) The binary number 11111 corresponds to 31 in base 10, i.e. one unit, one 2, one 4, one 8 and one 16. Adding these up gives us 31.

(c) The binary number 1010101 corresponds to 85 in base 10.

### Activity 1.5: Converting from base 10 to binary

(a) 1001. Meaning that 9 can be represented by writing a '1' in the 8 column, and a '1' in the 1 column.

(b) 100100. Meaning that 36 can be represented by placing a '1' in the 32 column, and a '1' in the 4' column.

(c) 1001001.

### Activity 1.6: Binary arithmetic

(a) 11+101= 3+5=8. This corresponds to the binary number 1000

(b) 1110-11= 14-3=11. This corresponds to the binary number 1011

(c) 100101*11=37*3= 111. This corresponds to the binary number 1101111

### Activity 1.7: Counting in binary

```
0000
0001
0010
0011
0100
0101
0110
0111
1000
1001
1010
1011
1100
1101
1110
1111
```

This gives a total of sixteen different values.

### Activity 1.8: Binary representation

(a) 16 bits – 65,536

(b) 32 bits – 4,294,967,296

(c) 3 bytes corresponds to 24 bits which can take on 16,777,216 different values.

# CHAPTER 2

# Logic gates and simple digital circuits

## OVERVIEW

The basic hardware elements that form a computer (gates) are very simple – not only in terms of their electronic circuitry, but also in terms of their functionality. A computer comprises an enormous number of such simple building blocks and in this chapter we introduce logic gates by reviewing their individual functionality and by providing some simple circuits that show how they can be interconnected in order to form useful functions.

<table>
<tr><td>Learning outcomes</td><td>On completion of this chapter you should be able to:</td></tr>
</table>

- Identify the function of various logic gates and draw their associated symbols

- Understand and write out truth tables for logic gates and simple circuits

- Distinguish between sequential and combinational circuits

- Understand the operation of basic sequential and combinational circuits

- Perform conversions between binary (base 2) and hexadecimal (base 16) and understand the advantages of representing binary in base 16.

## 2.1 Introduction

Computers are constructed through the interconnection of very large numbers of simple circuits (these are referred to as logic gates). In this chapter, we introduce several types of logic gate, focusing our attention on the most basic and most widely used devices. In Section 2.3 we briefly introduce two general types of digital circuit – these being referred to as combinational and sequential logic circuits. In the case of the former, a circuit's output is entirely determined by the combination of signals currently supplied to it. In contrast, sequential logic circuits produce output which is determined not only by the current logical state of the input signals, but also by the previous state of the circuit. In short, sequential logic circuits exhibit 'memory' and underpin the construction of, for example, a computer's main memory.

In Sections 2.4 and 2.5 we provide exemplar circuits that demonstrate the implementation of both combinational and sequential circuits and therefore provide an insight into the design of digital electronics.

Finally, in Section 2.6 we discuss the hexadecimal number base (base 16). As we discussed in the previous chapter, modern computers perform their computations on binary (base 2) numbers. Although binary may be the language of machines, from our point of view it is certainly a far from convenient method of expressing and writing down large numbers. However, binary numbers can be easily converted into base 16 and this provides a compact and convenient means by which we can express and represent strings of 1s and 0s.

## 2.2 Logic gates and truth tables

When we think of a computer, we often imagine it to be constructed from immensely complex circuits. In fact, a computer is essentially constructed through the use of many instances of simple building blocks. These building blocks are referred to as logic gates, or simply as 'gates'. A gate consists of a simple electronic circuit which has one or more inputs and one or more outputs. We interconnect these gates on a vast scale, and each is responsible for reacting in some way to the binary input values presented to it.

Perhaps it is surprising that something as complicated as a computer can be created by the interconnection of only a small number of different types of gate. In fact, as we will see later in this chapter, a computer can (in principle) be constructed using only one type of gate. Nevertheless, different types of gate are manufactured, and facilitate both the construction of a computer and its speed of operation. The availability of different types of gate relates therefore to convenience and performance rather than absolute necessity. The functionality of seven key logic gates is briefly outlined below.

- **The inverter – (NOT gate)**
- **The AND gate**
- **The NAND gate**
- **The OR gate**
- **The NOR gate**
- **The exclusive OR gate**
- **The buffer.**

## *The inverter – (NOT gate)*

The inverter (also commonly referred to as the NOT gate) is the simplest of all gates. As the word 'inverter' implies, the function of this gate is to invert the signal presented to it. It has one input and one output. If a voltage corresponding to a binary number 1 (this is also called a 'logic high') is presented to the input of an inverter, then the output will be a binary 0 (this is also referred to as a 'logic low'). Conversely, if a logic low is presented to the input, the output will be a logic high. In this way the inverter simply inverts the binary value presented to it. All gates are represented in circuit diagrams by means of means of different symbols. The symbol for an inverter is shown in Figure 2.1. You will note that there is a small circle at the output of the gate. Whenever you see such a circle, it indicates that the gate has an inverting function. In the small table provided on the right-hand side of Figure 2.1 we illustrate the functionality of the gate. This shows the two possible logic states that can be applied to the input, and the corresponding logic states produced at the output. A table that illustrates the logical function of a gate is referred to as a 'truth table'. Such tables are very convenient and can be used not only to show the logical operation of individual gates, but also to summarise the logical operation of circuits that are constructed from any number of gates.

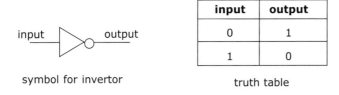

| input | output |
|-------|--------|
| 0 | 1 |
| 1 | 0 |

symbol for invertor              truth table

**Figure 2.1:** The symbol and truth table for an inverter

A gate is constructed on a silicon chip and consists of simple electronic components such as diodes and transistors. However, when the input state applied to the gate changes, it takes the components within the gate a certain time to react to these changes and so produce an output. Thus, if the input applied to a gate is changed, it takes a certain (very small) amount of time for this change to be reflected at the output. This delay in the reaction of a gate to an input change is referred to as the gate's 'propagation delay'. These are very small; typically a small number of nanoseconds (1 nanosecond equals $10^{-9}$ seconds). It would seem that such delays are of no significance, but we must remember that computers operate at extremely high speeds, and signals within a computer pass through enormous numbers of gates. Therefore even very small delays can be significant. It is not the delay associated with a single gate that ultimately counts, but rather the sum of all the delays associated with many gates that form circuits within the computer. In Figure 2.2 a simple circuit diagram is presented showing three inverters connected together. As may be seen, the output of the third inverter is connected back to the input of the first inverter. Suppose that when we turn the power on to this circuit, wire A happens to be at a logic high (you may equally assume that it happens to be at a logic low). The output from inverter 1 will then be at a logic low, consequently the output from inverter 2 will be at a logic high, and in turn the output from inverter 3 will be at a logic low. If we now work our way through the circuit again, we will see that wire A will again change state. In short, the circuit oscillates – each wire switches between being at a logic high, and a logic low. In principle, this circuit will produce a waveform as indicated in Figure 2.2. (This explanation of the action of the circuit is somewhat simplified. As we will later discuss, signals do not instantaneously propagate through gates – their passage takes a finite time. This complicates the operation of this simple circuit – although if certain requirements are met, the circuit will oscillate and produce the form of waveform indicated in Figure 2.2.).

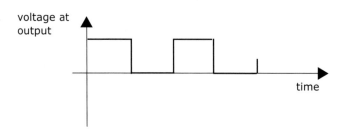

**Figure 2.2:** A simple oscillator that may, in principle, be formed using three inverters

**Activity 2.1**

### Propagation delay

Consider the circuit presented in Figure 2.2. Suppose that rather than using three inverters, five inverters are connected in a similar way. What effect is this likely to have?

**Activity 2.2**

### The action of an inverter

Consider the circuit shown in Figure 2.2. Suppose that it is constructed using an even rather than an odd number of gates. For example, you may consider a circuit comprising two, or four inverters, connected together in the manner indicated in Figure 2.2. How will this circuit behave?

## The AND gate

The function of the AND gate is slightly more difficult to understand than the inverter. The AND gate has more than one input (typically between two and eight inputs), and a single output. If any of the inputs are in a logic low state (binary 0), then the output will also be a logic low. This can be easily remembered as:

- **Any low gives a low.**

The symbol for an AND gate is given in Figure 2.3, together with a corresponding truth table. Here, an AND gate with two inputs (labelled A and B) is shown, and as can be seen from the truth table, if either of these inputs is a logic low then the output is also a logic low. Consequently, the output from the gate can only be a logic high if the inputs are all logic highs. As with an inverter, this functionality does not seem particularly complicated and it is difficult to imagine that such a simple circuit can be of such importance in the implementation of computer systems.  As with the inverter and all other gates, there is a propagation delay associated with the operation of the AND gate.

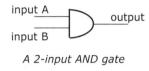

A 2-input AND gate

| A | B | output |
|---|---|--------|
| 0 | 0 | 0 |
| 0 | 1 | 0 |
| 1 | 0 | 0 |
| 1 | 1 | 1 |

Truth table

**Figure 2.3:** A two-input AND gate and its truth table

## The NAND gate

In Figure 2.4 the symbol for a NAND gate is provided, together with its associated truth table. Silicon chips containing NAND gates are readily available.  However, if one does not have access to a specifically manufactured NAND gate, it can be implemented by combining an AND gate with an inverter, see Figure 2.5.  The diagram illustrates the way in which a NAND gate can be implemented using an AND gate connected to an inverter (recall this is also referred to as a NOT gate).  In fact, the word NAND is created by bringing together the words 'NOT' and 'AND'.  Thus, a NAND gate is a 'NOT AND' gate. As you will see from the truth table provided in Figure 2.4, if any of the inputs of the NAND gate are at a logic low, then the output is a logic high.  This can easily be remembered as:

- **Any low gives a high.**

Consider for a moment the implementation of the NAND gate using a NOT and an AND gate, as shown in Figure 2.5.  Here, we have simply inverted the output from the AND gate, and a comparison of the truth table provided in this illustration with the one presented in Figure 2.4 shows that both circuits perform the same logical function.  However, since electrical signals must now travel through two gates this circuit will exhibit a greater propagation delay than would be the case if a single NAND gate were used.

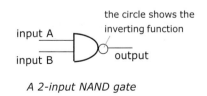

the circle shows the inverting function

A 2-input NAND gate

| A | B | output |
|---|---|--------|
| 0 | 0 | 1 |
| 0 | 1 | 1 |
| 1 | 0 | 1 |
| 1 | 1 | 0 |

Truth table

**Figure 2.4:** A two-input NAND gate and its truth table

As with the AND gate, a NAND gate has two or more inputs (typically between two and eight), and a single output. Referring to the symbol for the NAND gate which is illustrated in Figure 2.4, you will see that this symbol is the same as that used for the AND gate, but it has a small circle at the output. As indicated above when discussing the inverter, this circle indicates that the gate has an inverting function. By connecting together the inputs of a NAND gate, an inverter may be constructed. This is illustrated in Figure 6.6.

**Activity 2.3**

**A three-input NAND gate**

Draw up a truth table for a 3-input NAND gate.

| A | B | C | output |
|---|---|---|--------|
| 0 | 0 | 0 | 1 |
| 0 | 1 | 0 | 1 |
| 1 | 0 | 0 | 1 |
| 1 | 1 | 1 | 0 |

*Truth table*

**Figure 2.5:** A NAND gate implemented by using an AND gate and inverter

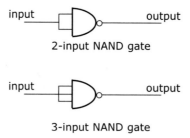

2-input NAND gate

3-input NAND gate

**Figure 2.6:** When the inputs of a NAND gate are connected together it acts as an inverter

## The OR gate

As with the AND and NAND gates, the OR gate has two or more inputs. The symbol for a two-input OR gate is given in Figure 2.7 together with the corresponding truth table.

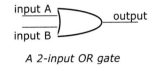

| A | B | output |
|---|---|--------|
| 0 | 0 | 0 |
| 0 | 1 | 1 |
| 1 | 0 | 1 |
| 1 | 1 | 1 |

*A 2-input OR gate*

*Truth table*

**Figure 2.7:** The symbol for a two-input OR gate and its truth table

In fact, an OR gate can be implemented using an AND gate and some inverters. Consider the circuit and truth table presented in Figure 2.8. As may be seen, each of the input signals passes through an inverter before being applied to the AND gate, and the output from this is also passed through an inverter. You should verify the truth table presented in this illustration, and with reference to the truth table given in Figure 2.7 confirm that this circuit performs the logical OR operation.

| A | B | C | D | E | output |
|---|---|---|---|---|--------|
| 0 | 0 | 1 | 1 | 1 | 0 |
| 0 | 1 | 1 | 0 | 0 | 1 |
| 1 | 0 | 0 | 1 | 0 | 1 |
| 1 | 1 | 0 | 0 | 0 | 1 |

*Truth table*

**Figure 2.8:** A two-input OR gate implemented using an AND gate and three inverters

**Activity 2.4**

**Building a two-input OR gate by means of NAND gates**

Draw a circuit diagram showing how a two-input OR gate could be implemented using only NAND gates.

## The NOR gate

The NOR gate derives its name from the 'NOT OR' designation. This means that it is an OR gate whose output is inverted. The symbol for a two-input NOR gate is provided in Figure 2.9. Here, you will see that this symbol is the same as that used for an OR gate, but is followed by a small circle which indicates its inverting function. A NOR gate has two or more inputs – most commonly between two and eight inputs are provided.

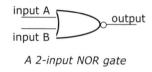

| A | B | output |
|---|---|--------|
| 0 | 0 | 1 |
| 0 | 1 | 0 |
| 1 | 0 | 0 |
| 1 | 1 | 0 |

*A 2-input NOR gate*

*Truth table*

**Figure 2.9:** The symbol for a two-input NOR gate and its truth table

**A three-input NOR gate constructed using only NAND gates**

Draw a circuit diagram showing how a three-input NOR gate could be implemented using only NAND gates.

## The exclusive OR gate

The name 'exclusive OR' is usually abbreviated to 'XOR' or 'EOR'. Again, this has two or more inputs and in the case of the two-input XOR gate, its functionality is the same as the two-input OR gate other than when the two inputs are a logic high. In this case, the output is a logic low. The symbol for a two-input XOR gate and its corresponding truth table are given in Figure 2.10.

As with other gates mentioned above, the XOR function can be implemented using other gates – as illustrated in Figure 2.11. Here, an XOR gate is constructed using a NAND gate, an OR gate and an AND gate. However, since we know that the OR and AND gates may be constructed using NAND gates, it follows that the XOR gate can be constructed using only NAND gates. In fact, most gates can be implemented using only NAND gates – and, in principle, a computer can be constructed from this single and very simple 'building block'.

| A | B | output |
|---|---|--------|
| 0 | 0 | 0 |
| 0 | 1 | 1 |
| 1 | 0 | 1 |
| 1 | 1 | 0 |

*A 2-input XOR gate*

*Truth table*

**Figure 2.10:** The symbol for an XOR gate and its truth table

A deeper insight into the functionality of an XOR gate can be obtained from the information provided in Figure 2.12. Here, one input is labelled as 'A' and the other as 'control'. As may be seen from the truth table provided in this illustration when the 'control' input is at a logic low, the output simply follows the input signal applied to 'A'. Thus, in this case if 'A' is a logic low – so too is the output. If we now apply a logic high to 'A', then the output also takes on this same logic state.

However, if the input labelled 'control' is a at logic high, then the gate acts as an inverter – the output state is a logic low when 'A' is a logic high and vice versa.

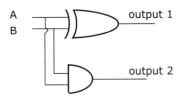

**Figure 2.11:** An XOR gate may be implemented using an AND gate, a NAND gate and an OR gate

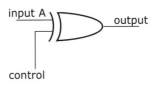

*A 2-input XOR gate*

**Figure 2.12:** The XOR gate may be considered to act as a 'programmable inverter'. When the input labelled 'control' is a logic low, then the output state is the same as input 'A'. However, if the 'control' input is a logic high, then the gate acts as an inverter.

## The buffer

The symbol and truth table for this gate are provided in Figure 2.13. As may be seen, the symbol used for the buffer has the same form as that used for the inverter, although the small circle used at the output of the inverter is missing. (Recall that this circle is used to indicate that the gate performs an inverting function.) In fact, as may be seen from the truth table, the buffer does not have any logical function – the input and output have identical logic states (a buffer has a single input and single output). It therefore appears that this device has little purpose – it simply relays to the output the logic state applied to the input.

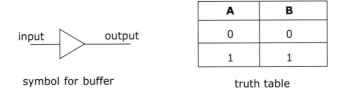

| A | B |
|---|---|
| 0 | 0 |
| 1 | 1 |

symbol for buffer          truth table

**Figure 2.13:** The buffer – here we show the circuit symbol and truth table.

However, within digital circuits the buffer has a very important function which relates to the interconnection of gates.

Gates are electronic devices which have one or more inputs to which we apply logic low and logic high signals. Typically, the former is represented by voltages close to zero volts and the latter by voltages close to 5 volts. (For example, in the case of a particular type (family) of logic gates (called the TTL LS series (Transistor-Transistor Logic Low-power Schottky)) a logic low applied to the input of a gate is represented by voltages in the range 0 – 0.8v, and a logic high by 2.8 – 5v. Another form of logic (CMOS) employs somewhat different voltages to represent logic low and logic high states). When we apply these voltages to the input(s) of a gate, a small electrical current will flow into the gate. This current must come from somewhere – it is in fact provided by the output circuit of the gate to which the input(s) of other gates are connected. Consider a circuit where the output of a NAND gate is connected to the inputs of six inverters. So as to correctly operate, each of these inverters will draw a small current from the NAND gate. However, there is a maximum current that the NAND gate can provide and if this is exceeded, the circuit will fail to operate. This limits the number of gates that can be connected to the output of a single gate and in this context we make use of the term 'fan-out' which refers to the maximum number of gates that can be directly driven by a single gate. For the TTL LS family of gates mentioned earlier, the maximum fan-out is 20.

A buffer is commonly used in situations in which we wish to exceed the maximum fan-out that can be supported by a single gate. By way of an example, suppose that we are using some form of logic gates that have a maximum fan-out of four (this would not be a very attractive form of gate) and that we wish a NAND gate to drive six other gates (inverters). If we simply connect these then we would exceed the fan-out limitation and the circuit would not operate correctly. However, by means of two buffers, we can solve the problem whereby the NAND gate drives the two buffers and each of these drives three inverters and so the maximum fan-out specification is not exceeded.

It is important to note that although the buffer serves no logical function, as with all logic gates, it does exhibit a propagation delay and therefore when the logic state applied to the input is changed, a short time will elapse before this change appears at the output.

## 2.3 Combinational and sequential circuits

The gates introduced in the previous section provide the essential building blocks from which the computer is constructed. These gates are fabricated in large numbers on the CPU chip and interconnected to provide the required functionality. They are also used in the implementation of memory and other devices within the computer.

Gates may be used to create circuits that are broadly divided into two categories:

- **Combinational logic circuits**
- **Sequential logic circuits.**

These are briefly summarised below:

- **Combinational logic**: A combinational logic circuit has outputs that are completely defined by the combination of input signals applied to the circuit. Thus, given a certain set of binary input values, the circuit will produce a certain result (output). For example, the AND, OR and NOT gates provide examples of combinational logic circuits.

As we will see in the next section, these may be interconnected to provide us with more complex combinational logic circuits

- **Sequential logic:** A sequential logic circuit differs from combinational logic in that the output(s) depend not only on the combination of inputs applied to the circuit but also on the sequence in which they occur (i.e. on some previous state). The concept of sequential logic will be familiar to you – but the name may not be. For example, a TV may have a single ON/OFF button, and the TV may be in one of two states: ON or OFF. The effect of pressing the ON/OFF button will depend on the state of the TV before the button is pressed. If, for example the TV is already turned on, then the effect of pressing the button will be to turn it off. Similarly, if the TV is turned off, then pressing the button will turn it on. Thus the output resulting from the input depends on where we are in the on/off sequence. Sequential logic circuits are constructed using the combinational logic gates of the sort described in the previous section.

## 2.4 Example combinational logic circuits

In this section we briefly examine some simple circuits constructed by means of the logic gates introduced in Section 2.2. Here, we will examine several circuits and draw up truth tables for them. All circuits discussed in this section fall within the 'combinational' category mentioned in the previous section.

Example circuit 1:

Consider the circuit provided in Figure 2.14. For all possible combinations of input, let us determine the corresponding outputs. This may be readily achieved by drawing up a truth table and including within this table the logic levels that appear on the connections between the gates (in this case there are two – labelled x and y in the illustration.

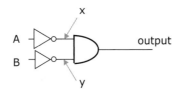

| A | B | x | y | output |
|---|---|---|---|--------|
| 0 | 0 | 1 | 1 | 1 |
| 0 | 1 | 1 | 0 | 0 |
| 1 | 0 | 0 | 1 | 0 |
| 1 | 1 | 0 | 0 | 0 |

**Figure 2.14:** Combinational logic example circuit

If we compare the input and corresponding outputs given in this table to the truth tables presented in Section 2.2, we will see that this circuit is acting as a NOR gate. Thus a NOR function may be implemented by means of two inverters and an AND gate.

**Activity 2.6**

### Circuit behaviour 1

Consider the circuit provided in Figure 2.15. Complete the truth table so as to show the output from the circuit for all possible combinations of input.

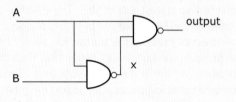

| A | B | x | output |
|---|---|---|--------|
| 0 | 0 |   |        |
| 0 | 1 |   |        |
| 1 | 0 |   |        |
| 1 | 1 |   |        |

*Truth table*

**Figure 2.15:** Combinational logic example circuit

**Activity 2.7**

### Circuit behaviour 2

Consider the circuit provided in Figure 2.16. For all possible combinations of input, determine the corresponding outputs. Hint: you should employ the same approach that was used in the previous activity and complete the truth table provided.

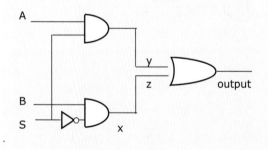

| A | B | S | x | y | z | output |
|---|---|---|---|---|---|--------|
| 0 | 0 | 0 |   |   |   |        |
| 0 | 1 | 0 |   |   |   |        |
| 1 | 0 | 0 |   |   |   |        |
| 1 | 1 | 0 |   |   |   |        |
| 0 | 0 | 1 |   |   |   |        |
| 0 | 1 | 1 |   |   |   |        |
| 1 | 0 | 1 |   |   |   |        |
| 1 | 1 | 1 |   |   |   |        |

*Truth table*

**Figure 2.16:** Combinational logic example circuit

Examine the truth table that you have drawn for Activity 2.7. Here, you will see that when the input 'S' is a logic low, then the output corresponds to whatever input signal is applied to 'B'. Conversely, when 'S' is a logic high, the output follows whatever signal is applied to input 'A'.

The type of circuit is referred to as a multiplexer and is widely used in digital electronics. In fact, in circuit diagrams a special symbol is often used to represent the multiplexer – as illustrated in Figure 2.17(a). In Figure 2.17(b) a diagram is presented which shows the functional behaviour of the multiplexer.

We can consider this device to act as a switch, with the position of the switch being determined by the value of the 'select' signal. Consequently, if the 'select' signal has one particular binary value, the output will be governed by the signal applied to one of the inputs (say 'input 1') and when the value of the 'select' signal is changed, the output will be driven by the binary values applied to the other input ('input 2'). In fact, multiplexers often have more than two inputs – perhaps eight or sixteen – in which case more than one 'select' signal is required. For example, in the case that a multiplexer has eight inputs, then three 'select' signals are required. This is because the three signals may take on $2^3=8$ different binary values and each of these values determines the particular input that will drive the output.

**Activity 2.8**

**A 16-line multiplexer**

Consider a multiplexer with 16 inputs and a single output. How many select wires (lines) are required to enable any of the inputs to be routed through to the output?

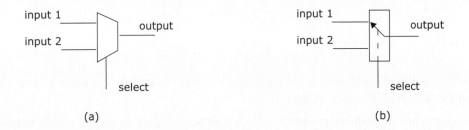

(a)                                          (b)

**Figure 2.17:** In (a) the symbol for a multiplexer is given and (b) indicates the effective action of this device.

## The half-adder

Here we briefly consider the creation of a circuit able to add together two binary digits (bits). Before we do this, let us briefly look at the process of adding binary numbers.

First, consider adding two 3-bit binary numbers. For example:

```
1  1  0 +
0  1  1
```

We start the addition process with the rightmost column (the least significant bits) and work our way to the left.

```
1  1  0 +
0  1  1
─────────
         1
```

As we add, we may need to carry. In this example, we begin by adding 0 and 1. What should we carry? Technically, you do not have to carry anything. However, when this process is implemented in hardware, we always need to define a carry value, which in this case is zero.

We therefore carry a 0 into the next column, and then add that column.

```
    0
1  1  0 +
0  1  1
─────────
      0  1
```

This time, when we add the middle column, we get 0 + 1 + 1 which sums to 0, with a carry of 1.

```
   1  0
   1  1  0 +
   0  1  1
──────────────
(1) 0  0  1
```

The final (leftmost) column adds 1 + 1 + 0, which sums to 0, and also generates a carry. We put the carry in parentheses on the left.

Typically, when we perform an addition of two k-bit numbers, we expect the answer to be k-bits. If the numbers are represented in binary, the result can be k+1 bits. To handle that case, we have a carry bit (the one written in parentheses above).

It makes sense to design a circuit that adds in 'columns'. Let us consider adding the rightmost column. We are adding two bits. Therefore the adder we want to create should have two inputs. It generates a sum bit for that column, plus a carry bit. So there should be two outputs. This device is called a half-adder.

- **Data inputs:** 2 (call them A and B)
- **Outputs:** 2 (call them SUM, for sum, and CARRY, for carry).

A circuit for a half-adder together with its associated truth table is presented in Figure 2.18 and uses an AND gate together with an XOR gate.

**Activity 2.9**

**The half-adder**

Verify the accuracy of the truth table presented in Figure 2.18 for the half-adder.

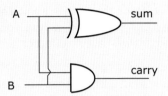

| A | B | sum | carry |
|---|---|-----|-------|
| 0 | 0 | 0 | 0 |
| 0 | 1 | 1 | 0 |
| 1 | 0 | 1 | 0 |
| 1 | 1 | 0 | 1 |

**Figure 2.18:** A half-adder and its associated truth table

As may be seen, a 'carry' value of 1 is generated only when both inputs are a logic high, and the 'sum' is zero when we add together two zeros or two ones (in this latter case a 'carry' is produced). This circuit is called a half-adder because although it produces a 'carry out' of the current arithmetic operation, it does not permit a 'carry in' from a previous arithmetic operation.

## 2.5 Example sequential logic circuits

In Section 2.3 we introduced the concept of the 'sequential logic' circuit. Here, the logic state(s) of a circuits output(s) depends not only on the present values of the inputs applied to the circuit but also the circuits previous state. In this section we provide several examples of circuits of this type.

Consider the circuit presented in Figure 2.19. As may be seen, this circuit employs 'feedback' since the outputs of the two NAND gates are 'fed back' to act as inputs. The two outputs are labelled Q and $\overline{Q}$ (generally expressed as 'Q bar'). The use of the 'bar indicates that the two outputs are always (or should be) in opposite logic states (if, for example Q is a logic low then $\overline{Q}$ will be a logic high).

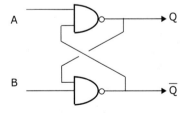

**Figure 2.19:** A simple example of sequential logic. This circuit is known as the 'RS bistable'.

Consider the case that A is a logic low and B a logic high. Using the same approach that was adopted in the previous section, we can readily determine the output states (recall that for a NAND gate 'any low gives a high'). Since input A is low, it follows that the output from the top gate will be a logic high (thus Q is high). Both inputs to the lower NAND gate are high, and so its output will be a logic low. Thus Q=high and $\overline{Q}$ =low. If we now change input A to a logic high state (leaving B unaltered), then this will have no impact on Q and $\overline{Q}$ (in fact we can say that the circuit 'remembers' its previous state).

Now consider the case that A is a logic high and B a logic low. Using the same reasoning as was used in the previous paragraph, it follows that Q will be a logic low and $\overline{Q}$ a logic high. If we now change input B to a logic high and leave A unaltered this will have no effect on the outputs. Again the circuit 'remembers' its previous state.

Unfortunately, if a logic low is applied to both inputs, then any subsequent change to either one of the inputs has an undefined impact on the circuit. This can be understood by examination of the circuit. If both inputs are a logic low, then the outputs from both NAND gates will be high. If we now change A and B to a logic high, we cannot predict the states of Q and $\overline{Q}$ – this will simply depend on slight differences in the propagation delays of the two gates and so the circuit cannot be viewed as being stable. Consequently, we must avoid simultaneously applying a logic low to both inputs.

The operation of this circuit can be summarised as follows:

- If A=0 and B=1 then Q=1 and $\overline{Q}$ =0. Call this state 1
- If A=1 and B=0 then Q=0 and $\overline{Q}$ =1. Call this state 2
- If we now make A=1 and B=1 then the circuit will retain its previous state (state 1 or state 2) – i.e. it will 'remember' its previous state.

Note that when A=0 and B=1 then Q=1 and $\overline{Q}$ =0. Similarly when A=1 and B=0 then $\overline{Q}$ =1 and Q=0. Thus the output from the circuit corresponds to the inverted input. When Q=1 and $\overline{Q}$ =0 the circuit is said to be 'set' and in the converse case (Q=0 and $\overline{Q}$ =1) the circuit is referred to as being in the 'reset' state. Additionally, when both inputs are a logic high the circuit is said to 'latch' (remember) the previous input.

As we have seen, the circuit can latch two input states (1,0 and 0,1) and the output is the inverted input. Since the circuit can exhibit two stable states it is referred to as a 'bistable' device and is generally called an 'RS latch' or 'RS bistable'. Here, the R and S indicate the set and reset conditions in which the circuit is able to exhibit stability.

**Activity 2.10**

### The RS bistable

Consider the circuit presented in Figure 2.20.

Here, the two NAND gates employed in Figure 2.19 have been replaced with two NOR gates. For this circuit, if A and B are both a logic high the input is said to be invalid. Thus there are three valid combinations of input 0,0; 0,1; 1,0. When the two inputs are a logic low, the circuit will latch the previously applied values (0,1 or 1,0).

When A=1 and B=0 and when A=0 and B=1, determine the logic states of Q and $\overline{Q}$ .

Does this device invert the input values?

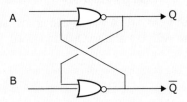

**Figure 2.20:** The implementation of a bistable using NOR gates

## The level-triggered D-type bistable

The simple form of circuit described above in which output is fed back to the circuit input underpins the operation of various forms of computer memory. Unfortunately, the circuit operates incorrectly when both inputs are in a logic low state, and so this condition must be avoided. One solution is to make use of two additional gates as illustrated in Figure 2.21. Here, we have only a single data input (D) and an additional input that is labelled 'clk' (a frequently used abbreviation for 'clock').

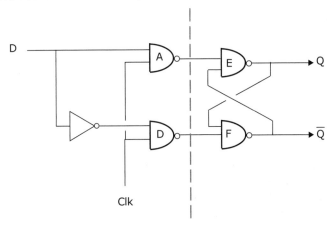

**Figure 2.21:** The level-triggered D-type bistable

Although at first sight this circuit may look complicated, its operation can be readily understood by remembering that the bistable (located to the right of the dashed line) may only be presented with three binary combinations (0,1; 1,0; 1,1). We aim to prevent it ever being simultaneously presented with two logic lows.

The clock ('clk') is used to enable data to be presented to the bistable and subsequently latched. When the clock is a logic low, then the output from gates A and B will be a logic high (recall that for a NAND gate 'any low gives a high') – in this situation input D has no effect. Thus both gates within the bistable (gates E and F) are presented with a logic high – this corresponds to the latched state.

Now consider the case in which the clock ('clk') is a logic high. If the input D is a logic low, the output from gate A will be a logic high and the output from gate B a logic low (this is because in the case of gate B, the value of D has been inverted and so both its inputs are in a logic high state). Thus the bistable receives 1,0 and so Q=0 and $\overline{Q}$ =1 (the reset condition).

If input D is a logic high, the output from gate A will be a logic low and from gate B a logic high. Thus the bistable is presented with 0,1 and so Q=1 and $\overline{Q}$ =0 (the set condition).

## Summary

- We apply either a logic high or low to input D when the clock is in a logic high state. The value of D sets or resets Q and $\overline{Q}$ . If now the clock changes to a logic low (before we remove the value applied to input D), the bistable will latch (remember) the value of the signal that was applied to input D. We have a memory device able to store one binary digit (bit).

This circuit is referred to as the 'level-triggered D-type bistable' and there are no circumstances (other than circuit failure) in which both of the inputs of the bistable will be simultaneously presented with a logic low. Thus the 'invalid' state is avoided.

The device is said to be 'level-triggered' since it is the binary value (level) of the clock that determines when the bistable is in the latched state. As we will see, many digital circuits employ an alternative approach in which they react to changes in the state of a signal (rather than to the absolute binary value). Such devices are said to be 'edge-triggered'. This can be readily understood by reference to Figure 2.22, which shows the variation of a digital signal (waveform) with time. As indicated, a 'level-triggered' device responds to the absolute binary value of a signal. This contrasts with the 'edge-triggered' device in which changes in the state of the waveform are of importance.

The waveform presented in this illustration is idealised in as much as the changes in state appear to occur instantaneously. However, in the case of a real signal these changes occupy a finite (although very small) time. The transition from a logic low to a logic high corresponds to the waveform's 'rising edge' and the converse to the 'falling edge'.

## *A register*

As we will discuss in Chapter 3, within a microprocessor there are a number of registers. These are each able to store one or more bytes, and support both the operation of the processor and the implementation of arithmetic and logical operations. Since the registers are implemented on the processor chip, they operate at very high speeds.

For our present purposes it is sufficient to note that registers are simply storage locations able to 'remember' one or more bytes. We can implement such a register by means of a set of D-type bistables (the number of bistables needed corresponds to the number of bits that are to be stored within the register). For simplicity, we will assume that a register is to hold (store) four bits, and a suitable circuit is illustrated in Figure 2.23. Here, you will notice that each bistable device is simply represented by a rectangle, each of which has two inputs ('D' and 'clk') and two outputs Q and $\overline{Q}$ . For the moment we will assume that these are 'level-triggered' devices of the sort that were illustrated in Figure 2.21.

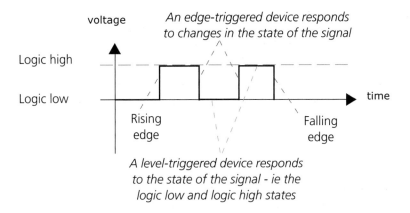

**Figure 2.22:** An idealised waveform. Circuits may react to the absolute binary state (voltage) of the signal or to changes in its state.

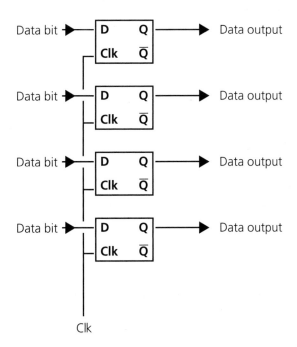

**Figure 2.23:** The creation of a 4-bit register using level-triggered D-type bistable

The circuit operates as follows:

1. The 'clk' signal goes to a logic high
2. The four bits that are to be 'remembered' are applied to the four inputs
3. The 'clk' goes to a logic low (thereby latching the data bits)
4. The input data is removed
5. The data outputs retain their state, thereby 'remembering' the values of the input data bits.

## 2.6 Hexadecimal

As discussed in Chapter 1, computers operate on binary numbers – 1s and 0s. Unfortunately, binary numbers tend to be quite large in terms of the number of bits (binary digits) needed to represent the decimal (base 10) equivalent. For example, to represent the base 10 number, 255, we need to use eight binary digits (11111111), and to represent the decimal number 64535 we need to use 16 binary digits. Writing down numbers in binary is in fact extremely tedious and it is easy to miss out a number – errors easily occur! A solution to this tedious process is to represent binary numbers not in base 2, but in base 16. Base 16 is generally referred to as 'hexadecimal'.

As we have seen, in base 2 we use only two symbols (0 and 1) and in base 10 we have ten symbols (0 through to 9). It follows therefore that in base 16 we will make use of sixteen symbols. As we only have numbers in the range 0 through to 9, we need six more symbols in order to represent a single hexadecimal digit. We do this by making use of six letters: A through to F.

Consequently, to represent a single hexadecimal digit we use 0 through to 9, and if the number is larger than 9 we make use of letters to represent the number, as follows:

| | |
|---|---|
| A = 10 | D = 13 |
| B = 11 | E = 14 |
| C = 12 | F = 15 |

So, for example if you were asked to represent the base 10 number 13 in hexadecimal, you would simply write the letter 'D'. By now, you are probably asking: what do we do if we wish to represent a base 10 number greater than 15 in hexadecimal? To answer this question, we need to consider what we do in base 10 when we want to represent a number larger than 9.

As you will recall, in base 10 when we wish to represent a number greater than 9, we make use of our set of ten symbols but place the symbols in different columns, and this gives them different values. For example, suppose we want to represent the number twenty-seven – we do so as follows:

| 10s | 1s |
|---|---|
| 2 | 7 |

This indicates that the number 2 is representing two times ten, and the number 7 is representing seven times one (i.e. the number of 'units'). Let us take another example. Suppose we want to represent three hundred and twenty-four as a number. We do so as follows:

| 100s | 10s | 1s |
|---|---|---|
| 3 | 2 | 4 |

This indicates that the number 3 is representing three times one hundred, the number 2 is representing two times ten, and the number 4 represents four times one. Thus, the position of digits within a number determines the way in which we interpret their values. Recall from our previous discussion that although we can represent the base 10 columns as we have done above (1s, 10s, 100s), a better way to think of this is to consider the columns as representing $10^0$, $10^1$, and $10^2$, etc (recall $10^0$ is defined as 1). So the column values in base 10 increase by factors of 10.

Similarly in base 2, the column values increase by factors of 2 (e.g. $2^0$, $2^1$, $2^2$, $2^3$, etc). Not surprisingly, therefore, in base 16 the column values increase by factors of 16, i.e.

   256s $(=16^2)$     16s $(=16^1)$     1s $(=16^0)$

Let us now take two cases. The first is the conversion of a binary number to base 16, and the second is the conversion of a base 16 number to binary. Most scientific calculators will perform conversions between number bases and consequently it is possible to carry out conversions without a proper understanding of what is going on. However, if you are going to be working with computers you will, at times, need to be able to quickly make conversions, and sometimes your calculator will not be to hand! It is a good idea therefore to be able to perform these conversions manually (but equally you should make sure that you can also carry out these conversions by means of your calculator).

### *Binary to hexadecimal:*

This conversion is illustrated in Figure 2.24 and in reading the text below you should closely follow the illustration. We take as an example the binary number 10110110. We begin by splitting this into groups of four digits as shown in the diagram. Each group of digits is then converted into base 10, thus 1011 converts to the base 10 number eleven, and the binary number 0110 converts to the base 10 number six. We then convert each of these numbers directly to their hexadecimal representation. In the case that the number (s) are no greater than 9, no action is necessary. However, in the example that we're using a conversion is necessary because the number eleven is larger than nine, and therefore cannot be represented by a single symbol (in base 10). You recall that for numbers bigger than nine we use letters in which A represents 10, B represents 11, etc. Thus, the number 11 that we have obtained in our conversion is represented by the symbol B. The lower four digits of the binary number produced the number 6. This is smaller than 9, and we do not need to worry about changing the symbol used. And so the result of the conversion is B6.

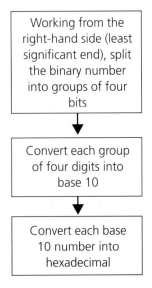

**Figure 2.24:** The conversion of a binary number into hexadecimal (base 16)

Consider a further example: suppose that we want to convert the binary number 11111111, to hexadecimal. Again, we split it into groups of four digits, i.e. 1111, and 1111. We then convert each of these groups of digits to their base 10 equivalent. (Verify that this is 15.)

We now simply represent the two 15s in their hexadecimal symbol equivalent, which you will recall is the letter F. Thus the binary number 11111111 equals FF in hexadecimal.

Only one difficulty can arise – perhaps the number of bits in the binary number is not an integer multiple of four. For example, consider the binary number 10010. Working from the right-hand side this splits into one group of four bits with a single bit (1) left over. To deal with this situation we pad out the number by inserting binary 0s to the most significant end and thereby enable the number to be split into groups of four bits. In the case of the above example, we would begin the conversion by adding three 0s; thus, 10010 would be written 00010010. This would then be split into 0001 and 0010. These groups are then converted to base 10 – giving us 12. Since both of these numbers are less than nine, the conversion is complete.

**Activity 2.11**

**Converting from binary to hexadecimal**

Following Figure 2.24 or otherwise, manually convert the binary number 11011111 to hexadecimal. Also perform this conversion using your calculator (or use the calculator provided on your computer.)

## *Hexadecimal to binary*

The process we use here is essentially the reverse of that used earlier. We take the symbols in the hexadecimal number and convert each into their base 10 equivalent. The process is illustrated in Figure 2.25. Suppose by way of an example we want to convert the hexadecimal number F4 to binary. The base 10 equivalent for the symbols are 15 and 4 respectively (recall from the beginning of this section that *F* in hexadecimal represents the base 10 number fifteen). We then draw up our base 2 columns as shown below, and place these two numbers within the columns (expressed in binary):

| 8s | 4s | 2s | 1s | | 8s | 4s | 2s | 1s |
|----|----|----|----| |----|----|----|----|
| 1 | 1 | 1 | 1 | | 0 | 1 | 0 | 0 |

Thus, the hexadecimal number F4 corresponds to the binary number 11110100.

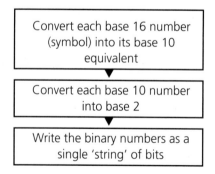

**Figure 2.25:** The hexadecimal-to-binary conversion process.

**Activity 2.12**

### Converting from hexadecimal to binary

Following Figure 2.25 (or otherwise), manually convert the hexadecimal number EA into binary. Also perform this conversion using your calculator.

**Activity 2.13**

### Converting from hexadecimal to base 10

Convert the hexadecimal number 4E to base 10.

## 2.7  Summary

In this chapter, we have introduced some of the basic 'building blocks' (logic gates) that are used in the implementation of the modern computer. As we have discussed, each type of gate performs a very simple and precisely defined function and gates may be combined to create combinational and sequential logic circuits. In the case of the former, a circuit's output is wholly defined by the binary values applied to it. In contrast, sequential circuits exhibit 'memory' and, as we have seen, this results in circuits whose output is not only determined by the current input signals but also by the circuit's previous state.

Both combinational and sequential logic circuits are used in the implementation of the computer, which comprises very large numbers of gates. These are fabricated on silicon chips – integrated circuits (ICs) – by means of automated production techniques. In fact, the invention of the transistor in the late 1940s and the development of IC fabrication techniques that has taken place since the early 1960s denote two of the most important technical advancements that underpin the operation of today's computers – enabling increasingly powerful machines to be implemented in an ever-more compact form.

In the next chapter, we begin to consider aspects of the computer's internal architecture and build on previous discussion presented in Chapter 1 in relation to the stored program architectural model.

## 2.8 Review questions

**Question 2.1** Some of the symbols used to represent logic gates have a small circle at their output. What is the reason for this?

**Question 2.2** Under what circumstances will the output from a NAND gate be a logic high?

**Question 2.3** What is meant by the term 'propagation delay' – as applied to logic gates?

**?** **Question 2.4** Explain the nature of combinational logic circuits.

**?** **Question 2.5** Is the RS bistable an example of a combinational or sequential logic circuit?

**?** **Question 2.6** What is the purpose of a register?

**?** **Question 2.7** What do we mean by the term 'rising edge' as applied to a digital waveform?

**?** **Question 2.8** Why do we make use of hexadecimal (base 16) when representing binary numbers?

## 2.9 Feedback on activities

### Activity 2.1: Propagation delay

The speed of oscillation will be reduced because the addition of two further inverters will increase the overall propagation delay of the circuit.

### Activity 2.2: The action of an inverter

This circuit will not oscillate. If the input to the first inverter is a logic high, the output from this inverter will be a logic low, and in turn the output from the second inverter will also be a logic high. This is fed back to the first inverter, thus confirming its state of input. The circuit will then continue in this state. If you assume that the input to the first inverter is a logic low, then you can use the same reasoning to determine that this state will continue. Only circuits of this type which comprise an odd number of inverters will oscillate.

### Activity 2.3: A three-input NAND gate

In the table given below, A, B and C denote the three inputs.

| A | B | C | output |
|---|---|---|--------|
| 0 | 0 | 0 | 1 |
| 0 | 0 | 1 | 1 |
| 0 | 1 | 0 | 1 |
| 0 | 1 | 1 | 1 |
| 1 | 0 | 0 | 1 |
| 1 | 0 | 1 | 1 |
| 1 | 1 | 0 | 1 |
| 1 | 1 | 1 | 0 |

## Activity 2.4: Building a two-input OR gate by means of NAND gates

See Figure 2.26.

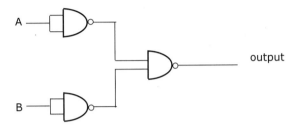

**Figure 2.26**: Building a two-input OR gate by means of NAND gates

## Activity 2.5: A three-input NOR gate constructed using only NAND gates

See Figure 2.27.

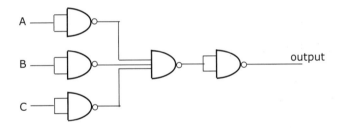

**Figure 2.27 :** A three-input NOR gate constructed using only NAND gates

## Activity 2.6: Circuit behaviour 1

| A | B | x | output |
|---|---|---|--------|
| 0 | 0 | 1 | 1 |
| 0 | 1 | 1 | 1 |
| 1 | 0 | 1 | 0 |
| 1 | 1 | 0 | 1 |

## Activity 2.7: Circuit behaviour 2

| A | B | S | x | y | z | output |
|---|---|---|---|---|---|--------|
| 0 | 0 | 0 | 1 | 0 | 0 | 0 |
| 0 | 1 | 0 | 1 | 0 | 1 | 1 |
| 1 | 0 | 0 | 1 | 0 | 0 | 0 |
| 1 | 1 | 0 | 1 | 1 | 1 | 1 |
| 0 | 0 | 1 | 0 | 0 | 0 | 0 |
| 0 | 1 | 1 | 0 | 0 | 0 | 0 |
| 1 | 0 | 1 | 0 | 1 | 0 | 1 |
| 1 | 1 | 1 | 0 | 1 | 0 | 1 |

## Activity 2.8: A 16-line multiplexer

Four select wires are needed. These may take on 16 different binary values thereby enabling any of the 16 inputs to be selected for output.

## Activity 2.9: The half-adder

No feedback required.

## Activity 2.10: The RS bistable

The circuit does not invert the inputs.

## Activity 2.11: Converting from binary to hexadecimal

Split into two groups of four bits: 1101 and 1111

Convert each to base 10: 13 and 15

Convert to hexadecimal 13=D and 15=F

Thus, 11011111=DF in hexadecimal.

## Activity 2.12: Converting from hexadecimal to binary

E=14 in base 10

A=10 in base 10 In base 2

14 equals 1110 In base 2

10 equals 1010

Thus, EA equals 11101010.

## Activity 2.13: Converting from hexadecimal to base 10

| 16s | units |
|-----|-------|
| 4 | E |

The 4 represents 4 'lots' of 16 and the E (=14) represents 14 units. Thus, the hexadecimal number 4E equals 4*16 + 14*1 = 78 in base 10. (The '*' denotes multiplication.)

# CHAPTER 3

# Using and accessing memory

## OVERVIEW

The modern computer makes use of different types of memory device. These devices differ in terms of their cost per unit of storage capacity, their overall capacity, and their speed. Furthermore, some types of memory device lose their contents when a computer is turned off or reset. In this chapter, we introduce several forms of memory.

**Learning outcomes** On completion of this chapter you should be able to:

- Describe the use of binary addresses for referencing memory locations

- Discuss the use of the address, data and control buses

- Describe the use of memory in a computer

- Identify the various types of memory used and compare their characteristics

- Describe the function of ROM, RAM and processor registers

- Understand the nature of machine code and the general characteristics of assembly language.

## 3.1 Introduction

In this chapter we introduce a number of the key concepts and techniques that underpin a computer's operation. We begin by briefly revising several of the ideas introduced in Chapter 1, and then consider the way in which the processor (CPU) is able to access particular (specific) memory locations. This leads to further discussion in Section 3.4 relating to the fetch-execute cycle, and here we briefly introduce the use of processor registers (these being storage locations within the CPU that are used by the processor to control its operation, and also for arithmetic and logical operations). In Section 3.5 we describe the interconnection of the processor with memory devices and introduce the use of the address, data, and control buses. Here, we discuss the way in which the processor is able to write to, or read from, particular memory locations.

In Section 3.6 we revisit the use of processor registers and describe the function of the program counter register (this is often given the abbreviation PC – not to be confused with the same abbreviation that is generally used when referring to the personal computer). Subsequently in Section 3.7 we consider machine code which takes the form of the low-level binary codes that can be understood and acted on by the processor. Here, it is important to remember that whatever programming language is used by us to create programs (e.g. Java, C or Visual Basic), program statements are ultimately converted into machine code prior to their execution by the processor.

In Section 3.8 we discuss two general types of memory device – specifically, random access memory (RAM) and read only memory (ROM). The former is often referred to as volatile memory since the instructions and data stored in memory of this type are lost when the power is removed. On the other hand, ROM does not lose (forget) its contents when the power is disconnected, and is therefore referred to as non-volatile memory. Finally, in Section 3.9 we briefly introduce the use of cache memory, which is able to operate at a higher speed than a computer's main memory, but which is more expensive in terms of price per unit of storage capacity.

## 3.2 Concepts and terminology

In this section, we present some basic ideas that will help you in studying subsequent sections where we describe the way that the central processing unit (CPU) is able to read instructions and data from memory, and write back to memory the results of the computational process. We begin by summarising some relevant points already mentioned in Chapter 1. A computer is able to execute a series of instructions and to store data during the computational process. We have seen that a set of instructions may be executed in three ways:

- **By sequence:** Here, a list of instructions are executed one after another (sequentially). By way of analogy, we consider following a recipe for making a cake, or a set of directions when driving to an unfamiliar destination.
- **By selection:** In this case, a computer can break away from following the sequential list of instructions according to something that 'happens' (a 'condition'). For example, consider an instruction of the form:

    If x = 10 do 'this' or else do 'something else'

    Here, we are putting a programming construct into words. The symbol 'x' represents a variable – a value perhaps read from memory – and the CPU checks to find out whether this variable equals ten. If it does equal ten, then it will follow some particular action, and if it does not equal ten a different action will be followed.

- **By iteration:** This corresponds to the processor (a word frequently used as an abbreviation when referring to the CPU) executing the same series of instructions time after time (e.g. repeatedly following the same recipe to make a number of cakes).

In Chapter 1 we indicated that all operations carried out by a computer are based upon mathematics, and the computer performs its calculations and logical operations in base 2 (binary). Here we only have two numbers, 0 and 1, which are referred to as a logic low and a logic high respectively. (A logic high is also referred to as 'true', and a logic low as 'false'.)

Also recall from Chapter 1 that each binary digit is referred to as a 'bit'. For example, consider the binary number 1100 (can you recall how to convert this to base 10? – the answer is 12.) This corresponds to four binary digits or bits. When a processor reads or writes from memory, it does not read or write *single* bits, but *groups* of bits. When we have a group of eight binary digits, this is referred to as a 'byte'.

Early microprocessors (a microprocessor is a particular form of processor) that appeared in the mid- to late-1970s and early 1980s were commonly referred to as 8-bit processors. This was because these microprocessors carried out their basic operation on groups of eight binary digits. Moreover, each memory location (we'll talk more about this soon) was usually able to store eight bits, i.e. one byte.

Modern processors are able to read from and write to memory (and operate on) larger groups of bits. For example, a processor may be able to read from memory a group of, say, thirty-two or sixty-four bits in one operation.

The phrase 'word length' is generally used to represent the number of bits upon which a processor can perform arithmetic operations. Consequently, for example, a processor may be said to have a word length of thirty-two or sixty-four bits.

In reading the last two paragraphs you may have wondered why we are using numbers such as thirty-two and sixty-four as opposed to exact multiples of 10. However, it is important to remember that although the use of multiples of 10 may be natural to us, the computer operates in binary and therefore our everyday number system is of less importance in the digital domain. Today's computers employ word lengths that are multiples of eight (i.e. integer multiples of one byte). In many ways this is simply a legacy of the computer's evolution, and there is nothing particularly special about the 8-bit grouping of binary digits.

## 3.3 Addresses

Let us suppose that we want to send a letter by mail to a friend. When we address the envelope, we must provide a unique address. For example, consider the following:

> Professor Smith,
> Department of Computer Science,
> University of the South Pole,
> Antarctica.

We hope that this is a unique address (and given the location of the address that is given here, this is certainly likely to be the case!). In the last line, we often specify a country (in this case a continent), in the line above that we specify an institution within the country, and above that the name of a department. Naturally, in the example we have just given, we are assuming that there is only one 'Professor Smith' within the department.

Similarly, when a processor wants to read from, or write to, a memory location, it has to provide a unique address. Unlike a postal address, this address is not specified in words (letters), but rather as a binary number. Each memory location within main memory has a unique numerical address as illustrated in Figure 3.1. (Recall from Chapter 1 that, during the execution of a program, software is temporarily stored in 'main memory' and this type of memory can support both read and write operations. However, the contents of main memory are usually lost when the computer is turned off or reset).

| Memory address | | |
|---|---|---|
| 00000000 | 01101111 | memory location 0 |
| 00000001 | 10110011 | memory location 1 |
| 00000010 | 11010101 | memory location 2 |
| 00000011 | 11111111 | memory location 3 |
| 00000100 | 10001011 | memory location 4 |
| 00000101 | 11101001 | memory location 5 |
| 00000110 | 10110011 | memory location 6 |

**Figure 3.1:** A series of memory locations. Each has a unique binary address. Here, for simplicity, we show an 8-bit address being used – normally addresses are much longer, typically 32 or 64 binary digits (bits). In this figure we illustrate each memory as storing 8 bits (1 byte).

In this figure you can see that within main memory there are a series of what we call 'memory locations', each one having a numerical address. The number of bits that can be stored within each location commonly equals the word length of the computer (although this is not always the case). Since computers operate in base 2 (binary), each address has a binary value. Older microprocessors used a 16-bit address, i.e., an address comprising sixteen binary digits. Today's processors commonly employ, for example, 32- or 64-bit addresses. Given that we use eight binary digits as an address, how many memory locations could we access? Recall Section 1.7, where we indicated that n binary digits can represent $2^n$ different values. Thus eight bits can represent $2^8 = 256$ different values and so an eight-bit address could be used to access 256 different memory locations.

**Activity 3.1**

**Memory addressing**

Suppose that we use a sixteen-bit address to access the main memory within a computer. Calculate how many memory locations can be directly accessed.

# 3.4 The fetch-execute cycle

As indicated in Chapter 1 the CPU (processor) reads instructions and data from memory, executes the instructions, and returns (when appropriate) data values to memory. Reading from memory is usually referred to as a 'fetch operation'. Consequently, we talk of a 'fetch-execute cycle'. When the processor reads instructions or data from memory, it places these within special storage locations known as 'registers'. These registers are located on the processor chip, and since they are physically at the heart of the computer, operations can be carried out upon their contents very rapidly. Different processors have different numbers of registers. The simpler microprocessors from the late 1970s and early 1980s contained only a very small number of registers (typically six to ten). Today's processors generally use many more registers (for example, thirty-two registers in the case of a popular processor called the 'MIPS processor'). As will be discussed in subsequent chapters (see also Section 3.6), registers serve a variety of purposes; some underpin the operation of the processor, and others are available to the programmer for arithmetic and logical operations. For example, a particular instruction may indicate that the contents of one register are to be added to the contents of another register, or that the value within a register is to be incremented (add 1) or decremented (subtract 1). Returning now to the fetch-execute cycle, consider for a moment Figure 3.2. Here we show four processor registers. External to the processor we have some main memory, and data and instructions are being fetched from this main memory to the processor. Following processing, data is being returned to the main memory, thereby completing the fetch-execute cycle.

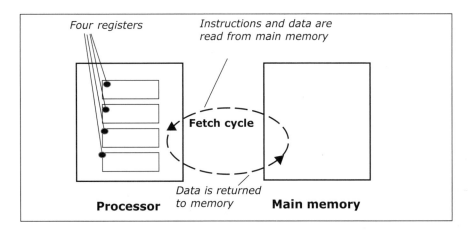

**Figure 3.2:** The processor reads instructions and data from main memory into registers. Some registers are available to the programmer for arithmetic and logical operations. Data may subsequently be returned to main memory.

**Registers within a processor**

Briefly explain why registers are important to the operation of a modern computer.

## 3.5 The connection between the processor and the main memory

Two main 'buses' are used to connect the processor with memory and other peripheral devices. A 'bus' is simply a collection of wires that are used for some common purpose. As outlined in Section 3.3, when we wish to access a particular memory location we must provide a unique address. This takes the form of a binary number and is passed to memory via what is called the 'address bus'. When we set up some binary number on this address bus, we are telling the memory device which location we are referencing. We will now want to either write data to the specified memory location, or read something from the location. The passage of instructions and data between the processor and the main memory takes place via what we call the 'data bus'. In the case of early microprocessors, sixteen wires were frequently used for the address bus, and eight wires for the data bus, as illustrated in Figure 3.3.

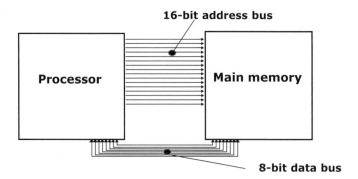

**Figure 3.3:** The processor and memory are shown connected via an address and data bus. The address bus illustrated consists of 16 wires, and the data bus comprises 8 wires. Usually larger buses are used. Drawing so many wires quickly becomes tedious, see Figure 3.4 for a simpler approach.

Modern processors use larger address and data buses, meaning that there are more interconnections between the processor and the memory. Drawing all the wires within an address or data bus soon becomes tedious and has little value. Consequently, we simply represent each group of wires by a pathway as indicated in Figure 3.4. Note that the processor tells memory which specific locations are being addressed. The address bus is therefore said to be 'uni-directional' since signals flow only in one direction – from the processor to memory (and other peripheral devices). However, in the case of the data bus, data may flow from the processor to memory (and other devices) and also from the memory (and other devices) to the processor. Consequently, the data bus is said to be 'bi-directional" because signals can flow along it in both directions.

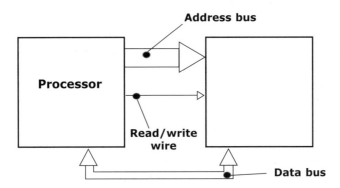

**Figure 3.4:** The address bus and data bus are drawn symbolically (rather than using detailed connections as employed in Figure 3.3). An additional interconnection is also shown – the read/write wire (R/W wire) – see text for details.

The 'other devices' mentioned in the last paragraph can be specialised chips that, for example, deal with communications to the outside world (e.g. input and output). However, we do not need to concern ourselves with these for the present.

Returning to Figure 3.4, we illustrate not only the data and address buses connecting the processor to main memory (remember that these buses simply represent groups of wires), but also an additional connection between the processor and the main memory, labelled the 'read/write wire'. This connection is used by the processor to tell the memory device whether the processor is wishing to carry out a 'read' or a 'write' operation.

## *Writing to memory*

When the processor wishes to write to a memory location, it sets up on the address bus a binary number corresponding to the address of the location it wishes to write to. It also sets up on the data bus a binary number corresponding to the value it wishes to write into the particular memory location. Additionally, it sets up an appropriate signal on the read/write wire, indicating that a write operation is to be performed. The memory device responds to the address appearing on the address bus, notes that a write operation is to be performed, and accepts the data (the binary number) which is present on the data bus and stores it at the indicated address location.

## *Reading from memory*

When the processor wishes to read from a memory location, it sets up on the address bus a binary number corresponding to the address of the location it wishes to read from, and a signal on the read/write wire indicating that a read operation is to be performed. The memory device responds to this, and outputs onto the data bus the binary value stored within the particular memory location. The processor reads whatever value appears on the data bus. Commonly, when a signal corresponding to a binary 1 (logic high) appears on the read/write (generally abbreviated to R/W) wire, this is interpreted as corresponding to a read operation. When a binary 0 (logic low) signal appears on the read/write wire, this is interpreted as corresponding to a write operation.

However, whilst this is usual, the opposite convention may be the case with certain processor architectures. The R/W wire provides us with an example of a 'control' signal that is used to support communications between the processor and peripheral devices such as memory. Other 'control' signals are also necessary. For example, during a read or write operation, a device must know that the processor has placed a valid address on the address bus. For this purpose, we may therefore make use of an additional control signal that has a certain (predefined) logic state when (and only when) a valid (meaningful) address has been set up on the address bus wires. For example, the 'valid memory address' control signal may take on a logic high state only when a valid address has been generated on the address bus. In this scenario, at all other times, the 'valid memory address' signal would be a logic low. Control signals are passed between the processor and peripheral devices via the 'control bus' – this being a group of wires used to enable and properly support communication. In Figure 3.5 we extend the model used in Figure 3.4 to show the interconnection of the processor and main memory using address, data, and control buses.

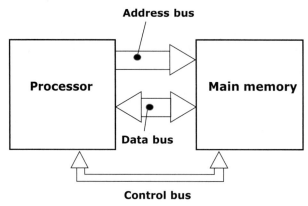

Figure 3.5: The interconnection of the processor and main memory via address, data, and control buses. Note that some of the wires within the control bus may be uni-directional (i.e. support signal transfer in only one direction) whilst others are bi-directional.

**Activity 3.3**

**Signal propagation**

Suppose that an electrical signal travels along a wire at one-third of the speed of light (i.e. at $\sim 10^8 ms^{-1}$). Determine the time taken in nanoseconds (1 nanosecond (1ns) = $10^{-9}$ seconds) for the signal to travel along an address bus, the wires of which are 50cm in length.

## 3.6 Processor registers

As previously indicated, within the processor there are a number of registers. Each is able to store up to a few bytes of data. To ensure its correct operation, some registers are used by the processor, and others can be manipulated by the programs running on the computer (i.e. they are general in their purpose). In the latter case, instructions are provided enabling algebraic and logical operations to be carried out upon and between registers. For example, the contents of one register may be added to the contents of a second register. This provides an example of a simple mathematical operation.

As indicated in Activity 3.3, electrical signals do not travel along wires at the speed of light – propagation speeds are somewhat slower. Consequently, it is desirable to minimise the length of the wires ('bus length') that connect the processor to peripheral devices such as memory. Since registers are located on the processor chip, the time taken for signals to pass to and from the registers is very short and so operations can be carried out on registers at a very high speed.

The EDSAC (Electronic Delay Storage Automatic Calculator) computer dates back to the late 1940s and employed a processor with a single general-purpose register. However, modern processors typically supply between 16 and 32 registers (for example, the MIPS processor is equipped with 32 registers, and the widely used Motorola 68000 provides 16). Patterson and Hennessy (Patterson, D.A., and Hennessy, J.L., *Computer Organization and Design: The Hardware /Software Interface*, Morgan Kaufmann Publishers, Inc., (1998)) provide interesting discussion in this area.

It is important to note that increasing the number of general-purpose registers is not necessarily beneficial:

- **Increases in the number of registers can increase the circuit complexity within the processor and the physical extent of the registers on the processor chip.** This can adversely impact on the time that it takes to access a register

- **Programs/programmers often do not take full advantage of the availability of a large number of general-purpose registers.** Thus some registers are not used to their full potential, or remain largely unused. The 'program counter' provides us with a convenient example of a register that is used to ensure the correct operation of the processor. An understanding of the purpose of this register is readily obtained through a simple analogy. Suppose that you were asked to copy down the list of binary numbers given below:

    11001
    10011
    11011
    11111
    01101
    11001
    10101
    01010
    11100
    01001
    11001
    11000
    10001
    10101

To ensure that you do not miss out a line of digits (or copy out the same line twice), you would probably use some sort of pointer to keep track. For example, you may use a ruler, pen or finger to indicate exactly where you are up to. Similarly, when executing a set of instructions the processor must keep track of where it is up to and the program counter stores the address of the instruction currently being executed.

The program counter (often abbreviated to PC) contains the address of the instruction currently being executed by the processor. If the contents of this register are lost (or corrupted) the processor would have no way of knowing the point at which it is up to in program execution – the computer would simply fail and have to be restarted.

This may give the impression that the contents of the PC are continuously incremented as the processor moves from one instruction to the next. This is often not the case because:

- Instructions frequently occupy more than a single memory location. This is because many instructions also have some associated data value. For example, an instruction may indicate to the processor that a particular register should be loaded with some particular binary value (the instruction may, for example, say load a register (that we will call 'register 1') with the binary number 11110011). In this case the instruction will generally be contained in one memory location, and the data value in the next memory location as illustrated in Figure 3.6. As a result, once the current instruction has been executed, the value held in the PC will be increased by two (thereby allowing it to 'point' to the next instruction as indicated in Figure 3.6).

- Recall from Chapter 1 and from Section 3.2 that a computer is able to execute a set of instructions in sequence, by selection and by iteration. An example of sequential execution is provided above. The execution of instructions by selection and by repeated iteration both require that at times the processor breaks away from sequential execution. For example, as you read this paragraph, you will read the words in the sequence in which they are presented. However, if you are asked to turn back a few pages and, for example, take another look at Section 3.2, you will then break away from your sequential reading of the words in this paragraph and pick up at another point in the book. In the same way, a program instruction may tell the processor to break away from the current flow of sequential instruction execution and move to a different point within the program. This is typically achieved using 'jump' or 'branch' instructions. In the next section we will discuss these instructions in a little more detail, but for the moment it is sufficient to note that when such instructions are encountered, they cause a new address to be loaded into the PC. This is illustrated in Figure 3.7.

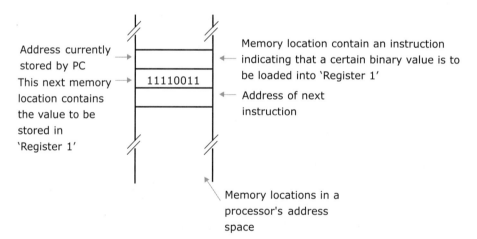

Address currently stored by PC

This next memory location contains the value to be stored in 'Register 1'

11110011

Memory location contain an instruction indicating that a certain binary value is to be loaded into 'Register 1'

Address of next instruction

Memory locations in a processor's address space

**Figure 3.6:** Here, we provide an example of an instruction that has an associated data value. In this simple example, the instruction occupies one memory location and the data value is contained in the next memory location. The execution of this instruction causes the value contained in the PC to be increased by two.

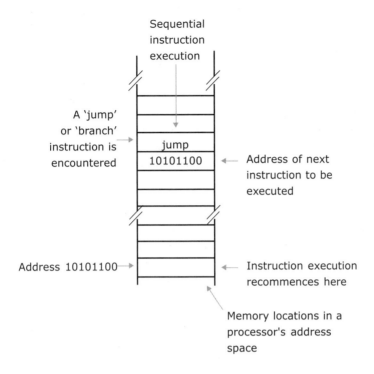

**Figure 3.7:** Here, a 'jump' or 'branch' instruction is encountered. Associated with the instruction is the address of the next instruction that should be executed. (For simplicity, we assume the use of an eight-bit address.) This address will be loaded into the PC and instruction execution will recommence from this memory location – as indicated.

## 3.7 Machine code

In Chapter 1, we emphasised that computers operate on binary numbers. If you have experience in programming, or are learning programming techniques, then in this respect you will be creating your programs in what are called 'high-level languages', such as Java, C, Fortran, Pascal, etc. These languages are said to be high-level languages because programs can be expressed by means of words. For example, some languages allow you to use the word 'print' when you wish to send a character string to the screen. The use of a natural language makes programs easier for us to understand. However, these high-level languages cannot be directly executed by a computer and so we may use a compiler (a special program) to convert the high-level language to a low-level language, and ultimately into 'machine code'.

Machine code is the name given to the code that can be directly executed by a computer and which takes the form of a series of binary numbers. These binary numbers may represent instructions or data. If you have any experience in compiling programs, you will know that ultimately an 'executable' file is created and it is this file that can be run on your computer, i.e. 'executed'. The executable file is the file containing the binary codes and data – the machine code. Naturally, for us to interpret very long series of binary numbers is a difficult undertaking, although not so very long ago this was routine. The process of understanding the long series of binary instructions found in an executable file can be made easier by representing the binary codes in their hexadecimal equivalent. Writing programs directly in low-level languages can, under certain circumstances, be advantageous, as it is possible for the programmer to create very efficient code that can be executed at high speed.

A machine code instruction is traditionally referred to as an 'operation code' (op-code) and any data employed by the instruction is referred to as the 'operand'. Some op-codes are self-contained and require no additional data. For example, an instruction may indicate that the contents of a particular register are to be incremented or decremented. Such an op-code requires no additional data values. Alternatively, consider an instruction that indicates that a certain value is to be loaded into a particular register. Here, we must not only supply the op-code which specifies the action to be taken, but also the binary value that is to be loaded into the register. For example, suppose that the op-code 10000110 indicates that a binary value is to be loaded into a certain register (we will assume the binary value is 10001000). In Figure 3.8 we illustrate the storage of this op-code and operand in memory and assume that the op-code resides at an arbitrary address 11001101 (as with previous examples and for simplicity, we assume the use of an eight-bit address).

The processor is assumed to have just completed execution of a previous instruction and the address of the next instruction to be executed is loaded into the PC (11001101). A memory read operation is then performed from address 11001101 and this is assumed to contain an instruction. The instruction is decoded and the processor 'realises' that an operand is associated with the instruction. A further memory read operation is performed (from the next memory location) and the operand obtained is loaded into the specified register. Having completed this instruction, the processor will then perform a read operation from memory address 11001111 where it will expect to locate the next op-code that it should execute.

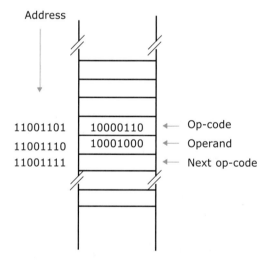

**Figure 3.8:** Here, an op-code (10000110) has an associated single byte operand (10001000). The title 'op-code' is traditionally used when referring to an instruction, and the word 'operand' is used when indicating data associated with an instruction.

As will be evident from the above, different instructions have varying numbers of associated memory read or write operations. In the simplest case, a 'self-contained' op-code (i.e. an op-code that has no associated operand) can be executed by a single memory read operation – the instruction is fetched from memory, decoded and executed. On the other hand, an instruction may require additional read and/or write operations – in which case the instructions will take longer to perform. Additionally, particular instructions may take on various forms. By way of a simple example, consider the 'jump' instruction introduced in the previous section:

- **Jump to an absolute address:** In this case the 'jump' instruction is represented by an op-code that indicates to the processor that the operand supplied with the instruction represents a specific memory address. This is illustrated in Figure 3.9.

- **Jump to a relative address:** In this case, rather than supply a specific memory address to which instruction execution should 'jump', we provide a value that indicates the number of memory locations that should be 'hopped over'. This scenario is illustrated in Figure 3.10. The difference between absolute addressing and relative addressing can be readily understood by a simple analogy. If when reading this book you are asked to turn to a certain page (e.g. page 10) – this would provide an example of the former. On the other hand, if you were asked to read material located three pages forwards or backwards from the current location, then this would provide an example of relative referencing. Here, it is important to note that relative addressing can be used to skip either forwards or backwards across the address space

- **Conditional jump:** In this case, the 'Jump' instruction may or may not be executed; its execution is conditional upon the results of some previously computed condition. This may be readily understood by continuing with the book analogy employed above. For example, you may be asked to assess your understanding of some topic. In the case that you understand the topic, then you simply read on, otherwise you are asked to turn back to a previous page where the topic is explained. Thus in the case of the conditional jump (which is often referred to as a 'branch' instruction) the results of some previous computation determine the action taken – the 'jump' may occur – or otherwise. The conditional 'jump' (or 'branch') operation may employ absolute or relative addressing

- **The unconditional jump:** In this case the 'jump' will always occur; unlike the previous point, it is not reliant on any previous computation. Both absolute and relative addressing may be employed.

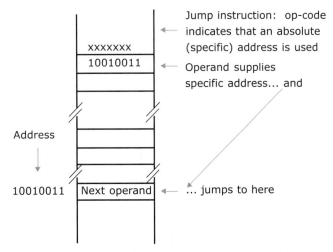

**Figure 3.9:** In this example, an absolute address (10010011) is supplied with the 'jump' instruction. Upon execution of this instruction the absolute address value is loaded into the program counter.

In this discussion we have referred to two different (indicative) addressing modes (absolute and relative). Processors support other 'addressing modes' and you are encouraged to obtain from your library or via the Internet a copy of the instruction sets supported by different processors (the instruction set details the set of instructions that are supported by a processor). From this information you will be able to learn of other addressing modes employed by specific processors.

Activity 3.4

### Machine code

Suppose that a processor employs the following op-codes:

B6 – load an 8-bit value into a register called 'register 1'. The value to be loaded (i.e. the operand) is contained in the next memory location.
A6 – load an 8-bit value into a register called 'register 2'. The value to be loaded (i.e. the operand) is contained in the next memory location.
D9 – add together the contents of 'register 1' and 'register 2' and place the result in 'register 1' (i.e. the contents of register 1 are overwritten).

Write the machine code (in binary) that will enable the hexadecimal values 22 and 4A to be loaded into registers 1 and 2 respectively and add their contents together, placing the result in 'register 1'.

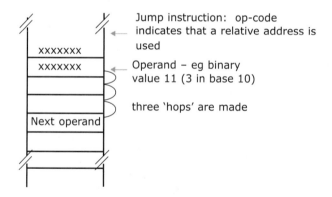

**Figure 3.10:** In this scenario, a relative address is associated with the 'jump' instruction. This indicates the number of 'places' (memory locations) (either forwards or backwards) that will be 'skipped' following the execution of the instruction. The use of this 'addressing mode' enables a 'jump' to either higher or lower addresses (i.e. forwards or backwards).

Writing programs in binary machine code is tedious and easily prone to error. Consequently, an alternative way of writing (expressing) such 'low level' programs is commonly employed. Rather than simply using the binary codes (as used in Activity 3.4), a special programming language (called 'Assembly Language') is employed. This enables op-codes to be written in the form of mnemonics, and symbols are used to express operands. For example, to increment the contents of a hypothetical register (that we will call 'register A') we may be provided with an instruction of the form 'INCA' (increment register A).

Recall that such an instruction does not require an operand – it is 'self-contained'. It can therefore be represented by a mnemonic and an operand is not needed. On the other hand, consider an instruction of the sort used in Activity 3.4 in which a particular binary value is loaded into a register (we will refer to this as 'register 1'). Here, we may employ an assembly language instruction of the form:

**LDR1 $3A**

The first part of this instruction (i.e. to the left of the space) is a mnemonic representing the op-code (and indicates a LoaD into Register 1). In this example, the value that is to be loaded (the operand) is the hexadecimal value 3A. The '$' sign is generally employed to indicate that a numerical value (expressed in hexadecimal) follows.

In Chapter 7 we take a more detailed look at assembly language, and for the moment it is sufficient to note that it provides us with a convenient means of representing machine code. It is also important to note that although it is certainly easier for us to understand programs written in this way (as compared to the use of machine code written in binary), an assembly language program cannot be directly executed by the processor – it must be turned into binary machine code form. This is achieved by means of a special program called an 'assembler', see Figure 3.11.

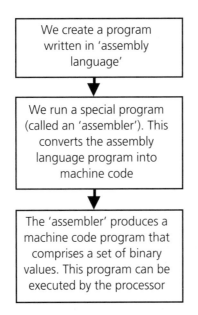

**Figure 3.11:** An 'assembler' is used to convert an 'assembly language' program into machine code

## 3.8 Volatile and non-volatile memory

In this section we briefly examine various forms of memory found in today's computer. As we have discussed, a memory device is able to store one or more bits at a set of uniquely addressable locations. In Figure 3.12 we illustrate the three buses connected to a memory device. The address bus is used to specify the address within the memory device that the processor wishes to access. The data bus enables the binary value(s) stored at the specified location to be accessed by the processor (a read operation), or permits the processor to write to the location (although as indicated below, not all forms of memory permit 'write' operations). The control bus passes the signals between processor and memory that permit the required communication.

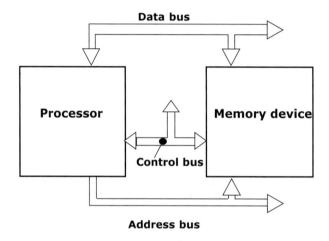

**Figure 3.12:** The address bus, data bus, and various control signals are connected to memory devices

Two general classes of memory chips are used in the modern computer. These are referred to as random access memory (RAM), and read only memory (ROM).

### *Read only memory (ROM)*

This type of memory will usually only support read operations. Generally, special hardware is used to write patterns of 1s and 0s to a ROM chip (these binary values representing instructions (op-codes) and/or data (e.g. operands)). The ROM retains these bit patterns even when the power is removed from the device (this is an essential difference between ROM and RAM; as indicated below, RAM devices lose their contents when the power is removed). The BIOS (Basic Input/Output Systems) program that executes on a personal computer when it is turned on is stored in a ROM chip. This program contains basic instructions and data needed when we turn on our computer, and since the contents of ROM are not lost when the power is removed, these instructions and data are always available to the computer (for further discussion on the BIOS see Chapter 8).

There are various forms of ROM, several types of which are briefly summarised here.

- **Programmable read only memory (PROM)**

  In the case of this form of memory, patterns of 1s and 0s are fused into the chip via a special apparatus known as a 'PROM programmer'. Once a PROM device has been programmed, its contents cannot be changed – the 1s and 0s are embedded on the chip

- **Electrically programmable read only memory (EPROM)**

  Functionally, this is similar to PROM but with one essential difference. Once the device has been programmed (via an 'EPROM programmer'), its contents can be erased and it can be reprogrammed. Erasure of contents is achieved by shining ultraviolet light through a small rectangular transparent (quartz) window located above the surface of the silicon chip. Typically, the chip is irradiated with ultraviolet light for around fifteen minutes and during this time the digital data stored within it is erased. It can then be reused

**Activity 3.5**

**Erasure of EPROM**

Once an EPROM has been programmed, a non-transparent label is used to cover the window that is located above the chip. Suggest a reason for this.

- **Electrically erasable programmable read only memory (EEPROM (E2PROM))**

  This is similar to EPROM. However, rather than using ultraviolet light to erase the contents of the chip, electrical signals can be used. Furthermore, it is possible to erase the contents of only certain memory locations and leave the contents of others intact. This is not possible with EPROM as the ultraviolet light erases the contents of the entire chip. Furthermore, specialist equipment is not needed in order to erase or write to memory locations. EEPROM can be written to without the need to remove the chip from the computer and specialist equipment is not required for device programming. EEPROM can therefore support both read and write operations but is classed as ROM rather than RAM. This is because EEPROM does not lose its contents when the power is removed. Furthermore, the time needed to write to locations within the device is much longer than in the case of RAM chips

- **Flash memory**

  This is similar to EEPROM, but these two types of device differ in terms of the physical mechanism used when data is written to the device. Flash EPROM and EEPROM differ in terms of erasure times, and the times needed to support read and write operations.

  NOTE: EEPROM and Flash EPROM cannot indefinitely sustain the read, erasure, and reprogramming cycle. Over time, this process damages the devices, which ultimately limits their lifetime.

## *Random access memory (RAM)*

The title 'random access memory' is used to indicate that the processor may address memory locations at random. This is in contrast to other (earlier) forms of memory (commonly referred to as 'bubble memory') in which the processor had to sequence (cycle) through memory addresses. Thus, in the case of RAM, any address within a device may be accessed directly – at random. This can cause confusion since ROM devices can also support random access for read operations. This type of memory device is able to support both read and write operations and is used as the 'main memory' within a computer.

However, when the power is removed (e.g. when the computer is turned off), RAM chips lose ('forget') their contents. There are a number of different kinds of RAM device and these differ in terms of speed, storage capacity and price. For example:

- **Dynamic RAM (DRAM)**

  This is the main type of RAM used in today's personal computers. This kind of memory device can be produced at low cost but performance is lower than some other types of RAM. Each bit is represented by charge stored within a memory cell (the quantity of charge representing the storage of either a binary zero or one). Over time this electrical charge drains away. As a result, the binary values stored in DRAM are gradually lost over time. This problem can be overcome by regularly refreshing the contents of each memory cell. (A 'memory cell' stores a single bit – thus eight memory cells are needed to store a byte.) This involves the use of special hardware which reads memory contents at regular intervals (i.e. before the stored charge has drained away to such an extent that 1s and 0s cannot be distinguished) and then writing the contents back to the memory cells (thereby restoring the charge to its original level). Typically, this refresh operation has to be carried out every few milliseconds (1 millisecond = $10^{-3}$ seconds). This means that separate refresh circuits are needed, adding to the complexity of the electronics. On the other hand, a memory cell can be implemented very simply, requiring only a transistor and capacitor (which stores the charge). As a result, DRAM is inexpensive, and integrated circuits of this type can store large volumes of data

- **Static RAM (SRAM)**

  Unlike DRAM, SRAM does not need to be regularly refreshed; memory cells retain their contents until they are changed by a write operation or until the power is removed from the device. The complexity associated with the refresh circuitry used with DRAM is therefore avoided. However, each memory cell is more complex and whilst DRAM requires only a single active component (transistor) per cell, SRAM requires 4 to 6 transistors. This increases fabrication costs and impacts on the storage capacity of an SRAM chip.

  As indicated above, one disadvantage of RAM is that when power is removed from a memory chip, the contents stored within the chip are lost. One solution is to equip the memory chip with a small battery so that when the main power supply is turned off, the device can continue to draw current from the battery. For this to operate correctly, it is vital that the memory device draws only a very small current from the battery, which is indeed the case for CMOS memory devices (CMOS is an acronym for 'complementary metal oxide semiconductor' and relates to the manner in which circuits are fabricated on the silicon chip). This approach provides 'non-volatile' RAM.

  When non-volatile RAM is implemented in a PC, a small lithium battery located on the motherboard usually supplies power and – unless the battery is soldered in place – its replacement is simple. This battery supplies power to several devices (such as the real-time clock chip, thereby ensuring that the time and date information are not lost when a computer is turned off) and to memory (RAM) in which system settings are stored. (In fact, if you set a power-on password, this is held in the CMOS memory. Removal of the battery for even a short period of time will force a re-set of the settings to the manufacturer's defaults, so overcoming the password. For this reason you should not rely on such a password!)

An important consideration in computer performance is the time that it takes to access memory (i.e. perform read or write operations). There are two issues that determine this time:

- **The time taken for signals to pass along the address, data, and control buses.** Here, the design of the bus is of critical importance and since electrical signals travel at a speed that is significantly less than the speed of light it is important to minimise the length of the wires that comprise the buses

- **Memory latency refers to the time that it takes for a memory device to respond to a read or write request.** This is usually quoted in nanoseconds. (Although for EEPROM the time needed to support a write operation may be more appropriately measured in microseconds or milliseconds.)

## A little mathematics – units

A nanosecond is $10^{-9}$ seconds: in other words, 1/1,000,000,000 seconds. This is a thousand times shorter than a millionth of a second. In human terms, it is an impossibly short period of time – but in computing terms it is an 'everyday' unit of time. Table 3.1 shows some of the powers of 10 and the associated names and symbols.

| Factor of 10 | Value | Prefix | Symbol |
|---|---|---|---|
| $10^{-12}$ | 0.000000000001 | pico | P |
| $10^{-9}$ | 0.000000001 | nano | N |
| $10^{-6}$ | 0.000001 | micro | μ |
| $10^{-3}$ | 0.001 | milli | M |
| $10^{-2}$ | 0.01 | centi | C |

**Table 3.1:** Fractional quantities and their associated names

The capacities of devices able to store binary data are typically quoted in terms of kilobytes, megabytes, and gigabytes. In Table 3.2 the meanings of these units are summarised. As can be seen, although a kilobyte in fact represents 1,000 bytes it is used approximately when referring to 1,024 bytes (i.e. $2^{10}$ bytes). Similarly although a megabyte accurately indicates one million bytes, it is approximated to 1,048,576 bytes (i.e. $2^{20}$ bytes).

| Power of 2 | Number of bytes | Symbol | Name |
|---|---|---|---|
| $2^{10}$ | 1,024 | Kbyte | Kilobytes |
| $2^{20}$ | 1,048,576 | Mbyte | Megabytes |
| $2^{30}$ | 1,073,741,824 | Gbyte | Gigabytes |

**Table 3.2:** Terms used when referring to the storage capacity of memory devices

Some decades ago Gordon Moore (one of the founders of Intel) made an interesting prediction based on what had happened up to that time with memory chips. Noticing that memory/ storage devices doubled in capacity every 18-24 months, he predicted that this would continue, leading to an exponential growth in size and hence computing power. Market trends have shown this to be generally true. This is known as Moore's Law.

However, in terms of current technologies, there is uncertainty as to how long this growth rate can continue.

Note: Moore's 'law' is not a law, it is simply a prediction, and is therefore incorrectly named! A more appropriate name would be Moore's Model.

### A little mathematics – what is exponential growth?

A series grows in an exponential manner when the next term in the series is obtained by the multiplication of a constant factor. For example, if you take a number, say 1, and multiply it by a factor, say 2, you get an answer of 2. If you then repeat this, the number grows slowly at the start but rapidly increases.

For instance: if you start with 1 and keep multiplying by 2, you get the series 1, 2, 4, 8, 16, 32, 64, 128, 256, 512, 1,024 and so on.

| Bricks & towns | Computer hardware | Computer software |
|---|---|---|
| Bricks: study what a brick is made of, how it is made, how strong it is, what it will cost. | 1s and 0s, simple digital circuits and how logical arithmetic can be performed with a circuit. | Boolean logic. |
| Walls: study how to mix cement, how to lay bricks to make a wall, how strong a wall is. | How a sequence of logical operations can be achieved with a circuit, how to add, subtract, perform logical AND and OR operations, etc. | How to perform arithmetic with simple numbers. |
| How to make several walls into a building with spaces for windows and doors, etc. How to build a roof. | How to store many logical instructions and feed them in sequence to a circuit that can execute them. | How to perform arithmetic with multiple digit numbers. |
| How to install all the services a building needs, water, electricity, gas, heating, etc. and to move in the carpets, furniture, etc. | How to accept human inputs by devices such as a keyboard and to display outputs using devices like a colour monitor. | How to handle data such as text and to edit it, i.e. move a sentence within a paragraph. |
| How to build a row of houses, provide street lighting, public access, etc. | How to provide a complete set of devices such as a mouse, keyboard, printer, CPU, etc. and to make them all connect correctly. | How to present a complete set of facilities in a word processor. |
| How to plan a town, provide libraries, shops, hospital, bus station etc. | A complete PC. | How to control the entire machine: the operating system. |

**Table 3.3:** An example of a function that grow exponentially. Note that the rate of increase is slow at the beginning but rises rapidly.

**Moore's Law**

Assume that the average size of a hard disk drive in a PC in the year 2000 was 10Gb. If Moore's Law were applied and continued until the year 2012, what would the average size be in that year?

Hint: Assume that Moore's Law indicates that the capacity should double every 1.5 years.

## 3.9 Cache memory

As we have indicated, latency in memory access is not only determined by the performance of memory chips, but also by the speed of the computer bus (in the modern computer, the time taken for electrical signals to propagate along the bus can make a significant contribution to latency).

Analysis of a large number of machine code programs (remember that all programs run as machine code in the CPU) reveals that most of the time the next instruction to be executed is held in memory next to, or very close to, the instruction currently being executed. This is known as 'spatial locality'. We can make use of this observation by providing a small amount of high-speed memory that is physically located close to (or even within) the processor. Such memory is referred to as 'cache memory' and naturally the processor can access such memory very quickly. When the processor reads an instruction from main memory, it brings into the cache memory other neighbouring instructions. Subsequently, when wishing to read the next instruction from main memory, it first examines the cache memory to see if it is already present. In the case that it is found, it may be accessed very rapidly. On the other hand, if it is not present in the cache memory, the processor will transfer it from main memory, together with other adjacent instructions.

The performance improvements that can be gained through the adoption of cache memory are further increased by the concept of 'temporal locality'. The examination of real programs in execution reveals that if an instruction has been recently executed by a processor, then it is likely that it will be executed again in the near future. The transfer of groups of instructions from main memory to a local high-speed cache memory takes advantage of this principle.

For this approach to provide real benefit, it must be possible for the processor to be able to rapidly determine whether or not an instruction or a data value is already within the memory cache. This is a vital consideration in the implementation of cache memory techniques and can introduce a number of complexities.

**Spatial locality**

Suppose that you were in the library researching material for a project that you have been asked to do for one of your courses. How would you make use of the concept of spatial locality?

## 3.10 Summary

In this chapter we have introduced a variety of concepts that underpin the operation of the modern computer. We have discussed computer operation in terms of the fetch-execute cycle, whereby the processor continually reads instructions (op-codes and operands represented in binary format) from memory, executes these instructions and where appropriate returns results to memory. Furthermore, we have considered several types of memory and have introduced the concept of processor registers. In this chapter we have also encountered Moore's Law (Model) in relation to the growth (in time) of computer storage capacity. Although this model has been reasonably accurate in its prediction of growth to date, great caution has to be exercised in using this to extrapolate future trends.

A processor is only able to execute machine code programs and whilst from the processor's perspective this may be an effective and efficient means of directing computational operations, programs written in this way are difficult for the human operator to understand. One solution is to develop programs using assembly language whereby binary codes are replaced with easily understood mnemonics. An assembler is then used to convert this form of program into machine code that in turn can be executed by the processor.

In the next chapter, we initially turn our attention to examining ways in which different types of number may be represented within a computer and this leads on to discussion of the representation of symbols such as alphabetic characters. Subsequently, we introduce the concepts of an interrupt-driven computer.

## 3.11 Review questions

**Question 3.1** Address and data buses play a pivotal role within a computer. Describe their purpose and in each case state whether they are uni-directional or bi-directional.

**Question 3.2** What is the purpose of an assembler?

**Question 3.3** Express 10 microseconds in nanoseconds.

**Question 3.4** How are the contents of an EPROM erased?

**Question 3.5** State the meaning of the terms 'op-code' and 'operand'.

**Question 3.6** What is the function of the program counter?

**Question 3.7** Explain the concept of temporal locality as applied to the execution of a program.

**Question 3.8** State one advantage and one disadvantage associated with the use of DRAM.

**Question 3.9** In assembly language the dollar ($) symbol is often used. What is this intended to indicate?

**Question 3.10** What is the meaning of the acronym EPROM?

# 3.12 Feedback on activities

## Activity 3.1: Memory addressing

A 16-bit address bus can address $2^{16}$ different memory locations.

## Activity 3.2: Registers within a processor

Some registers are used to support the operation of the processor and others are available to the programmer (and are used in support of arithmetic and logical operations). The transfer of binary values between registers and the manipulation of values held in the registers can be performed at very high speeds. The number and size of registers located on the processor chip varies between processor types.

## Activity 3.3: Signal propagation

$0.5 \times 10^{-8}$ seconds = 5 nanoseconds

## Activity 3.4: Machine code

10110110
00100010
10100110
01001010
11011001

## Activity 3.5: Erasure of an EPROM

Since normal lighting (e.g. fluorescent lighting or direct sunlight) contains a small portion of ultraviolet radiation, it is usual (after programming the device) to place a non-transparent label over the window so that the ambient ultraviolet light does not inadvertently erase the contents of the chip over time.

## Activity 3.6: Moore's Law

| Year | Size in Gbytes |
|------|----------------|
| 2000 | 10 |
| 2001.5 | 20 |
| 2003 | 40 |
| 2004.5 | 80 |
| 2006 | 160 |
| 2007.5 | 320 |
| 2009 | 640 |
| 2010.5 | 1,280 |
| 2012 | 2,560 |

### Activity 3.7: Spatial locality

Books in a library are usually classified (ordered/grouped) according to their general content. Consequently, books that cover similar topics tend to be located close together on the shelves. When researching your project, you will begin by identifying the area of the bookshelves that relates to the general topic that you are working on. It is likely that you will return to this area a number of times to access other books that are relevant to your writing. Here, you are making use of spatial locality in as much as you are accessing books that are in close physical proximity. As we have seen, in the context of a computer-spatial locality refers to the likelihood of the computer executing instructions and data that are stored in close proximity within main memory.

# CHAPTER 4

# The computer: an interrupt-driven mathematical machine

## OVERVIEW

The computer is a mathematical machine – all computation carried out within a computer takes the form of arithmetic or logical operations. In this chapter, we review several ways in which numbers can be represented within a computer, and also show how symbols (such as letters of the alphabet) are represented numerically. In addition, we introduce the use of interrupts – which perform a vital role in a computer's operation.

| Learning outcomes | On completion of this chapter you should be able to: |
| --- | --- |

- Describe ways in which signed (positive and negative) integers may be represented in a computer

- Describe the use of the normalised floating-point number representation within a computer

- Describe ways in which symbols may be represented in a computer

- Discuss the general techniques used in the implementation of an interrupt-driven machine

- Discuss forms of interrupts and interrupt priorities.

## 4.1 Introduction

In the first two sections of this chapter we consider the representation of several types of number within a computer. Up to this point we have focused on the representation of positive integer values (positive 'whole' numbers). In order to perform useful and wide-ranging functions, a computer must also be able to store and process negative integers and numbers that have a fractional (decimal) component. Furthermore, the computer must also be able to store (with a sufficient degree of precision) numbers that are either extremely small or extremely large. Such issues are discussed in Sections 4.2 and 4.3.

In Section 4.4 we turn our attention to the representation of symbols (such as letters of the alphabet), and here we introduce the ASCII character codes. This leads on to brief discussion in Section 4.5 relating to the means by which the processor is able to determine the manner in which operands and data should be treated. In this context it is important to remember that the processor has no inbuilt knowledge of what we are trying to achieve, nor the meaning that we assign to the operands and data that are to be processed. After all, the digital world knows only of the logic high and logic low states – the binary ones and zeros – and it is up to the programmer to ascribe meanings to these states and ensure that they are operated upon in the desired manner.

In Sections 4.6 and 4.7 we introduce the use of 'interrupts' within a computer. These provide a system whereby the processor is able to efficiently determine when peripheral devices such as the hard and floppy disk drives require attention and underpin computer communication.

## 4.2 Representing positive and negative integers

In previous chapters we confined our discussion to the representation of positive integers. For example, the base 10 number 27 may be represented as the binary value 11011. If this number were to be stored within an 8-bit register, then we would simply pad it out by inserting leading zeros, i.e. 00011011. By way of a further example, consider the base 10 number 15. This would be represented within an 8-bit register as the binary value 00001111.

If we have a binary number comprising N bits, then this may represent $2^N$ different values. For example an 8-bit number may represent $2^8$ (=256) different values ranging from zero through to 255.

A computer must be able to deal with both positive and negative numbers, and one simple approach to the representation of negative numbers is to dedicate one bit to indicate a number's sign. This may be achieved as indicated in Figure 4.1 where we show one bit (the left-most bit) as indicating the sign (positive or negative), and the remaining bits as indicating the magnitude (size) of the number. In this scenario, we could adopt the convention that if the sign bit is a zero then the number is positive, and if the bit is a one, then a negative number is indicated. (This convention is arbitrary. Equally, a zero could be used to indicate a negative number, and a one to indicate a positive number. Two examples of this approach are illustrated in Figure 4.2.)

The use of a sign bit gives rise to the number zero being represented in two ways – see Figure 4.3. Consider a binary number comprising N bits (one of these bits representing the number's sign, and N-1 bits the number's magnitude). This enables $2^{N-1}$ different binary values to be represented (the '-1' arises because the number zero is represented in two different ways).

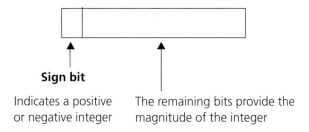

**Sign bit**

Indicates a positive
or negative integer

The remaining bits provide the
magnitude of the integer

**Figure 4.1:** The representation of positive and negative numbers by means of a
'sign' bit. We may, for example, adopt the convention that if the sign bit is a
binary *zero* then the integer is *positive*, whilst if the sign bit is a binary *one*
then the number is *negative*.

In the early days of computing, the implementation of the electronic circuits that comprise the
computer was a difficult and laborious task. Consequently, one key objective of the computer
designer was to minimise the number of logic gates needed to perform computational
(arithmetic) operations. Although the representation of positive and negative binary numbers
in machine code programs using a 'sign' bit (and associated magnitude bits) is logical, it means
that addition and subtraction operations have to be carried out by largely separate hardware.
In essence, it becomes necessary to implement hardware for the addition of numbers, and
different hardware for their subtraction. Designers therefore sought alternative solutions and
developed number representation schemes that would permit both addition and subtraction
operations to be performed by the same hardware. Below we review the use of the 2s
complement approach.

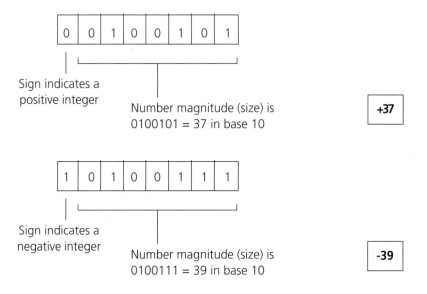

Sign indicates a
positive integer

Number magnitude (size) is
0100101 = 37 in base 10

+37

Sign indicates a
negative integer

Number magnitude (size) is
0100111 = 39 in base 10

-39

**Figure 4.2:** The representation of positive and negative integers
using a 'sign' bit

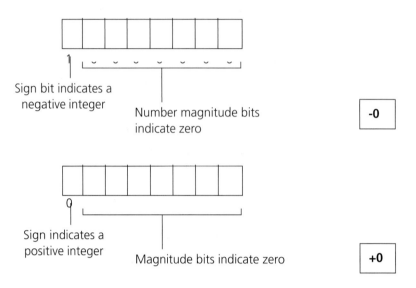

**Figure 4.3:** The use of a 'sign' bit results in the number *zero* being represented in two different ways (as +0 and –0). This is non-optimal.

## Twos complement arithmetic

Rather than employing a 'sign' bit to indicate whether a number is positive or negative, an alternative approach is to encode the negativity of a number within the number itself. In this context and when working in the binary number base, we make use of what is called a number's '2s complement'.

Although at first sight this may seem complicated, in practice the technique is very simple. Below we provide two techniques that may be used to obtain the 2s complement of an integer:

The first approach may be summarised as follows:

- Change all 1s in the number to 0s; change all 0s to 1s; and add 1.

By way of example, consider the binary number 10101. We begin by changing 1s to 0s and 0s to 1s (i.e. inverting the bits). (The process of swapping 1s to 0s and 0s to 1s is referred to as calculating the 1s complement of a binary number.) Thus we obtain 01010. We then add 1 and this gives 01011. Thus, the 2s complement of 10101 is 01011.

The second approach is even simpler and can be summarised as follows:

- Inspect the number starting at the right-hand side (least significant end). For all bits to the left of the first '1' that you encounter, change all 1s to 0s and all 0s to 1s.

Taking the first example used (10101), the first digit is a one. We leave this unchanged and swap all ones and zeros located on its left-hand side. This gives the same result as above – 01011.

Let us try employing these two approaches on two more example numbers:

## Example 1

Find the 2s complement of the binary number 11001100.

- Using the first approach, we swap 1s and 0s – thereby obtaining 00110011. We then add one – this gives: 00110100.
- Using the second approach, we move along the number for the right-hand side and make no changes until we encounter the first '1'. Subsequently, we swap (invert) 1s and 0s. Thus the first three bits are not changed and all others that are a '1' become '0', and all that are '0' become '1'. This gives: 00110100.

## Example 2

Find the 2s complement of the binary number 11000000.

- Using the first approach, we swap 1s and 0s – thereby obtaining 00111111. We then add one – this gives: 01000000.
- Using the second approach, we move along the number for the right-hand side and make no changes until we encounter the first '1'. Subsequently, we swap 1s and 0s. Thus the first seven bits are not changed and the eighth bit becomes a zero This gives: 01000000.

NOTE: If you calculate the 2s complement of a number and then repeat the process on this result, you obtain the original number. This provides a convenient method of checking your arithmetic. For example, consider the number 1100110. If we take the 2s complement of this number (using either of the above methods), we obtain 0011010. If we take the 2s complement of this number, we obtain 1100110 – the original value!

---

**Activity 4.1**

### The 2s complement technique

Calculate the 2s complement of each of the following binary numbers:

(a) 1101010

(b) 1000011

(c) 1110000

(d) 1010100

It is recommended that in each case you employ both of the methods introduced above.

---

In order to subtract one binary number from another, we can make use of 2s complement arithmetic. Let us suppose that we wish to perform the following calculation:

$$A - B = C.$$

Where A and B represent two binary numbers each comprising N bits. We simply calculate the 2s complement of B (we will refer to this as B') and then compute:

$$A + B'$$

In other words, by first taking the 2s complement of B, the subtraction of B from A can be performed using addition!! There is however one small complication – when performing subtraction operations, the result is sometimes negative. However, when we use the 2s complement approach the sign of the answer (positive/negative) may be determined from the value of the carry (overflow) that occurs. Let us take a couple of examples and see how this works in practice:

### Example 1: Calculate the binary subtraction 11001 – 10011, using the 2s complement approach

Before we begin, it is convenient to convert both these binary values to base 10 and see what answer we should obtain for the subtraction. Recall from Chapter 1 that 11001 equals 25 (base 10) and 10011 equals 19 (base 10). The subtraction is 25 - 19 = 6 and therefore in base 2 the answer that we obtain should equal 110. (For convenience, we may add two leading zeros so that the result comprises the same number of bits as the two original numbers, i.e. 00110).

Now let us try the 2s complement approach. In this question A = 11001 and B = 10011. We begin by finding the 2s complement of B (10011) which is 01101 (we will call this B'). We now add A and B' together, see Figure 4.4.

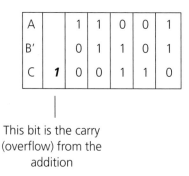

This bit is the carry
(overflow) from the
addition

**Figure 4.4:** Performing subtraction using 2s complement arithmetic

As may be seen, we obtain a result of 00110 with a carry (overflow) of one. If the overflow bit is a one, then this indicates that the result is positive – if there is no overflow (i.e. the carry/overflow bit is zero) then the result is negative.

Recall from above that when we performed this calculation in base 10, we obtained an answer of 6 (binary 110). Thus the 2s complement approach provides the correct result. (Note: to obtain the magnitude of the answer, we discard the overflow bit).

### Example 2: Calculate the binary subtraction 110010 – 111010, using the 2s complement approach

As with the previous example, it is instructive to convert both of these binary values to base 10 and see what answer we should obtain for the subtraction. Recall from Chapter 1, 110010 equals 50 (base 10) and 111010 equals 58 (base 10). The subtraction 50 - 58 = -8 (i.e. a negative answer).

Now let us try the 2s complement approach. In this question A = 110010 and B = 111010. We begin by finding the 2s complement of B (111010) which is 000110 (we will call this B'). We now add A and B' together, see Figure 4.5.

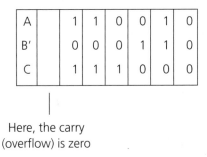

| A | 1 | 1 | 0 | 0 | 1 | 0 |
|---|---|---|---|---|---|---|
| B' | 0 | 0 | 0 | 1 | 1 | 0 |
| C | 1 | 1 | 1 | 0 | 0 | 0 |

Here, the carry
(overflow) is zero

**Figure 4.5:** Performing subtraction using 2s complement arithmetic

As may be seen, we obtain a result of 111000 with a carry (overflow) of zero. As shown above, this indicates that the result is a negative number.

Recall from above that when we performed this calculation in base 10, we obtained an answer with a magnitude of 8 (binary 1000), and negative in sign. However, the 2s complement method that we have used gives us an answer of 11100. Something seems to have gone wrong!

The answer that we have obtained is a negative value and as such, in order to find the actual magnitude (size) of the result we need to take its 2s complement. The 2s complement of 111000 is 001000 and in base 10 this equals 8. Thus the 2s complement technique has provided the correct answer.

For convenience, the overall technique is summarised in Figure 4.6 and an important point to remember about this method is that it permits both the addition and subtraction of binary integers to be performed by a single hardware unit that performs only addition operations.

## 4.3 Dealing with non-integer numbers

So far we have confined our discussions to the representation within a computer of positive and negative integers ('whole' numbers). In this section, we briefly consider ways in which we can represent and manipulate numbers that have a fractional/decimal component (e.g. 3.142). We begin by summarising some basic maths.

### A little mathematics: Exponents – base 10

Consider the following expression:

$3.24 \times 10^2$.

The power (2) is referred to as the exponent whilst the number appearing on the left-hand side (3.24) is called the mantissa. This expression evaluates as follows:

$3.24 \times 10^2 = 3.24 \times 100 = 324$.

An alternative way of viewing this is to say that the exponent (power to which 10 is raised) indicates the number of places the decimal point should be shifted (a positive exponent indicating that the decimal point should be moved to the right). Thus, in the case that the exponent is 2, the decimal point is shifted two places to the right and so 3.24 becomes 324. Similarly, consider 527.23456 x 10³. Here the exponent is 3 and therefore the decimal point is shifted three places, giving 527234.56.

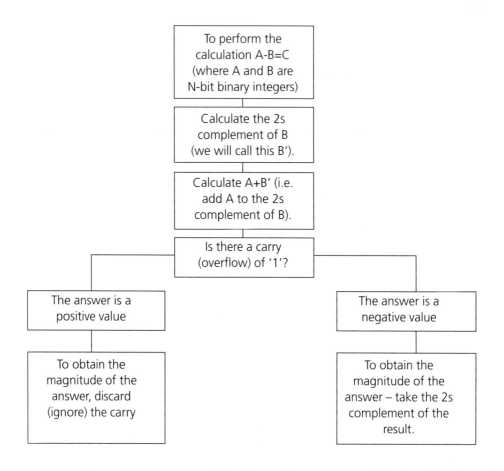

**Figure 4.6:** A summary of the 2s complement approach for the subtraction of two binary integers

**Subtraction using 2s complement arithmetic**

Perform the following binary subtractions using 2s complement arithmetic:

(a) 1010 – 0110

(b) 1100 – 1000

(c) 10011 – 11000

In the case that the exponent is negative (i.e. 10 raised to a negative power), the decimal point is shifted to the left. Consider, for example:

$327.24 \times 10^{-2}$

This evaluates to:

$$327.24 \times 10^{-2} = 327.24 \times \frac{1}{10^2} = 327.24 \times \frac{1}{100} = 3.2724$$

Alternatively, we can simply move the decimal point two places to the left so that 327.24 becomes 3.2724 (the decimal point is shifted to the left since the exponent is negative).

For convenience, in Table 4.1 we summarise the value of some positive and negative exponents of 10. Note that by definition any number that has an exponent of zero evaluates to 1 (e.g. $4^0=1$, $7^0=1$ and $10^0=1$).

| | | |
|---|---|---|
| $10^3$ | 10x10x10 | 1000 |
| $10^2$ | 10x10 | 100 |
| $10^1$ | 10 | 10 |
| $10^0$ | | 1 |
| $10^{-1}$ | $\frac{1}{10}$ | 0.1 |
| $10^{-2}$ | $\frac{1}{10 \times 10}$ | 0.01 |
| $10^{-3}$ | $\frac{1}{10 \times 10 \times 10}$ | 0.001 |

**Table 4.1:** Some positive and negative exponents of 10

Frequently, in science and engineering, numbers that have a fractional/decimal component (i.e. non-integer numbers) are expressed in scientific notation. This involves writing a number in the following form:

$M \times 10^e$

Where M represents the *mantissa* and e the *exponent*. M has a value that lies between 1 and 10. For example, consider the number 36,742. This may be expressed in scientific form as:

$3.6742 \times 10^4$

As may be seen, we have arranged for the mantissa to lie between one and ten and the exponent indicates that the decimal point will (when the expression is evaluated) shift the decimal point four places to the right.

## Activity 4.3

**Scientific form**

Express the following numbers in scientific form:

(a) 3,674

(b) 86.792

(c) 0.0034

## A little mathematics: Exponents – base 2

In the above discussion we considered numbers expressed in base 10. However, computers operate in base 2 and therefore in order to understand the way in which these machines are able to deal with non-integer values, we need to extend our discussion to encompass elementary base 2 arithmetic.

In Chapter 1, we introduced the binary number base but confined our discussion to integer values. However, as with base 10 numbers, binary numbers may also have fractional parts. For example, consider the binary value:

1101.101

This is a non-integer binary number and includes a '.' Since we are now working in the base 2 number system, this is referred to as a 'binary point' rather than as a 'decimal point' Recall from Chapter 1 that in the case of a binary number the 'column' values to the left of the binary point increase by factors of 2:

| 8s | 4s | 2s | 1s |
|----|----|----|----|
|    |    |    |    |

We now need to supplement this with the equivalent column values that lie to the right of the binary point. These are indicated below:

| Column values | 8s | 4s | 2s | 1s | 0.5s | 0.25s | 0.125s |
|---|---|---|---|---|---|---|---|
| Column values expressed as powers of 2 | $2^3$ | $2^2$ | $2^1$ | $2^0$ | $2^{-1}$ | $2^{-2}$ | $2^{-3}$ |
| Exemplar binary number (non-integer) | 1 | 1 | 0 | 1 | 1 | 0 | 1 |

From this table it is evident that the exemplar binary number 1101.101 converts to base 10 as:

8 + 4 + 1 + 0.5 + 0.125 = 13.625

Recall from the earlier point that in base 10, multiplying a number by 10 raised to some integer exponent (e.g. $4.36 \times 10^2$) results in the decimal point being shifted (the direction of shift and the number of places being determined by the sign and value of the exponent). This also occurs in base 2 – with one significant difference. Rather than using 10 raised to the power of some exponent, we use 2 raised to the power of an exponent. Thus, for example, to shift a binary point two places to the right we multiply by $2^2$, and to shift three places we multiply by $2^3$.

This matter can cause some confusion for when the decimal number 2 is converted to binary it is represented as 10, and we need to continually remember that we are working within the binary and NOT the decimal domain.

By way of example, consider the binary number 10101.1 and suppose that we wish to express this in such a way that the binary point lies immediately before (i.e. to the left) of the left-most bit (i.e. .101011). This task is illustrated in Figure 4.7.

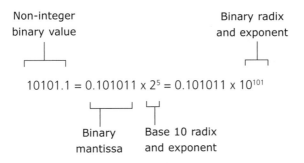

Non-integer
binary value

Binary radix
and exponent

$$10101.1 = 0.101011 \times 2^5 = 0.101011 \times 10^{101}$$

Binary
mantissa

Base 10 radix
and exponent

**Figure 4.7:** Changing the format of a binary number. Note: the term 'radix' is commonly used when referring to the number which is raised to the integer power (in this case it is the base 10 value 2 (=10 in base 2).

In scientific notation (referred to above), the number is said to be 'normalised', meaning that the mantissa lies between 1 and 9.999…. In a similar way, binary numbers can also be normalised by writing them in the format used in Figure 4.7. There is one difference between the normalisation of base 10 numbers (as adopted by scientists and engineers) and the normalisation of binary numbers. This relates to the range of values within which the mantissa must lie. In base 10 this range is limited to being between 1 and 9.9999…, in base 2 the range is from binary 0.1 to 0.1111… (which corresponds in base 10 to 0.5 to 1).

**Activity 4.4**

**Normalising binary numbers**

Express the following binary numbers in normalised form:

(a) 1101.1

(b) 100010.01

(c) 1.001001

Having briefly reviewed the underlying mathematics, we can now turn our attention to the storage of non-integer numbers (i.e. real numbers with a fractional/decimal component) within a computer.

Perhaps the most obvious way of storing numbers of this type is to employ a binary point that has a fixed position within the number. For example, consider the use of 8 bits (one byte) for the storage of such numbers. As illustrated in Figure 4.8, we can assume that the binary point is always located at a certain position – we have arbitrarily assumed that this is midway (i.e. between the 4th and 5th bits).

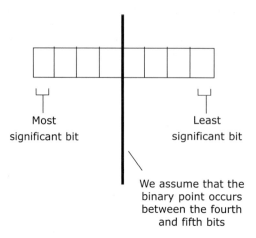

We assume that the
binary point occurs
between the fourth
and fifth bits

**Figure 4.8:** The use of a binary point that is located at a fixed (pre-defined)
location within a binary number. We do not need to include the actual binary
point ('.') within the number, as we know where it occurs.

This provides a very simple approach to the representation of non-integer numbers and, for
example, numbers represented in this way can be added together using the same hardware
employed for the addition of integer numbers.

Unfortunately, there are also disadvantages to this approach. For example, consider an 8-bit
number that employs the fixed binary point scheme, and let us continue to assume that the
point is located between the 4th and 5th bits. The largest value that can be represented clearly
occurs when all the bits are set to a '1' (i.e. 1111.1111). In base 10 this corresponds to
15.9375. Therefore, this approach enables the 8 bits to represent numbers in the range 0 to
15.9375. Recall that when 8 bits are used to represent an unsigned integer they may indicate
values in the range 0 to 255. Consequently, the fixed binary point scheme reduces the
maximum range of values that may be represented, and in order to increase this range we are
forced to increase the number of bits that comprise the number.

Although increasing the number of bits provides a possible solution, it is certainly non-optimal,
especially because we often wish to represent extremely large (or extremely small) numbers.
Consider the scientist working at the sub-atomic level who wishes to perform computations on
quantities such as the charge and mass of electrons and protons, and the astrophysicist whose
computations involve the masses of stars and their distance apart. To cater for these extreme
cases via the fixed binary point scheme, a large number of bits would be required and often
these would remain unused. For example, when used to represent sub-atomic measurements
the numbers to the right of the binary point (i.e. able to represent small values) would be most
relevant. Conversely, for the astrophysicist, the numbers to the left of the binary point
(enabling the representation of large values) would be crucial.

**Activity 4.5**

**The fixed binary point scheme**

The radius of the moon is approximately 1,737km. By converting this number to
binary (or otherwise), determine the number of bits needed for its representation as
an unsigned integer.

A more effective and versatile means of representing non-integer numbers is to use the 'normalised floating point' format. This follows (and builds on) the approach outlined in the maths review presented earlier in this section. Consider the binary number 1100110.1. As we have discussed, this can be represented in the form:

$$0.11001101 \times 10^{111}$$

This is commonly referred to as the 'normalised floating-point' format and can be stored within a computer by simply assigning bits to represent the mantissa and the exponent. Note: the radix is *always* 2 (i.e. binary 10) and therefore we do not need to include it within the number's representation.

In Figure 4.9(a) we illustrate how a normalised floating-point number may be represented. This format does not accommodate both positive and negative numbers, and this deficiency can be overcome by including a sign bit, as shown in Figure 4.9(b).

One further complication arises in that not only must we accommodate positive and negative values of the mantissa, but we must also make provision for positive and negative exponent values. This can be achieved in several ways (for example by means of a sign bit, or by using the 2s complement scheme described previously). However, a different scheme is normally employed and this involves the use of a 'biased' exponent. This approach operates as follows:

- We add to any exponent that we wish to represent a value ($k$) that usually equals $2^{n-1}$.
  Here, $n$ represents the number of bits designated to the representation of the exponent.

This can be readily understood by means of a simple example. Let us suppose that we assign 3 bits for the representation of the exponent (i.e. n=3). The value of $k$ is given by $2^{3-1} = 2^2 = 4$ and this value is added to any exponent that we wish to represent. The process is illustrated in Table 4.2. As may be seen from this table we have mapped each of the exponents that we may wish to represent in such a way that they are recorded as positive values.

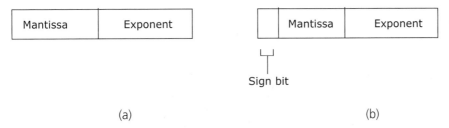

(a)                                                      (b)

**Figure 4.9:** In (a) we illustrate a scheme for representing normalised floating
point numbers. This does not make provision for accommodating both
positive and negative values. However, this may be accomplished through
the inclusion of a 'sign' bit as indicated in (b).

Many processors are unable to deal directly with floating-point numbers and therefore two possible approaches may be adopted:

- We develop programs that undertake floating-point arithmetic
- We add special hardware, specifically a 'floating-point co-processor' which is a special integrated circuit designed to carry out floating-point arithmetic.

| Exponent (that we wish to represent) | Biased exponent (that we store) |
|:---:|:---:|
| -4 | 0 |
| -3 | 1 |
| -2 | 2 |
| -1 | 3 |
| 0 | 4 |
| 1 | 5 |
| 2 | 6 |
| 3 | 7 |

**Table 4.2** The 'biased' exponent approach for a simple situation in which we record the exponent using three bits. Here, $k=4$.

## 4.4 Character representation: ASCII

So far, we have confined our discussion to the representation of numbers within a computer. However, for many applications (such as a word-processing activity) the computer must also be able to handle symbols (such as characters of the alphabet, punctuation characters, and the symbols that we use to represent numbers). As we have seen, the digital world knows of only two states – logic high and logic low (binary 1 and binary 0). Consequently, in order to process characters we must represent them numerically as binary codes.

The technique most widely employed for the representation of symbols is based on the use of ASCII codes (ASCII is an acronym for the 'American Standard Code for Information Interchange'). This standard was originally developed by the American National Standards Institute. Traditionally, it is based on the use of seven bits to represent each character, as illustrated in Table 4.3. (An alternative coding scheme is known as EBCDIC (Extended Binary Coded Decimal Interchange Code).)

Here, for example, the character 'A' is represented by the hexadecimal number 41. The character 'B' is represented by the hexadecimal number 42. Non-symbolic functions (control functions) are also represented – for example, the 'return' key by the hexadecimal number 0D.

| Decimal | Hex | Binary | Value |
|---|---|---|---|
| 000 | 000 | 00000000 | NUL (Null char.) |
| 001 | 001 | 00000001 | SOH (Start of Header) |
| 002 | 002 | 00000010 | STX (Start of Text) |
| 003 | 003 | 00000011 | ETX (End of Text) |
| 004 | 004 | 00000100 | EOT (End of Transmission) |
| 005 | 005 | 00000101 | ENQ (Enquiry) |
| 006 | 006 | 00000110 | ACK (Acknowledgement) |
| 007 | 007 | 00000111 | BEL (Bell) |
| 008 | 008 | 00001000 | BS (Backspace) |
| 009 | 009 | 00001001 | HT (Horizontal Tab) |
| 010 | 00A | 00001010 | LF (Line Feed) |
| 011 | 00B | 00001011 | VT (Vertical Tab) |
| 012 | 00C | 00001100 | FF (Form Feed) |
| 013 | 00D | 00001101 | CR (Carriage Return) |
| 014 | 00E | 00001110 | SO (Serial In) |
| 015 | 00F | 00001111 | SI (Serial Out) |
| 016 | 010 | 00010000 | DLE (Data Link Escape) |
| 017 | 011 | 00010001 | DC1 (XON) (Device Control 1) |
| 018 | 012 | 00010010 | DC2 (Device Control 2) |
| 019 | 013 | 00010011 | DC3 (XOFF) (Device Control 3) |
| 020 | 014 | 00010100 | DC4 (Device Control 4) |
| 021 | 015 | 00010101 | NAK (Negative Acknowledgement) |
| 022 | 016 | 00010110 | SYN (Synchronous Idle) |
| 023 | 017 | 00010111 | ETB (End of Trans. Block) |
| 024 | 018 | 00011000 | CAN (Cancel) |
| 025 | 019 | 00011001 | EM |
| 026 | 01A | 00011010 | SUB |
| 027 | 01B | 00011011 | ESC (Escape) |
| 028 | 01C | 00011100 | FS (File Separator) |
| 029 | 01D | 00011101 | GS |
| 030 | 01E | 00011110 | RS (Request to Send) |
| 031 | 01F | 00011111 | US |
| 032 | 020 | 00100000 | SP (Space) |
| 033 | 021 | 00100001 | ! |

.../cont

**Table 4.3:** The ASCII codes

| Decimal | Hex | Binary | Value |
|---------|-----|----------|-------|
| 034 | 022 | 00100010 | " |
| 035 | 023 | 00100011 | # |
| 036 | 024 | 00100100 | $ |
| 037 | 025 | 00100101 | % |
| 038 | 026 | 00100110 | & |
| 039 | 027 | 00100111 | ' |
| 040 | 028 | 00101000 | ( |
| 041 | 029 | 00101001 | ) |
| 042 | 02A | 00101010 | * |
| 043 | 02B | 00101011 | + |
| 044 | 02C | 00101100 | , |
| 045 | 02D | 00101101 | - |
| 046 | 02E | 00101110 | . |
| 047 | 02F | 00101111 | / |
| 048 | 030 | 00110000 | 0 |
| 049 | 031 | 00110001 | 1 |
| 050 | 032 | 00110010 | 2 |
| 051 | 033 | 00110011 | 3 |
| 052 | 034 | 00110100 | 4 |
| 053 | 035 | 00110101 | 5 |
| 054 | 036 | 00110110 | 6 |
| 055 | 037 | 00110111 | 7 |
| 056 | 038 | 00111000 | 8 |
| 057 | 039 | 00111001 | 9 |
| 058 | 03A | 00111010 | : |
| 059 | 03B | 00111011 | ; |
| 060 | 03C | 00111100 | < |
| 061 | 03D | 00111101 | = |
| 062 | 03E | 00111110 | > |
| 063 | 03F | 00111111 | ? |
| 064 | 040 | 01000000 | @ |
| 065 | 041 | 01000001 | A |
| 066 | 042 | 01000010 | B |
| 067 | 043 | 01000011 | C |
| 068 | 044 | 01000100 | D |
| 069 | 045 | 01000101 | E |
| 070 | 046 | 01000110 | F |
| 071 | 047 | 01000111 | G |
| 072 | 048 | 01001000 | H |
| 073 | 049 | 01001001 | I |
| 074 | 04A | 01001010 | J |
| 075 | 04B | 01001011 | K |
| 076 | 04C | 01001100 | L |
| 077 | 04D | 01001101 | M |
| 078 | 04E | 01001110 | N |
| 079 | 04F | 01001111 | O |
| 080 | 050 | 01010000 | P |

| Decimal | Hex | Binary | Value |
|---------|-----|----------|-------|
| 081 | 051 | 01010001 | Q |
| 082 | 052 | 01010010 | R |
| 083 | 053 | 01010011 | S |
| 084 | 054 | 01010100 | T |
| 085 | 055 | 01010101 | U |
| 086 | 056 | 01010110 | V |
| 087 | 057 | 01011111 | W |
| 088 | 058 | 01011000 | X |
| 089 | 059 | 01011001 | Y |
| 090 | 05A | 01011010 | Z |
| 091 | 05B | 01011011 | [ |
| 092 | 05C | 01011100 | \ |
| 093 | 05D | 01011101 | ] |
| 094 | 05E | 01011110 | ^ |
| 095 | 05F | 01011111 | _ |
| 096 | 060 | 01100000 | ` |
| 097 | 061 | 01100001 | a |
| 098 | 062 | 01100010 | b |
| 099 | 063 | 01100011 | c |
| 100 | 064 | 01100100 | d |
| 101 | 065 | 01100101 | e |
| 102 | 066 | 01100110 | f |
| 103 | 067 | 01100111 | g |
| 104 | 068 | 01101000 | h |
| 105 | 069 | 01101001 | i |
| 106 | 06A | 01101010 | j |
| 107 | 06B | 01101011 | k |
| 108 | 06C | 01101100 | l |
| 109 | 06D | 01101101 | m |
| 110 | 06E | 01101110 | n |
| 111 | 06F | 01101111 | o |
| 112 | 070 | 01110000 | p |
| 113 | 071 | 01110001 | q |
| 114 | 072 | 01110010 | r |
| 115 | 073 | 01110011 | s |
| 116 | 074 | 01110100 | t |
| 117 | 075 | 01110101 | u |
| 118 | 076 | 01110110 | v |
| 119 | 077 | 01110111 | w |
| 120 | 078 | 01111000 | x |
| 121 | 079 | 01111001 | y |
| 122 | 07A | 01111010 | z |
| 123 | 07B | 01111011 | { |
| 124 | 07C | 01111100 | | |
| 125 | 07D | 01111101 | } |
| 126 | 07E | 01111110 | ~ |
| 127 | 07F | 01111111 | DEL |

**Table 4.3:** The ASCII codes

The use of a 7-bit code enables $2^7 = 128$ different characters, symbols and control codes to be represented. Although this is sufficient for use in many countries, problems occur when we seek to embrace countries that employ alternative alphabets. As a result, additional bits are needed to support larger numbers of symbols.

**Activity 4.6**

**ASCII codes**

Write out in hexadecimal the ASCII codes used to represent the word 'Computer'.

## 4.5 Representation of data and instructions

In previous sections, we discussed the representation of instructions (op-codes), operands and data within a computer. As we have seen, operands and data may take on various forms. For example:

- An operand (or data value) may represent **an address** that is to be acted on in some way by the op-code
- An operand (or data value) may represent **a numerical unsigned integer value** on which arithmetic and/or logical operations are to be performed
- An operand (or data value) may represent **a numerical signed integer value** on which arithmetic and/or logical operations are to be performed
- An operand (or data value) may represent **a numerical value represented in normalised floating-point form** on which arithmetic and/or logical operations are to be performed
- An operand (or data value) may represent **an ASCII code.**

The processor is simply an electronic 'machine' – it has no intelligence and simply obeys a set of machine code instructions. Consequently, the processor has no 'common sense' or 'instinctive knowledge' concerning the task to be carried out, and we certainly cannot assume that the processor has any understanding of the meaning that we ascribe to operands and data. The programmer must therefore define the way an operand is to be handled.

For example, the op-code value defines the instruction that is to be obeyed, and may also define the significance of the operand (e.g. a certain op-code value may indicate that the contents of a particular memory address (that is defined by the operand associated with the op-code) are to be incremented).

An op-code may allow the contents of a particular register to be written to a certain address (the address being defined by the operand associated with the op-code). As will be discussed in Chapter 6, this may result in the value written to the address being sent to a peripheral device, such as a printer. In this case, the value written to the address would typically be an ASCII code that would be interpreted by the printer and acted upon. In this scenario, the processor has no knowledge that the data value written to the address represents a symbol – to the processor it is simply another numerical value. The actual meaning ascribed to this value is determined by the form of additional hardware systems.

## 4.6 Interrupts

In our previous discussions we have focused on the ability of the processor to read a series of instructions and data from memory, execute the instructions, and return to memory the results of the operations carried out. In this way, the processor executes a 'program'. There is little value in this activity unless it is possible for the processor to communicate with its surroundings. Consequently, a major aspect of computer operation concerns its ability to input instructions and data from the physical world and output the results of the computational process. (This input/output activity also includes, for example, reading from and writing to storage media such as the hard disk). In this section we focus our attention on aspects of the input process, and in this context we will introduce the 'interrupt' system.

To best understand how interrupts work it is helpful to use an analogy. Imagine that while you are reading this page somebody knocks at your door, or calls you on the phone. In short, they 'interrupt' you in your studies. What would you do? Perhaps before answering the phone, or going to the door, you would quickly write down on a piece of paper the number of the page that you are currently reading, or even put a mark in the margin of the book to indicate the sentence you are up to. In this way, when you have finished talking to the caller on the phone, or dealing with the person at the door, you can most easily pick up from where you left off. Perhaps if you do not write down the page number you will find it difficult to quickly return to your studies and pick up from where you left off – you may simply have forgotten exactly where you were up to!

Input to a modern computer is strongly based upon an interrupt system, and the underlying principle of this approach can be readily understood by reference to the above analogy. In Figure 4.10 we illustrate a processor that is linked to main memory. In this diagram we also represent an input device. This could take the form of, for example, a keyboard – but to simplify matters we will suppose that it is a switch. This switch is connected to a special connection on the processor chip, and when pressed it generates a signal that causes the processor to detect an 'interrupt condition' (i.e. the logic state of the interrupt pin is momentarily changed).

We assume that before the switch is pressed, the processor is executing some program. This is equivalent in the analogy given above to you studying your notes. We press the switch and this causes an 'interrupt' signal to be applied to the special connection on the processor (this is equivalent to the phone ringing, or somebody knocking at the door). It causes the processor to stop executing its current program, and to execute a different program which we have created to tell the processor what to do when the interrupt occurs (i.e. when the switch is pressed). This program is called an 'interrupt service routine' (ISR). Once the processor has executed this special program, it will go back and continue with the task (program) it was undertaking prior to the switch being pressed. The question is: how does the processor know where it was up to in the execution of this program when the interruption occurred? Using our analogy again, this is equivalent to returning to your studies and picking up from where you left off; you might have noted the number of the page that you were studying before you were disturbed from your work. In the case of a processor, when it experiences an interrupt it stores the contents of all its registers in a designated place in memory. Once it has serviced the interrupt, it reads back from memory the register values that it previously stored. In this way, it can pick up from exactly where it left off. Had it not saved the register contents before servicing the interrupt, then they would have been over-written when executing the interrupt servicing routine and consequently lost. Obviously, this would have meant that, having serviced the interrupt, the processor would have had no indication of the state it was in prior to undertaking this task (e.g. the contents of the program counter would have been lost). The events that take place when an interrupt occurs are summarised in Figure 4.11.

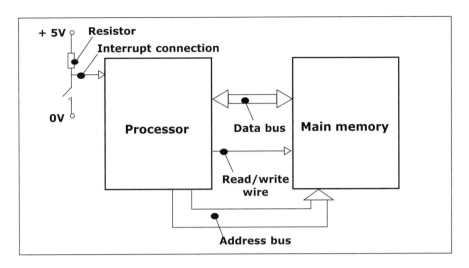

**Figure 4.10:** Showing the application of an interrupt to a processor.  Normally, with the switch open, the interrupt connection is at ~5V – a logic high. When the switch is pressed, the interrupt connection changes from being at ~5V to being at 0V – i.e.  it goes from a logic-high to a logic low. Subsequently, it returns to the logic high state.  The brief change to the logic-low state causes the processor to follow the 'interrupt sequence'.

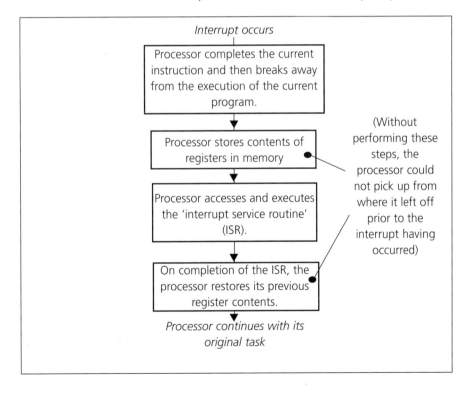

**Figure 4.11:** Illustrating the events that take place when an interrupt occurs. Note that if the contents of the registers (i.e.  the 'context' of the current program) are not saved prior to the interrupt being serviced, then it is not possible to resume normal activity once the interrupt service routine has run to completion.

## 4.7 Interrupt priorities

Here, we introduce a slight complication to the model described in the previous section and for a moment will return to the analogy used above. Imagine that you are studying these notes when somebody knocks at your door, i.e. causes an 'interrupt'. You write down where you are up to in your studies, and then respond to the person at the door. While you are talking, the phone rings. This represents a second interrupt occurring while you are 'servicing' the first. Do you stop talking to the person at the door and answer the phone, or do you ignore the phone until you have finished dealing with the person at the door? Here, you need to 'prioritise' the tasks. Perhaps the person at the door has an extremely serious and important message. Your discussion could be so vital that you may choose to ignore answering the phone until you have finished talking to this person. Alternatively, the person talking to you at the door may simply be trying to sell you a vacuum-cleaner, and you are expecting an extremely important phone call! In this case, you would break off from talking and answer the phone.

This analogy applies to computers. It is possible (and often happens) that while the processor is servicing an interrupt, other interrupts occur. There are all sorts of peripheral devices able to generate interrupts. Examples include the hard disk drive, the CD drive, the keyboard, and the mouse. In software we (or rather the operating system running on your computer) assign 'priorities' to all these possible sources of interrupt. If, when servicing an interrupt, a higher priority interrupt occurs (i.e. a more important interrupt) then the processor will break off from servicing the current interrupt, store the status of all its registers in a designated place in memory, and then service the higher priority interrupt. Once this has been dealt with, the processor will restore the contents of its registers and continue to service the lower-priority interrupt. Once this has been done, it will return to executing its original program. This is illustrated in Figure 4.12.

Computer technology is frequently used in control applications. Computer systems used specifically for control are often called 'embedded controllers'. Such systems respond to externally generated interrupts, and when an interrupt occurs from a particular source, a particular part of an interrupt service routine is executed. Suppose that we have an embedded controller in an aircraft, and that this controller is responsible for a whole range of functions. Two of its functions will be as follows:

- Monitor cabin temperature and adjust this temperature when necessary
- Monitor aircraft engines and continuously measure hydraulic pressures, temperatures, and of course check for fire.

Clearly, only a very poorly designed aircraft would make a single embedded controller responsible for both routine and critical measurement, but for ease of discussion we will assume this to be the case.

Suppose that a fire broke out in one of the engines; naturally, it is critical that the pilot be informed of this (via an alarm) immediately. However, at the time that the fire breaks out, the processor may be occupied in monitoring and adjusting the cabin temperature. This may keep it busy for some tens of seconds – clearly, we do not want to delay the pilot receiving the alarm simply because the embedded controller is busy dealing with passenger comfort! This provides us with an example of how interrupts can be used.

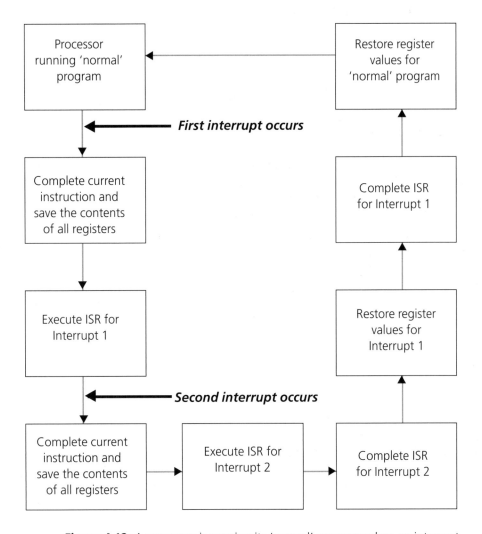

**Figure 4.12:** A processor is running its 'normal' program when an interrupt
occurs (Interrupt 1). It stores registers (the 'context' of this 'normal' program)
and begins to run the 'interrupt service routine' (ISR) for Interrupt 1. Whilst
this is executing, a second higher priority interrupt occurs (Interrupt 2). The
processor breaks off from servicing Interrupt 1, stores registers (the 'context'
of the interrupt service routine for this interrupt) and runs the ISR for Interrupt
2. On completion it restores the context of Interrupt 1 and runs the ISR for
this interrupt. Once this is completed, it restores the context of its original
('normal') program and returns to running this code (from the point at which
it broke off when Interrupt 1 occurred).

Special 'transducers' (devices that convert physical stimuli such as temperature and pressure
into electrical signals) are fitted to the engines. When critical conditions occur, such as over-
temperature, lack of hydraulic pressure, or fire, the relevant transducer is able to generate an
interrupt signal that is passed to the processor in the embedded controller. Additional
hardware informs the processor as to the source of the interrupt. Thus, the processor may be
monitoring and controlling the cabin temperature when it receives an interrupt from, for
example, the transducer monitoring engine temperature. It immediately breaks off from what
it is doing and executes a special interrupt service routine whereby it will provide a signal to the

pilot warning of over-temperature in a particular engine. As it is doing this, suppose that fire breaks out! Since we have instructed the processor that the fire condition is of greater importance (i.e. a higher priority) than the over-temperature condition, the processor will break off from what it is doing and immediately execute another interrupt service routine that will provide the pilot with an alarm indicating that a highly critical condition has occurred. Perhaps as part of this interrupt service routine, the embedded controller would also activate fire-extinguishers in an attempt to put out the fire. However – as an aside – it is interesting to consider whether we would allow the embedded controller to automatically activate the fire extinguishers. The problem is that transducers can provide incorrect information, and furthermore, software may be flawed. We therefore have to decide whether we are going to trust the computer system or whether we want to keep the pilot in the loop and give him a moment to glance out of the window to verify that there are in fact plumes of smoke emanating from the engine!

**Activity 4.7**

### A disadvantage of interrupts

Identify one disadvantage associated with the use of interrupts.

Below we briefly introduce two general categories of interrupt. These are as follows:

- **Non-maskable interrupts.** These are interrupts that can occur at any time and cannot be disabled. Non-maskable interrupts are therefore used for important events such as the monitoring of engine conditions in the example described above

- **Maskable interrupts.** These are interrupts that can be disabled (ignored) when more critical events are taking place. By way of a humorous analogy, suppose that in the case of the embedded controller used on an aircraft we also extend its duties to include monitoring the buttons used by passengers to attract the attention of the cabin crew. Naturally, should an engine fire break out, we would want the embedded controller to deal exclusively with this critical event and not be distracted by having to inform cabin crew that a particular passenger wants attention as their supply of peanuts is running low! In such a case, we would obviously wish to disable interrupts generated from non-important (non-critical) sources to allow the embedded controller to deal exclusively with interrupts occurring in respect of life-threatening conditions. Signals from the engines would – in this analogy – give rise to non-maskable interrupts, and those from passengers and the cabin temperature control system would make use of maskable interrupts.

The elegance of the interrupt technique becomes more apparent when we contrast this method with an alternative approach that involves 'polling'. Let us briefly return to the analogy used above and modify it a little. Suppose that while studying at home you are expecting a visitor to arrive. We will assume that from the location in which you are working, you cannot hear the doorbell ring. As a result (and because you do not want to miss the caller when he or she arrives), you must regularly break off from your studies and go to the door to check if anybody is waiting there. Here, you will need to strike a careful balance, as illustrated in Figure 4.13.

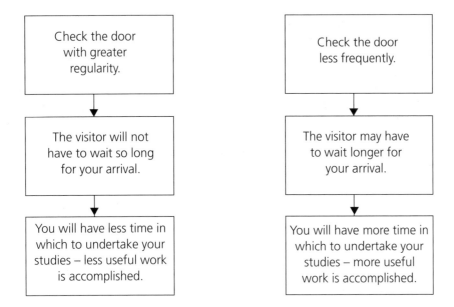

**Figure 4.13:** Balancing the time taken for checking if an event has occurred against the need to perform routine work

The process of checking to see if an event has occurred is referred to (in the context of computing) as 'polling'. As can be seen from Figure 4.13, increasing the frequency at which polling takes place reduces the average time for which the visitor must wait, but also reduces the amount of routine work (in this analogy studying) that you are able to achieve. This problem is exacerbated when we increase the number of devices that must be polled. In the case of the current analogy, suppose that the visitor may arrive at one of ten or twenty possible doors (you have a large house!). You must now poll each of these doors at regular intervals. This occupies more time and so detracts from the routine work that you are able to perform.

The use of the interrupt approach makes routine polling unnecessary. The processor does not have to check to see if a particular event has occurred – it is notified via an interrupt signal.

Many computer architectures handle interrupts by means of an 'interrupt controller'. This approach is illustrated in Figure 4.14. In this simplified diagram we show a processor connected to an interrupt controller via the address and data bus. The interrupt controller is also able to generate an interrupt signal that is applied to the 'interrupt request' connection on the processor. Four possible sources of interrupt are also shown. This simplified model operates as follows:

- The processor writes to a register(s) located within the interrupt controller and assigns priorities to each of the four possible sources of interrupt. This task is carried out when the processor 'configures' the interrupt controller. We assume that a lower priority interrupt cannot 'interrupt' a higher priority source of interrupt.

- When an interrupt occurs, the interrupt controller verifies that this is the highest priority interrupt currently being handled. If this is the case, then the interrupt controller applies an interrupt signal to the processor. The processor completes its current instruction, saves the contents of its registers in a designated area of memory, and executes the interrupt service routine. One of the first tasks carried out by the interrupt service routine is to communicate with the interrupt controller and identify which one of the four possible interrupt sources is responsible for the interrupt that has occurred (i.e. which of these four sources is requiring attention). The processor then carries out the appropriate task(s)

- If, while the processor is servicing an interrupt, a higher priority interrupt occurs, then the interrupt controller will notify the processor of this event by generating a further interrupt signal

- If, while the processor is servicing an interrupt, a lower priority interrupt occurs, then this will not be acted upon until the higher priority interrupt has been serviced.

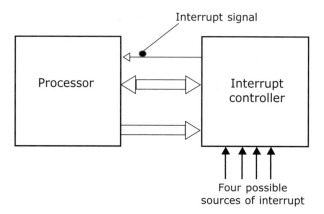

**Figure 4.14:** A simplified model of a processor connected to an interrupt controller integrated circuit. Four possible sources of interrupt are indicated.

In the above discussions, we have assumed that when an interrupt occurs the processor completes the current instruction and then automatically saves the contents of all of its registers to a designated region in memory. However, not all processors save registers automatically, and therefore for certain processors the saving of registers is a task that must be carried out by the programmer prior to entering the interrupt service routine.

## 4.8 Summary

We are able to represent various forms of numbers and symbols within a computer. In this chapter we have focused on the storage of signed integers and numbers that have a fractional component.

In relation to the representation of the former, we have introduced the use of 2s complement arithmetic, and for the latter the normalised floating-point approach has been described. Although the processor operates wholly on numbers and manipulates these numbers by means of arithmetic and logical operations, we can also represent symbols (such as the letters of the alphabet) within the computer. Here, we make use of codes that associate with each symbol a numerical value, and the processor has no knowledge of the actual meaning that we ascribe to these codes.

In the second part of this chapter we have introduced the polling and interrupt techniques that may be used to facilitate communication between peripheral devices and the processor. Although the interrupt approach has several advantageous characteristics, it is important to remember that each time an interrupt occurs the contents of the processor registers must be saved prior to executing the interrupt service routine (ISR), and restored upon exit from this routine. This process occupies a finite time and represents an undesirable (but unavoidable) overhead that is associated with interrupt handling.

# 4.9 Review questions

**Question 4.1** Write down the 2s complement of the binary number 110100.

**Question 4.2** What do we mean when we refer to a number's exponent?

**Question 4.3** Suppose that you determine the 2s complement of a binary number and that you the repeat the process on the value obtained (i.e. you take the 2s complement twice). What is the overall result?

**Question 4.4** State one advantage associated with the use of the 2s complement representation of an integer.

**Question 4.5** Following an interrupt, state the events that immediately occur.

**Question 4.6** State the meaning of the abbreviation NMI.

**Question 4.7** Within the context of computing, what is meant by the term 'polling'?

**Question 4.8** Distinguish between maskable and non-maskable interrupts.

**Question 4.9** State the meaning of the abbreviations ASCII and EBCDIC.

**Question 4.10** With reference to Table 4.3 determine what mathematical operation should be performed on an upper-case letter (A, B, C, etc.) to convert it into its lower-case equivalent (a, b, c, etc.).

# 4.10 Feedback on activities

**Activity 4.1: The 2s complement technique**

(a) 0010110

(b) 0111101

(c) 0010000

(d) 0101100

**Activity 4.2: Subtraction using 2s complement arithmetic**

(a) 1010 – 0110 becomes 1010 + 1010 = 10100. The left-most bit is the carry (overflow) and since an overflow of '1' has occurred, the answer is positive. The overflow is discarded and the answer is 0100.

(b) 1100 – 1000 becomes 1100 + 1000 = 10100. The left-most bit is the carry (overflow) and since an overflow has occurred, the result is positive. The overflow is discarded and the answer is 0100.

(c) 10011 – 11000 becomes 10011 + 01000 = 11011. Here, there is no carry (or, more accurately, the carry bit is zero) and therefore the result is deemed to be negative. To get the magnitude of the result, we take the 2s complement of 11011 which is 00101.

### Activity 4.3: Scientific form

(a) $3.674 \times 10^3$          (b) $8.6792 \times 10^1 = 8.6792 \times 10$          (c) $3.4 \times 10^{-3}$

### Activity 4.4: Normalising binary numbers

(a) $1101.1 = 0.11011 \times 2^4 = 0.11011 \times 10^{100}$

(b) $100010.01 = 0.10001001 \times 2^6 = 0.10001001 \times 10^{110}$

(c) $1.001001 = 0.1001001 \times 2 = 0.1001001 \times 10^1$

### Activity 4.5: The fixed binary point scheme

1,737 converts to 11011001001. Thus 11 bits are needed.

Note: the following approach is included for interest.

Alternatively, for those who enjoy a little mathematics (!) we can regard the binary column values as forming a geometric progression: 1,2,4,8,16,12... The first value (a) in the progression is 1 and the common ratio (r) is 2. Basic mathematics indicates that the sum $(S_n)$ of such a series is given by:

$$S_n = \frac{a\left(1-r^n\right)}{1-r}$$

We can therefore write:

$$S_n = \frac{a\left(1-r^n\right)}{1-r} \geq 1737$$

Thus:

$$\frac{1\left(1-2^n\right)}{1-2} \geq 1737$$

Solving for $n$, we obtain $n \geq 10.7$ – indicating that 11 bits will be needed.

### Activity 4.6: ASCII codes
(Remember that the first character is a capital letter!) 43 6F 6D 70 75 74 65 72

### Activity 4.7: A disadvantage of interrupts

When an interrupt occurs, the contents of the processors' registers must be saved prior to the execution of the ISR. At the end of the execution of this program, the contents of the registers must be restored. Saving and restoring registers involves a number of memory access operations and therefore occupies a finite time. In the case that interrupts occur with great frequency, this time becomes significant and detracts from the amount of 'useful work' carried out by the processor (i.e. although saving and restoring registers is a vital exercise, it represents a 'housekeeping' task and is therefore viewed as an 'overhead' associated with interrupt handling).

# CHAPTER 5

# Storage devices and data transfer issues

## OVERVIEW

The modern computer uses various forms of secondary storage media – such as the hard disk, the floppy disk, the CD-ROM. In this chapter, we focus upon distinguishing between these different forms of storage device. We also introduce serial and parallel communication techniques, and distinguish between synchronous and asynchronous buses.

**Learning outcomes** On completion of this chapter you should be able to:

- Identify two main categories of storage devices

- Describe the main characteristics of primary and secondary storage devices

- Describe the underlying principles of operation of key storage devices

- Discuss issues relating to serial and parallel data transfer

- Discuss issues relating to synchronous and asynchronous communication.

## 5.1 Introduction

Modern computers employ a hierarchy of storage devices which may be broadly divided into two categories: 'primary' and 'secondary' systems. In Section 5.2, we distinguish between these two general classes of digital storage, and consider the reasons for incorporating different types of media within a computer. In fact, these devices differ in terms of the speed at which they are able to support read and write operations, and in the cost per unit of storage capacity. Additionally, unlike secondary storage devices, primary storage systems (such as main memory (RAM)) generally lose their contents when the power is removed.

In Section 5.3 we discuss the underlying principles of operation of two forms of secondary storage device, specifically the hard and floppy disk drives. These record digital data through the magnetisation of a material, and in Section 5.4 we turn our attention to devices that use optical storage techniques.

In Section 5.5 we distinguish between serial and parallel interfaces. In the case of the former, data transfer is achieved by transmitting bits sequentially along a single interconnect (transmission medium such as a wire). In contrast, parallel interfacing enables groups of bits to be transferred at the same time (in parallel) via a set of interconnections. Finally, in Section 5.6 we introduce asynchronous and synchronous communication techniques.

## 5.2 Primary and secondary storage: capacity, speed and cost

We can loosely divide memory and other storage facilities into two broad categories. These offer 'primary storage' and 'secondary storage' capabilities. Primary storage refers to systems from which the processor is able to directly read instructions and data, and to which it is able to directly return the results of its computation. In short, primary storage devices are an integral part of the fetch/execute cycle. Both main memory (RAM) and cache memory represent forms of primary storage device. As discussed in Chapter 3, cache and main memory differ in terms of speed and the cost per unit of storage capacity. They are both able to directly support read and write operations carried out by the processor, but do not retain their contents once the machine is turned off. Devices such as flash memory, the hard disk, floppy disk, and writable optical disk, provide us with examples of secondary storage devices. These offer larger storage capacity than primary storage devices, but operate more slowly. When the power to the machine is turned off, these types of storage device retain their contents. On the modern computer, the hard disk forms the main secondary storage device. The performance of the hard disk has increased dramatically over the last twenty years: not only have hard disk drives become physically much smaller, but they are able to store much more data and support read and write operations at higher speeds. Computers employ a hierarchy of storage media. Devices used at each level within this hierarchy differ in various respects, especially in terms of:

- **Storage capacity**
- **Speed** at which they are able to support read and write operations
- **Price** per unit of storage capacity.

In general, storage devices that operate at higher speed (i.e. that support shorter access times and demonstrate low access latency) are more expensive. As a result, the computer designer attempts to develop a storage hierarchy that offers satisfactory performance at a reasonable price. In Figure 5.1 we illustrate such a storage hierarchy.

As may be seen from this illustration, the registers within the processor operate at the highest speed – their storage capacity is limited to a number of bytes.  Indeed, significantly increasing the number of registers located on the processor chip would be likely to compromise their overall speed of operation (i.e. increase the access latency).  Cache memory appears next in the storage hierarchy.  The technology used in the implementation of this form of high-speed storage is expensive and this limits the amount of cache that can be economically included within a computer.  Naturally, so as to make optimal use of this form of storage it is vital that it be located as close as possible to the processor chip.  The modern computer contains different levels of cache memory – these operate at different speeds.  Traditionally, Level 1 cache memory was located on the processor chip itself, Level 2 cache being external to the processor.  Modern processors often support both Level 1 and Level 2 caches on the processor chip.  Level 1 cache operates at the highest speed and is the first to be searched.  If the required material is not found to be present, Level 2 cache is then searched.   Recall from Chapter 3 that electrical signals propagate along wires at a finite speed and therefore it is important to keep the address, data and control buses as short as possible.

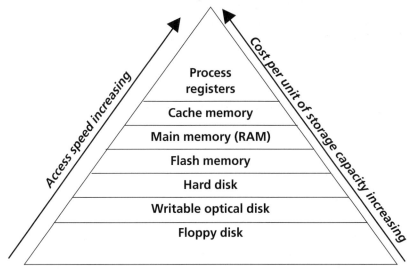

**Figure 5.1:** A typical storage hierarchy encountered in the modern PC

Main memory (RAM) offers the largest volume of primary storage with access times of the order of 10 to 50 nanoseconds (remember that 1 nanosecond = $10^{-9}$ seconds).  In recent years the price per unit of RAM storage capacity has dramatically decreased, while at the same time performance has increased.  In order to support the storage of very large volumes of digital data (an integral requirement for the modern computer), other forms of storage medium are needed.  Program instructions and data stored on secondary storage media cannot be read/executed directly by the processor, but must first be loaded into main memory.

Some key characteristics of secondary storage devices are:

- The ability to store very large volumes of digital material at a cost-effective price
- Access times are slower than primary forms of storage
- Digital data is not lost when the power is removed
- Some forms of secondary storage media can be readily removed from the computer and transported to other machines (e.g. the floppy disk and flash memory devices).

In the following two sections we briefly examine the operation of the hard disk, floppy disk and optical disc.

**Primary and secondary storage devices**

State two forms of primary storage device and two forms of secondary storage device. In each case, indicate in relation to the modern desktop computer which device you would expect to offer the highest storage capacity.

## 5.3 Secondary storage using magnetisation

In this section we consider secondary storage devices that operate on the principle of the magnetisation of a medium. Specifically, we briefly examine the hard disk and floppy disk. Subsequently, in Section 5.4 we turn our attention to media in which optical techniques are used for the recording of binary data.

### *The hard disk*

In the early 19th century, research pioneers such as Oersted, Ampere and Faraday were investigating a remarkable and mysterious discovery – electricity. It was found that when this invisible form of energy flows close to some types of metal, the metal becomes magnetised. Furthermore, and even more amazingly, when a magnet is moved about close to a conductor, an electrical current is induced into the conductor. In short, a flow of electricity can magnetise some metals (see Figure 5.2(a)) and a moving magnetic field can generate electricity (see Figure 5.2(b)). These two phenomena underpin the operation of the hard and floppy disks. In both cases a flow of electricity is used to magnetise small metallic particles to produce magnetisation in one of two directions (the existence of two states enables the storage of a binary one and a binary zero) – a write operation. Similarly, the motion of the magnetised 'grains' of material close to a conductor (coil of wire) results in electricity flowing in the wire. The direction in which the electricity flows depends on the orientation of the magnetic field associated with each 'grain' of magnetic material, i.e. whether it is representing a binary one or zero. This constitutes a read operation.

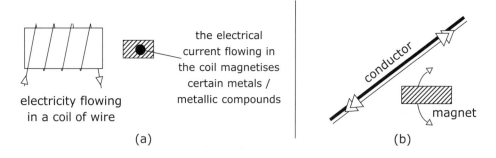

electricity flowing in a coil of wire

the electrical current flowing in the coil magnetises certain metals / metallic compounds

conductor

magnet

(a)

(b)

**Figure 5.2:** In (a), when electricity flows in a wire, a field is generated and this can magnetise certain metals/metallic compounds. Here, a coil of wire is depicted (this approach increases the field produced by the current). The direction of magnetisation depends on the direction in which the current flows in the wire. In (b) a magnet is moved about close to a conductor and this induces a current. The direction in which the current flows depends on the orientation of the magnet and its direction of movement. Note: electricity is induced only when the magnetic field changes, in size or direction. A static magnetic field does not induce electricity.

Essential components within a hard disk unit are illustrated in Figure 5.3, and a photograph of a disk assembly is provided in Figure 5.4.  As can be seen from these illustrations, the hard disk consists of a series of disks or platters mounted on a common driveshaft.  Typically, modern disks have diameters in the range 1.8 to 5.25 inches, and their rotational rate is typically in the range of 60 to 150 rotations per second.  (Although higher rates of rotation are sometimes encountered.)  The disks are formed from aluminium and the two surfaces of each disk are coated with either a ferric oxide material or a metal alloy.  The underlying technique used to record binary 1s and 0s on the surface of the disk relies upon the magnetisation of the surface coating.  This is achieved by means of read/write heads, one of which is positioned adjacent to each disk surface.  These read/write heads essentially fly across the surface of the disk, being separated from it by a remarkably small distance – of the order of one millionth of a metre.  The spacing between the read/write head and the disk's surface is critical, and it is remarkable that this precise spacing can be achieved in a reliable way.  Were a read/write head to be in physical contact with the surface of a disk, the surface coating would be rapidly eroded.

### The hard disk drive – speed of motion

*Activity 5.2*

Consider a hard disk drive that employs platters six inches (15.25mm) in diameter which rotate at 900 rpm (revolutions per minute).  Calculate the maximum speed at which the read/write heads travel over the surface of the disk.

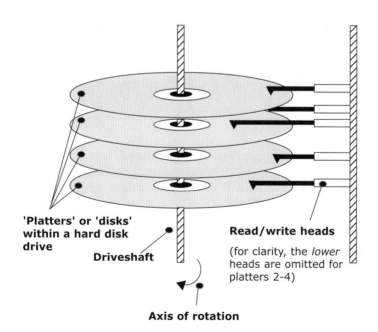

**Figure 5.3:** This diagram shows the main components within the hard disk drive.  A number of read/write heads are able to simultaneously write to, or read from, a set of rotating disks.  An actuator is used to move the heads across the surfaces of each disk.  This moves all of the heads together, i.e. they all lie at the same radial distance from the axis of rotation.

Given the close proximity of the read/write head to the disk's surface, even the smallest contaminants such as a fingerprint, or minute dust particles, can have catastrophic consequences and cause what is called a 'head crash'. If this occurs, it can result in total failure of the device.

Activity 5.3

**Head spacing**

Suggest a reason why it is necessary to reduce as much as possible the spacing between a read/write head and the surface of the disk.

**Figure 5.4:** A hard disk removed from its sealed container. A disk platter can clearly be seen, together with a read/write head located on the left side above the platter. The actuator that moves the heads lies in the upper left corner of the unit.

As indicated in Figure 5.4, there is a read/write head adjacent to each disk surface. Within the head is a minute coil of wire and when current is passed through this coil, locations on the adjacent disk's surface can be magnetised and thereby 1s and 0s recorded. The read/write heads are attached to a common 'actuator' and this enables the read/write heads to be moved across the disk's surface, i.e. from the periphery towards the centre and vice versa. Here, it is important to note that all read/write heads move together – they are not individually driven. Vinyl records, which for many years provided an essential approach to recording music, employ a spiral recording technique (a single track along which music is stored gradually spirals towards the centre of the record). The recording technique used for both hard and floppy disks is somewhat different from this approach. Consider a single disk surface. As shown in Figure 5.5, data is recorded on the disk in a series of tracks or concentric rings (each track lies at a certain radius from the axis of rotation). The read/write head can be positioned over a track, and then data can be either written to or read from the track.

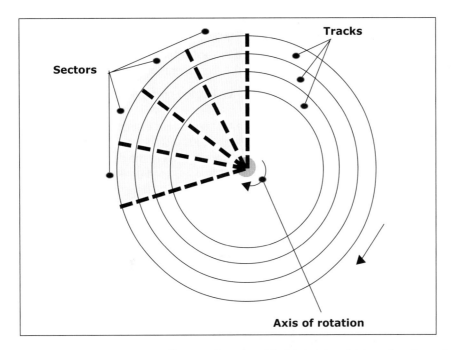

**Figure 5.5:** Here we illustrate in a simplified form the division of a platter into tracks and sectors. A set of concentric tracks are defined to which data may be written (or from which data may be read). Each track is divided into a series of sectors – all sectors are used to store the same volume of digital data. It is important to note that tracks and sectors are not physically cut or otherwise marked out on the disk's surface – they are simply defined by the localised magnetisation of the disk surface.

The use of multiple read/write heads (and multiple disks (platters)) enables data to be written simultaneously to more than one disk. Here, two more technical terms need to be introduced:

- **The cylinder:** the tracks on each disk and which are at an equal radius from the centre of the disk are said to form a cylinder. Thus all tracks within the same cylinder may be written to or read from in parallel (at the same time)
- **The sector:** each track is divided into a series of sectors (see Figure 5.5). All sectors are able to store the same amount of digital data. As is apparent from the diagram, sectors towards the periphery of the platter are larger in extent and therefore could offer to store greater amounts of data. Modern drives exploit this opportunity by dividing tracks that lie further from the rotational axis (i.e. that have a greater circumference) into a greater number of sectors. This increases storage capacity but adds complication to the control system.

Individual bits are not read from, or written to, the disk drive, but rather we read or write groups of bits. The smallest group of bits that can be written is called a 'block' (this corresponds to a sector) and typically a block may contain, say, 512 bytes.

Let us suppose that we wish to read a file from a hard disk. The processor will provide the hard disk controller (hardware specifically responsible for disk operations) with information concerning the identity of the file that it wishes to access. In turn, the disk controller will use information stored on the hard disk to relate the identity of the file that we wish to access to its physical location on the platters. This will involve identifying the cylinder number (and thus obtaining information on the tracks where the file can be found), and the sector numbers indicating at what point (or points) on a track the blocks that comprise the file may be found.

Once this information has been obtained, the read/write heads will be moved to be positioned over the appropriate set of tracks. Subsequently, it is likely that it will be necessary to wait for a very brief amount of time as the disk rotates and the appropriate sector comes around. Once the sector appears under the read/write heads, the read operation can commence.

In principle, the sectors to which a file is written are located next to each other (contiguously) along one or more tracks. Over time and as the disk fills, a file will often be stored in physically non-contiguous sectors (i.e. the sectors become scattered). For example, let us suppose that a file (File A) is written to a disk and occupies 20 contiguous sectors (i.e. 20 sectors that lie next to each other along a track). Over time, other files are written to the disk and as a result the sectors that lie on either side of those occupied by File A are used up (File A becomes 'hemmed in' on both sides). At some time later, File A is deleted and the 20 sectors can now be reused. Suppose that we now wish to store on the disk a file that will occupy 21 sectors. We may:

- Find a space on the disk in which there are at least 21 contiguous sectors that are free
- Place 20 of the sectors in the space that became free when File A was deleted and store the 21st sector elsewhere.

Problems occur if we always seek to place files within physically contiguous sectors (especially when we are dealing with large files and as the amount of free space is reduced). Consequently, files will often be located in sectors that are not necessarily physically contiguous. This enables us to efficiently utilise space that becomes available when files are deleted. Naturally, this scheme requires that a record (log) is maintained indicating the whereabouts of all sectors that constitute a file.

**Note**

- Placing a file in physically contiguous sectors reduces the time that it takes to store the file on the disk (and the time needed to read the file from the disk). Requiring that a file is always placed in physically contiguous sectors leads to inefficient use of disk space. This inefficiency increases with time (as more disk space has been used and more files deleted) and is particularly of concern when dealing with larger files.

Clearly, when we read from, or write to, a hard disk there are a number of latencies (or delays) that occur. The first of these corresponds to the need to move the read/write heads to the appropriate set of tracks (cylinder) – the 'seek' time (Tseek). The second is called the 'rotational latency' (Trot) and corresponds to the time we must wait in order that the relevant sector passes beneath the read/write heads. When using your computer, you may sometimes hear a slight sound from the hard disk during read or write operations. This is the noise made by the actuator responsible for moving the read/write heads to the appropriate cylinders.

Additionally, there is the settling time (Tset) that corresponds to the time taken for the head to stabilise when it reaches the intended track (e.g. this takes into account any overshoot). Finally, there is the time taken to perform the desired read/write operation – the time for which the read/write head is actively performing the storage or retrieval operation (the 'active' time (Tact)). Thus the overall time (T) may be expressed as:

$$T = T_{seek} + T_{rot} + T_{set} + T_{act}$$

Naturally, we wish to reduce delays as much as possible, and so the heads should move as fast as is practical, and similarly (to reduce the rotational latency) the disks should rotate at the highest possible speed.

**Activity 5.4**

**Rotational latency**

A disk rotates at 3,600rpm.

Determine the average rotational latency.

Encoding techniques are used to convert data that is to be written to a disk into a form that ensures that it may be read back correctly. Consider, for example that we wish to store on a disk a set of binary 1s or a set of binary 0s. If these were written directly into a sector, we would produce a region along a track of uniform magnetic field, i.e. each binary value would be recorded in a manner that is identical to its neighbours along the track, see Figure 5.6.

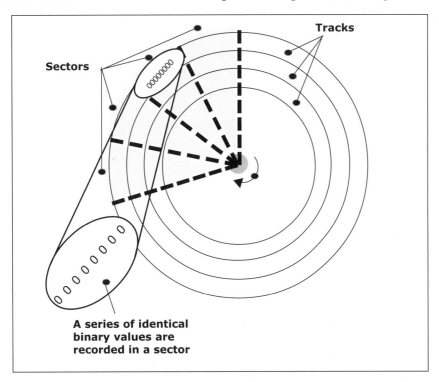

**Figure 5.6:** The result of directly storing a series of identical binary values on a disk. The read head is only sensitive to changes in field strength and therefore no 'read' signal is produced. Encoding techniques must therefore be employed.

As indicated earlier in this section, electricity is induced into a conductor by a magnetic field only when there is a change in the field strength – if the magnetic field is static, electricity is not induced. Consequently, if we directly record a series of identical binary states in a sector, their associated magnetic fields will be the same and no electricity will be induced into the read head as it passes over them. Some form of encoding technique must therefore be employed.

One simple encoding technique is the 'non-return to zero' approach. Here, every time there is a change in magnetic state, it is assumed to indicate the storage of a binary one. Thus if we wished to store the bit sequence 111 and the previous bit stored on the disk was a zero, we would write the encoded bit string 101 to the disk.

Laptop computers may be purchased that contain physically small hard disks with the capacity to store many gigabytes of data (a gigabyte is $1,024^3$ bytes – note that this is an approximation as 'giga' means $10^9$, whereas $1,024^3$ is somewhat larger than this).

This miniaturisation of hard disk technologies is a relatively recent occurrence and in the early 1980s the typical storage capacity of a hard disk would have been of the order of 72 megabytes. Furthermore, such disk units were quite large – just a little smaller than a shoebox. Earlier still, hard disks were built in such a way that it was readily possible to remove the disk assembly and replace it with another. However, this is no longer a possibility, given the very close spacing that exists between the read/write head and the disk's surface, and the consequent need for absolute cleanliness. Today's hard disk drive assemblies are constructed within sealed units and require clean-room conditions for their assembly or repair (although repairs are not really practicable in terms of repair cost versus replacement price).

If you have an unwanted hard disk drive assembly, you might try opening it – but do remember that once you have opened the case, it will not work again! Unfortunately, in an attempt to dissuade users from opening disk drives, unusual screws are often used which are difficult to undo. In such a case it may be necessary to use a drill to remove the screw heads.

**Activity 5.5**

**Hard disk performance**

Describe two latencies associated with a read or write operation to a hard disk.

## The floppy disk

Floppy disks were originally designed to provide a means of loading programs into early computers (i.e. in the 1960s), following a computer being turned on or reset. With the proliferation of the PC and workstation, they provided a means by which data and programs could be conveniently transferred between machines and via which small amounts of material could be backed up (for storage in a secure location). The original floppy disk, first developed in the 1960s, was housed in a sleeve that was eight inches square. Subsequently, the 5¼-inch disk was developed and then the 3½-inch disk became the standard (it is said that this size was chosen by measuring the typical size of a shirt pocket!). The underlying physical operation of a floppy disk is similar to that of the hard disk.

Unlike the hard disk that employs ridged platters, the floppy disk is constructed from a single disk formed from a flexible material (Mylar) that is coated with a magnetic surface material, such as ferric oxide. As with the hard disk, a read/write head is used to write binary data to a series of concentric tracks. However, the floppy disk does not employ precision engineering, and the requirement that it should be possible to remove and insert disks within the disk drive means that the mechanical components operate in a more rudimentary manner. The read/write head used in a floppy disk does not (as is the case with the hard disk) fly over the disk's surface, but is in surface contact. Over time, the read/write head can therefore erode the surface layer (and so give rise to a bad disk) and the head itself is gradually contaminated by particles that have come off the disk's surface. This means that the read/write head should be cleaned from time to time.

As the read/write head is in contact with the surface of the disk, the high rotation speeds employed by the hard disk cannot, in the case of the floppy disk, be achieved. Typically, a floppy disk rotates at 360rpm (six rotations per second), and so the rotational latency is significantly longer than that associated with the hard disk. The format used in reading and writing data to a floppy disk closely follows that used in the case of a hard disk. Specifically, data is written to a series of concentric tracks that are divided into sectors, and the minimum unit of data that can be written is again referred to as a 'block'.

**Activity 5.6**

**Hard disk capacity**

Determine the storage capacity of the hard disk connected to your computer, and the amount of unused (free) space currently available.

# 5.4 Secondary storage using optical techniques

In this section, we briefly consider the operation of systems that employ optical techniques for the storage of digital information. At the present time, the four most commonly used forms of optical storage device are:

- **The CD-ROM:** optical discs of this type contain prerecorded digital data. This data is loaded onto the disk at the time of manufacture – it cannot be deleted or overwritten. The capacity of a CD-ROM is approximately 600MB (megabytes (1,024$^2$ bytes))

- **The writable CD (CD-R):** a user may write to this type of media, but once written, the contents cannot be deleted or overwritten. This is also referred to as a 'WORM' – 'write once, read many (times)'

- **The Re-writable CD (CD-RW):** this type of optical disc can support both read and write operations, although the reading speed is higher than the writing speed. This is usually indicated by manufacturers, who may quote figures such as 8x32. The ratio of these numbers provides us with an indication of the relative read/write speed (i.e. 32/8 = 4, indicating that the device can be read four times faster than it is able to perform write operations)

- **Digital versatile disc (DVD):** these optical discs are able to store very large amounts of digital data (some gigabytes). As a consequence of their enormous storage capacity they are now the preferred media for the storage of video images and support the desktop computer's increasing role as a multimedia machine.

These different types of compact disc are all underpinned by optical storage techniques. Writing to a disc is achieved through the use of a highly focused laser beam that is able to change the properties of the disc at the point at which the beam impinges upon it. The beam in fact changes the reflectance characteristic of the disc material – where the disc is 'burned' by the laser, a spot that is non-reflective is created. In other regions the disc is reflective. The difference between reflective and non-reflective locations upon the disc corresponds to the storage of digital values (0s and 1s).

You will recall that in the case of the hard disk, data is stored along a set of concentric circular tracks and we contrasted this to the spiral storage technique used for the older audio recordings (vinyl or gramophone records). Interestingly, the compact disc does not use the concentric ring storage format, but rather the single spiral track approach. Along this spiral track, digital data is stored in the form of changes in the reflectance property of the CD material. In the case of the gramophone record, the direction of recording is from the periphery towards the axis of rotation.

In contrast, the CD operates from the centre outwards. It is interesting to note that although we usually consider that the underlying techniques used for the storage of data on the writable and re-writable CDs are optical, this is a slight misnomer. In fact, the focused laser beam heats the disk material at the point of contact, and it is this heat that changes the optical characteristics of the disc. Consequently, it is more accurate to consider the underlying physical technique used for the recording of data on a CD as thermal, rather than as optical.

The optical technique used for reading from a CD is illustrated in Figure 5.7. The electromechanical systems used for both writing to, and reading from, a CD have to operate with great accuracy. For example, the optics required to read data from the CD must accurately follow the spiral track as the CD rotates. In principle – since whilst the CD is being read no mechanical read head is in contact with the CD – the CD should provide a very reliable form of storage. However, the surface of a CD is very easily marked (e.g. scratched) and as a consequence considerable emphasis is placed upon error detection and correction. Special electronic hardware is used for this purpose within the CD controller, and in principle this hardware should be able to detect and often recover contaminated data. The error detection and correction mechanism naturally slows down the rate at which data can be retrieved from the CD. Both reading and writing speeds for a CD are less than those associated with a hard disk.

**Activity 5.7**

**Hard disk and compact disc formats**

'The hard disk and compact disc have the same data storage format.'

Briefly discuss the accuracy of this statement.

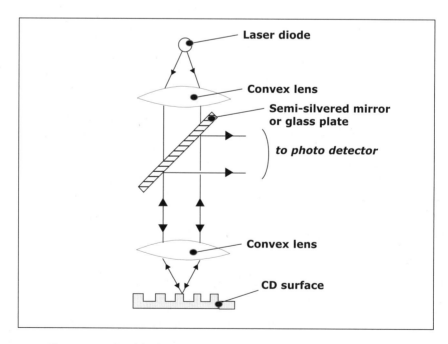

**Figure 5.7:** Simplified schematic illustrating the principle of operation of a CD read mechanism

Figure 5.7 illustrates how light from a laser diode is collimated and passes through a tilted, semi-silvered mirror or glass plate. Subsequently, the light is focused by a lens onto the CD. Depending upon whether the light impinges upon a 'pit' or 'bump' (corresponding to a 1 or a 0), the light is reflected or not. In the case of light that is reflected, it travels back through the lens and is reflected to the right by the semi-silvered mirror (or glass plate). The function of the semi-silvered mirror/glass plate is therefore to direct reflected light to the right-hand side where another lens would be used to focus the beam onto a photo detector. This converts the light into an electrical signal. In practice, more efficient optical arrangements would be used.

## 5.5 Serial and parallel interfaces

Typically, when a processor wishes to read information from the outside world, it performs a read operation from a special address within its address space. Similarly, when outputting to the physical world, it writes to a certain address. At these addresses, special hardware responsible for performing input/output operations is located. Thus, for example, if a computer wishes to output a character to a device such as a printer, it will write the character to an address where an input/output controller is located. The input/output controller (I/O controller) will then pass the character to the printer.

Two types of interconnect are widely used to link between I/O controllers and peripheral devices - namely, the serial and parallel interfaces. We briefly look at each of these in turn below.

- **Serial interface:** in the case of a serial interface, data to be sent from the I/O controller to the peripheral device is transmitted along a single wire (communication medium). Since the bits propagate down the wire sequentially, this is referred to as a 'serial interface'

- **Parallel interface:** in the case of the parallel interface, the peripheral device is linked to the I/O controller by a number of connections. If, for example, we decide that we wish to transmit individual bytes from the I/O controller to the peripheral device (e.g. a printer), then we would arrange to have eight wires connecting the two (together with one or more additional connections. One of these connections would be used to ensure that both devices share a common 'earth' connection (i.e. that they are both referenced to the same voltage level – this defines zero volts)). In this way, the eight binary digits forming the byte can be transmitted simultaneously, i.e. in parallel. Serial connections tend to operate at lower speed than do 'equivalent' parallel interfaces. Since parallel interfaces require more physical connections between the I/O controller and the peripheral device, parallel interfaces tend to be used for short distance interconnects. In summary, serial connections offer lower speed but are economical over longer distances than parallel interconnects.

Most interfaces include techniques that can be used to detect any corruption of transmitted data and may even allow for the correction of errors in the transmitted data stream. In the simplest case this is achieved through the inclusion of additional bits. These are referred to as 'parity bits' and their function is to provide an indication as to whether an error has occurred. In more advanced schemes, the inclusion of additional parity bits enables the possibility of error correction.

Peripheral devices such as printers normally have their own memory. This special memory is known as a 'buffer'. The inclusion of a buffer allows bursts of data to be transmitted at a speed greater than can be actually managed by mechanisms within the peripheral device. The printer provides us with a simple example of a peripheral device that employs its own memory (a buffer). Data can be transmitted to the printer along a parallel connection much faster than the printer can actually print this data. Consequently, by using a buffer it is possible to transmit an amount of data at high speed. This data is temporarily stored in the printer's buffer, and is gradually printed.

When the contents of the buffer have been printed (or nearly all printed), the peripheral device tells the computer that it is ready to receive more data. Naturally, for this scheme to operate correctly, the interconnect between the computer and the printer must support communication in both directions, i.e. it must be bi-directional. Data is transmitted in batches to the printer and the printer sends a signal back to the computer when it is ready to receive more data. This process of bi-directional cooperation is referred to as 'hand-shaking'.

Data buffering by a printer is something that you may have observed on your own computer. If you start printing a long file and for some reason stop the print job (i.e. cancel the printing task in Windows), you will generally find that even though the computer indicates that the print task has been cancelled, the printer will continue to print for some short time afterwards. This is now easily understood as we can see that the printer will carry on printing (after the print task has been cancelled) because it has data remaining in its buffer. It will continue to print until the contents of the buffer have been emptied.

**Activity 5.8**

**Data transfer to peripheral devices**

Explain in your own words why peripheral devices such as printers employ a buffer.

The speed at which a serial or parallel interconnect operates is measured in terms of the number of bits per second. For example, a standard modem typically operates at $56\text{kbit.s}^{-1}$. Alternatively, a 'baud rate' may be quoted. For most purposes the baud rate may be considered as representing the bit rate. (In fact, bit rate and baud rate do have a different meaning: the former defines the number of bits flowing per second and the latter the switching speed. Usually, this difference is not of great significance.) Thus a link operating at a 110-baud rate may be considered to transmit 110 bits per second (this was the operational speed typically used in the 1960s and 70s to link computers to mechanical teletypes and other forms of operator terminal).

## 5.6 Signal transfer

At present most telecommunication systems employ digital signal transmission techniques. Digital signals have a greater immunity to noise than do their analogue equivalent. (A digital signal can exist in only certain states (e.g. a logic low and a logic high). In contrast an analog signal can be continuous and in principle exist in an unlimited number of states. A sinusoidal curve (e.g. $y = \sin x$) provides us with an example of a continuous function and thereby an analog signal.) Furthermore, digital signals can be processed directly by computer hardware without the need to convert between the analog and digital domains (see Chapter 6).

When we consider transmitting data across an interconnect, we must consider detailed issues relating to its passage – this defines the 'protocol' at the lowest level. For example, should we transmit the data as one continuous 'bit stream' or should we fragment the data into smaller groups (or blocks) of data? In a previous section we briefly considered the transmission of data between a computer and printer. Here, we discussed the transmission of data in bursts to the printer and its temporary storage within a buffer (memory area) built into the printer. Similarly, in this context we also considered both parallel and serial data flow together with 'hand-shaking'.

In Figures 5.8 and 5.9 we illustrate the parallel and serial forms of interface and these two transmission modalities are summarised below:

- **Parallel transmission:** a group of bits are sent at the same time.  Each bit is transmitted along a separate path – see Figure 5.8
- **Serial transmission:** a group of bits are sent one after another along the same path, see Figure 5.9.  This reduces the number of physical connections needed.

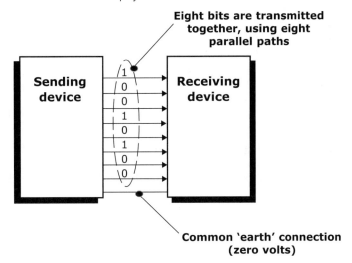

**Figure 5.8:** An 8-bit parallel data transmission interface

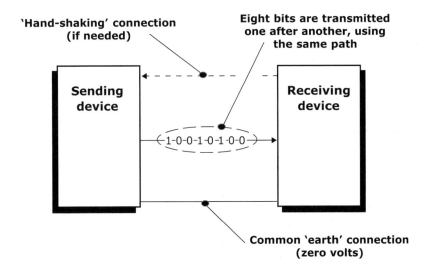

**Figure 5.9:** A serial data transmission interface (a 'hand-shaking' connection may, or may not, be needed – see text for discussion)

The movement of a stream of bits from one device to another via a medium using serial transmission requires a considerable amount of co-ordination between the two devices.  In particular, a means of ensuring synchronisation is required (i.e. some timing alignment to enable the faithful reception of data at the receiving end).

Two common techniques used for this purpose are **asynchronous** and **synchronous** serial transmission. These processes are illustrated in Figures 5.10 and 5.11 and are briefly summarised below.

Let us suppose that we wish to transmit bits in 'chunks' (i.e. groups of a few bits at a time) along a serial connection, see Figure 5.10(a). We must employ a scheme that addresses several issues, specifically:

- How does the receiver know where a group of bits start?
- How does the receiver know where a group of bits end?
- How does the receiver know how often (frequently), and when, it must sample the signal so as to detect each bit that is transmitted within a group?

The first issue is addressed by adding one or more 'start bit(s)', see Figure 5.10(b). Here, we arbitrarily assume that when no data is being transmitted, the transmission wire is in a logic-high state. The start bit is represented by a transition to a logic low and this bit has a certain defined duration. The receiver then knows that a certain number of data bits will follow. At the end of their transmission, one or more stop bit(s) are used to return the transmission medium to a logic-high state.

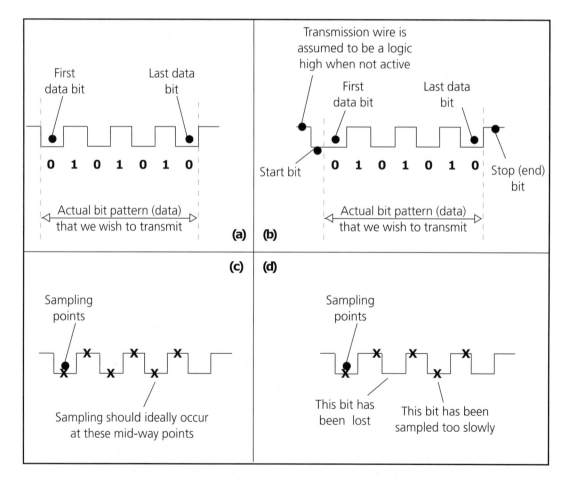

**Figure 5.10:** The transmission of a group of data bits. The recipient must sample these bits at the correct rate

Of course, the receiver must sample the signal at an appropriate rate so as to accurately detect each data bit. Ideally, this sampling occurs in the manner depicted in figure 5.10(c) and each bit is sampled at the its 'mid-way' point. If the sampling is not carried out at the appropriate rate, then errors can be introduced – as indicated in Figure 5.10(d).

The rate at which data is output onto the serial interconnect (wire) is determined by a 'clock' located at the transmitting end. Within a computer (or digital hardware system), a clock is a digital signal that repeatedly changes from a logic high to a logic low (and back again) at a regular rate – see Figure 5.11. The clock is used for all timing operations and is the 'heartbeat' of the system.

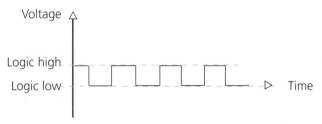

**Figure 5.11:** A clock signal comprises a regular transition between logic-high and logic-low states

The rate at which the receiver samples the incoming flow of bits along the serial interconnect is also defined by a clock signal. Here, two different approaches may be adopted:

- **Asynchronous communication:** in this case both the transmitting hardware and the receiving hardware employ separate clock signals. At the receiving end, the arrival of the start bit is used initiate signal sampling and the clock defines the sampling rate. However, since the clocks used at the transmitting and receiving end run asynchronously, we cannot assume that they operate at exactly the same frequency (indeed they will not do so). Imagine for a moment two conventional clocks or watches. Even if we accurately synchronise them, over time there will be differences in the time that they indicate. Since digital signals generally operate at high frequencies, small differences in timing can have a major impact and cause errors to occur.

In the case of the transmission of data along an asynchronous serial interconnect, we use the start bit to initiate the sampling process and assume that during the time that it takes to transmit a small group of data bits, the error in the timing of the two clocks will be so small as to be unimportant. Naturally, if we were to transmit larger groups of bits, timing errors could be more problematic. The transmission process is summarised in Figure 5.12.

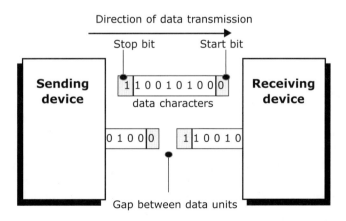

**Figure 5.12:** Asynchronous serial communication. Both the transmitter and receiver employ separate clocks

- **Synchronous transmission:** This does not require the use of the pre-agreed start and stop bits associated with asynchronous transmission. Here a common clock is employed from which both the sending node and the recipient obtain timing information. This process is illustrated in Figure 5.13. The clock determines the rate at which data (bits) are transmitted and also the rate (and time) at which the recipient samples the transmission medium. In some implementations the clock is transmitted along a separate cable. In the case of synchronous communication, data can (in principle) flow continuously between the transmitting and receiving parties – unlike the asynchronous model discussed above, there is no need to divide the data into a series of small 'chunks'.

Buses within a computer may operate synchronously or asynchronously. Although the use of a single common clock may appear to be a particularly elegant approach, this technique can prove problematic – especially when the communication occurs at a very high speed (rate of data exchange). Recall that signals travel along wires at a finite speed that is somewhat less than the speed of light. Consequently, if we transmit a common clock signal to a number of devices that are connected to a synchronous bus, each will receive a slightly different version of the clock – see Figure 5.14. As may be seen from this illustration the clock signals that arrive at the two peripheral devices are delayed (in this context we refer to them as being subjected to a 'phase shift'). As we increase the rate of data transmission (and the frequency of the clock signal) these phase shifts can be problematic and in such cases it is vital that the length of the wires used for the interconnect (bus) are kept to a minimum. (The extent of the phase shift is directly proportional to the length of the interconnect.)

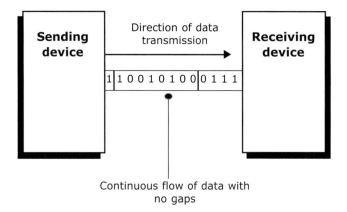

**Figure 5.13:** Synchronous data transmission. Here, the transmitter and receiver share a common clock

## 5.7 Summary

As we have seen, the computer designer attempts to devise a memory hierarchy which demonstrates an appropriate balance between capacity, performance and cost. Similarly, so as to maximise performance, great attention must be directed towards the design of the internal buses that connect components within the computer. Unfortunately, obtaining the ideal (optimal) design is generally impossible – different types of application place different demands on the computer hardware and a machine that is optimised for one sort of task may prove non-optimal when used for other activities. For example, a program written to solve a problem in engineering or computational physics may utilise a vast number of floating-point calculations.

In these circumstances the design of the processor/floating-point processor would strongly influence the computer's ability to efficiently execute the program. Alternatively, a program may perform very few floating-point operations but may require a vast number of disk accesses (referred to as 'disk I/O' operations). In this case, the performance of the hard disk and disk interface would play a crucial role in determining the efficiency of the computer when executing the program.

Clearly, it is far from easy to quantify (with accuracy) the precise gains that will be achieved by, for example, doubling the amount of cache and main memory or by developing a processor that makes available to user programs more registers. Unfortunately, this problem is exacerbated by computer manufacturers and vendors who characterise computer performance using a range of numerical parameters (such as the processor clock speed and size of memory cache) but provide purchasers with little information on how these parameters should be interpreted.

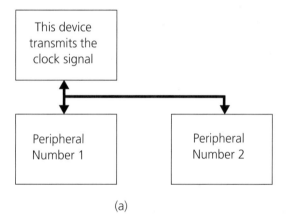

(a)

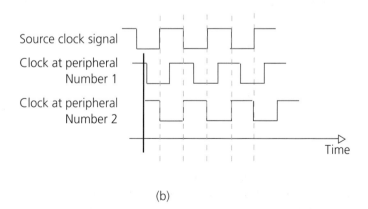

(b)

**Figure 5.14:** Here, we assume that peripheral device Number 1 is closer to the source clock than peripheral device number 2. As may be seen from (b) the clock signal received by peripheral device Number 1 is slightly delayed. This clock received by peripheral device Number 2 is subjected to even greater delay. This delay between signals is referred to a 'phase shift'.

## 5.8 Review questions

**Question 5.1** Explain why the modern hard disk is fabricated within a sealed container.

**Question 5.2** Consider the following storage devices: the hard disk, the floppy disk, and the CD-ROM. Of the three, which would you expect to normally provide the greatest storage capacity, and which would you expect to provide the least storage capacity? Similarly, which do you think would provide the highest read/write speed, and which would you expect to provide the lowest read/write speed?

**Question 5.3** Why is it important that the hard disk should rotate at the highest possible speed?

**Question 5.4** In the context of the hard disk, what is meant by the term 'cylinder'?

**Question 5.5** Why does a hard disk employ a plurality of platters and read/write heads?

**Question 5.6** Within the context of the hard disk and floppy disk, what do you understand by the term 'block'?

**Question 5.7** Within the context of data transfer, what do you understand by the term 'hand-shaking'?

**Question 5.8** What is the main difference between parallel and serial transmission?

**Question 5.9** State one way in which synchronous transmission differs from asynchronous transmission.

**Question 5.10** By means of a suitable example and diagram, explain what is meant by the term 'phase shift'.

## 5.9 Feedback on activities

### Activity 5.1: Primary and secondary storage devices

Two examples of primary storage device are cache memory and main memory. Main memory offers a much larger storage capacity than does cache memory. The hard disk and floppy disk represent two forms of secondary storage device. The hard disk provides a much larger capacity for storage than does the floppy disk.

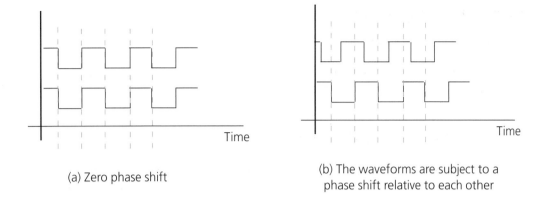

(a) Zero phase shift

(b) The waveforms are subject to a phase shift relative to each other

**Figure 5.15:** In (a) the two clock signals have zero phase shift (the rising (and falling) edges occur at the same time).  However, in (b) this is no longer the case – there is a phase shift.

### Activity 5.2: The hard disk drive – speed of motion

The maximum speed occurs when the read/write head is located at the periphery of the disk. In this location the circumference of the disk is ~19 inches (calculated using circumference = $2\pi r$).  At 900 rpm this gives 9,500 inches per minute and this converts to ~16 miles per hour.

### Activity 5.3:  Head spacing

The strength of the magnetic field generated by a 'permanent' magnet or by a conductor through which a current is flowing rapidly falls off with distance.  Therefore, to enable the surface coating to be magnetised using only small currents and to allow the read/write head to detect the relatively weak magnetic fields stored on the disk, the gap between each head and the surface coating must be minimised.

### Activity 5.4:  Rotational latency

A rotational rate of 3,600rpm equals 3,600/60 rotations per second (= 60).  Thus one rotation occurs in 1/60 seconds.  The average rotational latency corresponds to one-half a revolution i.e.  ½ .1/60 =8.3ms.  (Average equals ½ (max.  latency + min.  latency).)

### Activity 5.5:  Hard disk performance

The first latency concerns the time it takes for the read/write head to be located above the appropriate track on the disk's surface.  This corresponds to the time it takes for the actuator to move the read/write head across the surface of the disk.  The second latency is known as rotational latency and corresponds to the time it takes for the relevant sector to move so as to pass beneath the read/write head.  In the worse case, this corresponds to just less than the time for one rotation of the disk.  Naturally, the faster the disk rotates, the shorter will be the rotational latency.  As we discuss, floppy disks rotate more slowly than do hard disks, and this therefore considerably increases rotational latency.

### Activity 5.6: Hard disk capacity

If you are using a Microsoft Windows-based machine, you may obtain this information by selecting the following from the 'Start' menu icon (located at the bottom left of the screen): Programs Accessories/System Tools/Drive Space.

Then select the 'physical disk' (typically, drive C) option.

### Activity 5.7: Hard disk and compact disc formats

This statement is incorrect since the hard disk is formatted so as to provide a series of concentric tracks to which data can be written. On the other hand, the compact disc uses a single spiral track that spirals from the centre of the disk towards its periphery.

### Activity 5.8: Data transfer to peripheral devices

The use of a buffer enables data to be temporarily stored at the receiving end of a data transfer link. In this way, 'chunks' of data may be transmitted at a high speed across the link. Each of these is temporarily stored and acted upon by the receiver. For example, a printer may employ a buffer. The data transfer link can then be used to transmit groups of characters (or other printable material) at high speed. These are temporarily stored in the printer and acted upon (printed). Once the buffer becomes empty or nearly empty), a request is made by the printer for the next batch of characters to be sent to it.

# CHAPTER 6

# Interfacing to the physical world

## OVERVIEW

To serve a useful purpose, a computer must be able to take input from the physical world, perform calculations, and output the results of the computational process. In this chapter, we focus upon the input/output process, and examine ways in which a computer takes input from its surroundings and also the techniques used in displaying to the operator the results of the computation. In this context, we introduce the concept of the event-driven display.

| Learning outcomes | On completion of this chapter you should be able to: |
| --- | --- |

- Discuss the need for both input and output devices

- Describe the operation of analogue-to-digital and digital-to-analogue converters

- Distinguish between various forms of interaction device

- Discuss the operation of the 'pixmapped' graphics display and cathode ray tube

- Discuss the use of several display metrics.

## 6.1 Introduction

If it is to serve a useful purpose a computer must be able to accept commands, programs, and data from the physical world and output the results of the computational process. This requires the machine to interface not only with other hardware devices, but also with the human operator. In previous chapters we have largely confined our discussions to the internal architecture of the computer; we now turn our attention to some of the techniques that permit the computer to communicate with its surroundings.

As previously discussed, digital signals are an intrinsic part of computer operation and exist in two states (the logic high and logic low). However, often in the physical world, signals are continuous and can – at least in principle – exist in an infinite number of states. We refer to such signals as 'analogue signals', in order to distinguish between them and their digital counterparts. The first two sections of this chapter deal with the conversion of signals between the analogue and digital domains. Here, we introduce the digital-to-analogue and analogue-to-digital converters, and in Section 6.4 we briefly consider the sampling of an analogue waveform.

In Sections 6.5 and 6.6 we describe hardware devices that enable the human operator to interact with the computer. We begin by briefly examining several interaction tools, specifically the keyboard, mouse and joystick, via which the user can input commands and data to the computer. Subsequently, we discuss the computer display and introduce the 'bitmapped' ('pixmapped') graphics techniques and raster scan. Despite the increasing popularity of thin panel displays, traditional cathode ray tube (CRT) based systems continue to be widely used and are able to offer very high performance at a competitive price. Furthermore, the operation of the CRT-based display is more easily understood than the liquid crystal and gas plasma equivalents. For these reasons we focus our discussion on the CRT-based display. Finally, in Section 6.7 we describe several metrics that can be used to characterise display performance.

## 6.2 Digital-to-analogue conversion

An electronic device (integrated circuit) known as a digital-to-analogue converter (DAC) is used to convert digital (binary) signals generated by a computer into an analogue form. Such signals may then be used to control, for example, non-digital devices (such as motors, actuators, audio amplifiers). The DAC therefore enables a computer (or other digital system) to output signals in an analogue form to the outside world.

You may recall from previous chapters that a digital signal can exist in only certain states. In the case of the modern computer, all operations are carried out on binary values and so a signal within a computer can exit in only two states: a logic high and a logic low. Some earlier computers operated in other number bases. For example, in the case of the Analytical Engine designed by Charles Babbage in the mid-19th century, the machine was intended to operate in base 10 (so a signal could exist in 10 possible states). In contrast, a true analogue (continuous) signal has the ability (at least in principle) to exist in an infinite number of states. In practice, if the analogue signal is obtained through the conversion of a digital signal, the number of states that the former can occupy is limited.

A DAC is illustrated schematically in Figure 6.1. This device is known as an 8-bit DAC since it is able to convert 8-bit binary values into their analogue equivalent. As you will recall from Chapter Two, an 8-bit binary number may take on $2^8$ (256) different values. Consequently, in the case of the DAC in the diagram, the output signal may only take on 256 different values. By way of example, suppose that the output from the DAC is amplified to have a voltage range of 10 volts (i.e. 0 to 9 volts).

If we use an 8-bit DAC, the smallest step in voltage that we can generate will be 10 divided by 256 which equals approximately 0.04 volts. The output from a DAC is not therefore a truly continuous analogue signal, but comprises a number of voltage 'steps'. The size of these voltage 'steps' may be reduced by either reducing the voltage range generated by the DAC, or by increasing the number of bits used in the conversion process (e.g. use a 16-bit (rather than an 8-bit) DAC).

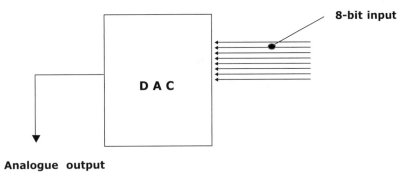

**Figure 6.1:** Representation of an 8-bit digital-to-analogue converter. This device converts the binary value that is applied to it into an analogue signal

Activity 6.1

### Digital-to-analogue conversion accuracy

Suppose that we use a 12-bit digital-to-analogue converter and the output from this device has a voltage range of 10 volts. What is the smallest change in voltage that we can produce?

In Figure 6.2, a DAC is used to convert a digital signal into analogue form. This signal is amplified and applied to a loudspeaker. In this way the computer is able to generate simple sounds.

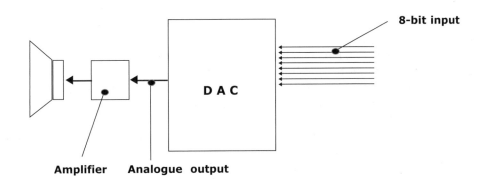

**Figure 6.2:** A DAC is used to generate an analogue signal. This is amplified and applied to a loudspeaker. In this way, digital signals may be used to generate simple sounds

The basic principle of operation of a DAC is straightforward and is based on the summation of signals. By way of a simple example, consider the case of a 2-bit DAC as illustrated in Figure 6.3. We assume that the least significant bit is referred to as 'A' and the most significant bit as 'B'. For simplicity we will assume that this is able to generate an output voltage in the range 0-3 volts. The outputs obtained from the DAC for each combination of input values are shown in Figure 6.3.

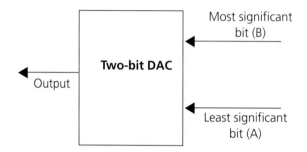

| B | A | Output (volts) |
|---|---|---|
| 0 | 0 | 0 |
| 0 | 1 | 1 |
| 1 | 0 | 2 |
| 1 | 1 | 3 |

**Figure 6.3:** A two-bit DAC with an output in the range 0-3 volts

As may be seen, the output may be calculated as:

$$\text{Output} = 2B + A$$

By way of a further example, consider the case of an 8-bit DAC. We will assume that the least significant bit is denoted $D_0$ and the most significant as $D_7$. The output is given by:

$$\text{Output} = D_0 + 2D_1 + 4D_2 + 8D_3 + \ldots\ + 128D_7$$

In practice, we create a set (series) of signals whose relative values increase by a factor of two. The number of signals we produce corresponds to the number of bits to be applied to the DAC. We then multiply each of these signals by the corresponding bit value and sum the results. For example, in the case of a 2-bit DAC, we generate two signals – a base signal (x) and a second signal 2x. These are then multiplied by their corresponding bit values. For example, suppose that we were converting the binary value 10 using a 2-bit DAC, we would multiply x by 0 and 2x by 1. The result is then summed:

$$\text{Output} = x.0 + 2x.1 = 2x$$

In Figure 6.4, we illustrate a circuit of a 2-bit DAC. On the right-hand side of this diagram an operational amplifier is shown (the triangle). A detailed understanding of this powerful device is unnecessary, and for our purposes it is sufficient to note that when connected as shown (i.e. with resistor 'R'), (a resistor is a simple electrical component that 'resists' the flow of electrical current. The 'resistance' of a resistor is measured in ohms. When a current (I) flows through a resistor (with resistance R), there is a voltage V across the resistor such that V = I.R (Ohm's Law). Thus if a current of 2 amperes (amps) were to pass through a resistor with resistance of 4 ohms, a voltage of 8 volts would appear across the resistor. Resistors are found in most electrical appliances and can be fabricated within integrated circuits) voltages emanating from any number of sources and that are applied to connection 'L' will be added together and their sum will appear at the amplifier's output.

Resistors R1 and R2 generate the two signals (voltages) – x and 2x referred to above. On the left-hand side of the diagram, two switches (S1 and S2) are shown. These represent the hardware used in the multiplication of the signals with the binary (bit) values applied to the DAC. Each switch may be in one of two positions:

- If the switch connects the resistor (e.g. R1) to 0 volts, then the signal delivered by the resistor to connection 'L' is zero
- If the switch is in the opposite position, then the signal presented to connection 'L' by the resistor will be x (as defined above).

For simplicity, in the illustration we have indicated the use of simple mechanical switches. In the case of an actual DAC, these switches are entirely electronic and are implemented using transistors.

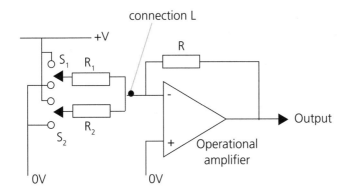

**Figure 6.4:** The implementation of a simple 2-bit DAC. See text for discussion.

## 6.3 Analogue-to-digital conversion

Electronic devices known as analogue-to-digital converters (ADCs) are used to convert continuous analogue signals to their digital (binary) equivalent values (i.e. they serve the opposite function to the DAC and are used to input signals into the computer). Typically, an ADC permits a voltage that, for example, may take on any value between say 0 and 5 volts, to be converted into a representative binary number. As the analogue voltage applied to the ADC varies, so does the binary number generated by the device.

The ADC therefore permits continuous analogue signals to be represented within the digital domain of the computer. An 8-bit ADC is illustrated schematically in Figure 6.5. An analogue signal is applied to the device and this is converted into an 8-bit binary number. The number of bits available for the representation of the analogue signal is referred to as the 'precision' of the device. Since an 8-bit binary number may take on $2^8$ (256) different values, the input signal (which is continuous, i.e. in principle may take on any voltage) can only be represented in the digital world by 256 different values.

Commonly, ADCs provide 8, 12, 16 and even 24-bit precision. As the precision offered by the ADC increases, the conversion speed per unit cost is reduced. Low-precision converters offer high speed at low price.

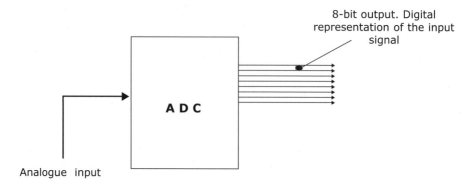

**Figure 6.5:** A schematic representation of an analogue-to-digital converter. The analogue voltage applied to the converter is turned into an 8-bit binary value

Let us consider in a little more detail the significance of the precision offered by an ADC: consider an 8-bit ADC. As indicated above, its output may take on any one of 256 different values. Let us assume that the input signal may take on values between 0 and 5 volts. Thus, in principle, the minimum change in input signal that may be detected by the ADC is given by 5 divided by 256, which equals ~0.02 volts. Within this context we often refer to the 'quantisation error', this representing the difference between the actual voltage applied to the ADC and the value that is represented by the converter. The quantisation error is given by:

$$Q = \frac{1}{2}\left[\frac{V}{precision}\right]$$

... where V represents the range of voltage across which the ADC operates and the precision corresponds to the number of different digital values that may be generated by the ADC (as we have just seen, in the case of an 8-bit ADC, the precision is 256).

A number of approaches may be adopted in the implementation of ADCs. Below we briefly outline one technique in which an ADC is implemented using a DAC and some additional hardware, see Figure 6.5. As may be seen from this illustration, the output from the digital-to-analogue converter is applied to an electronic device known as a 'comparator'. This compares the output from the digital-to-analogue converter with the input signal (the input signal is the one that we wish to convert into a digital form). The technique operates as follows (we assume the use of an 8-bit digital-to-analogue converter but the approach can be generalised to support other levels of precision):

1. The computer applies to the DAC the mid-range value, i.e. the value that is halfway between 0 and 255 (binary 01111111). This results in a DAC output voltage midway between the upper and lower values that it is able to produce

2. The comparator compares the input signal to the voltage produced by the DAC. If the voltage produced by the DAC is greater than the input signal, then the comparator will produce a logic high. Alternatively, if the voltage produced by the DAC is less than the input signal, then the comparator produces a logic low

3. The output from the comparator is sampled by the computer. If the computer reads a logic high, then the computer can determine that the DAC has produced a voltage bigger than the input signal. So as to produce an output from the DAC that more closely equates to the input voltage, it applies a new binary value to the DAC. This value is halfway between 0 and 127 (i.e. half of the value that was previously applied).

4. If the computer reads a logic low from the comparator, then it 'knows' that the output from the DAC is less than the input signal. It therefore applies to the DAC a value that is halfway between 127 and 255

5. The process is repeated and gradually the voltage generated by the DAC gets closer and closer to the input signal. This is achieved by repeating the steps described in (3) and (4) above

6. The process ends when changing the least significant bit applied to the DAC results in the comparator switching its output state. In this case the bit pattern applied to the DAC provides the closest possible representation of the input voltage (i.e. the smallest possible error for a given precision of DAC).

This technique is known as 'successive approximation conversion'.

**An alternative to successive approximation**

As an alternative to the approach described above, we could simply begin by presenting to the DAC a bit pattern comprising all zeros. We would then repeatedly increment this value and continually check for a change in the output state of the comparator. The conversion process would stop when the output from the comparator changes state. In this case the output from the DAC would be in the form of a ramp (or 'staircase'), see Figure 6.7. Suggest one reason why this approach is less efficient than the successive approximation method outlined above.

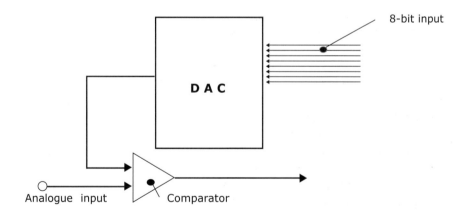

**Figure 6.6:** Here, we illustrate that a digital-to-analogue convertor can be used to implement an analogue-to-digital convertor. Additional hardware is, however, required in the form of a comparator. This device compares the analogue input voltage with the output from the digital-to-analogue convertor. See text for details.

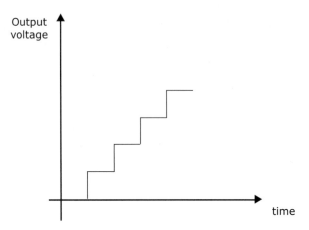

**Figure 6.7:** Repeatedly incrementing the binary value applied to a DAC produces a ramp ('staircase') output signal

## 6.4 Signals

As we have discussed, computers operate in the digital domain and signals (voltages) exist in two states – the logic high and the logic low. In contrast, signals generated outside the computer (and other digital systems) are often referred to as 'analogue' – meaning that at least, in principle, they can occupy an infinite number of states. In Figure 6.8 we illustrate a repetitive analogue signal which is in the form of a sinusoid. In order to most readily discuss the properties of such a signal we employ certain important terms:

1. **Peak amplitude (or simply 'amplitude'):** As indicated in Figure 6.8, the peak amplitude measures the maximum height attained by the waveform relative to the horizontal axis. In the case that a signal takes the form of an electrical disturbance, the amplitude is usually measured in volts

2. **Peak-to-peak amplitude:** As indicated in Figure 6.8, the peak-to-peak amplitude measures the distance between the maximum and minimum heights attained by the signal, i.e. the distance between the 'crest' and the 'trough'. The peak-to-peak amplitude is often twice the value of the peak amplitude

3. **Wavelength:** This is used to indicate the length of a complete cycle of oscillation of a repetitive signal. As may be seen from Figure 6.8, the wavelength corresponds to the distance between two identical points on the waveform. This may be readily measured by, for example, finding the distance between two neighbouring peaks

4. **Frequency:** This provides us with information on the temporal characteristics of a repetitive signal. The frequency indicates the number of complete oscillations of a signal that occur each second. Frequency is measured in hertz (Hz)

5. **Periodic time:** Again this provides information on the temporal characteristics of a waveform. The periodic time is the time taken for a waveform to undergo a complete cycle of oscillation. Frequency (f) and periodic time (T) are related by the expression:

$$f = \frac{1}{T}$$

Having loosely described various metrics that are used to characterize a repetitive waveform, we now briefly turn to the issue of signal sampling. Let us suppose that we wish to convert an analogue signal into a digital form. Naturally, a vital question concerns how often the ADC should sample the signal.

For example:

- If the signal is sampled **too slowly**, information contained within the signal will be lost
- If the signal is sampled needlessly **too often**, we will end up with more samples than are necessary. This will increase the amount of storage space that the samples occupy within the computer. Furthermore, the processor will waste time in performing computations on unnecessary samples.

In short there is an optimum rate at which a particular waveform should be sampled in order that (a) no information contained in the waveform is lost, and (b) that we minimise the number of samples and so maximise the efficiency with which we use a computer's storage facilities and computational resources.

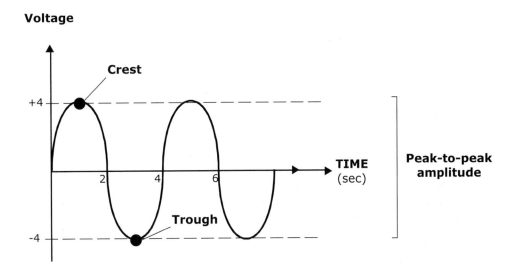

**Figure 6.8:** A sinusoidal waveform. Here, we indicate various measurements that are used in the characterisation of a waveform. Note: the 'crest' indicates the highest point reached by the wave, and the 'trough' the wave's lowest point.

**Activity 6.3**

**Waveform parameters**

Consider the waveform illustrated in Figure 6.9. Determine:

(a) The amplitude

(b) The peak-to-peak amplitude

(c) The frequency.

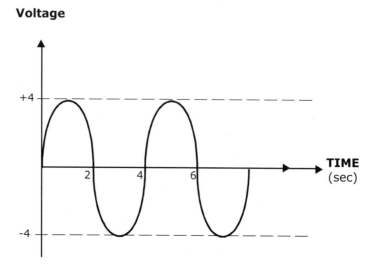

**Figure 6.9:** A repetitive sinusoidal waveform – see Activity 6.3

**Activity 6.4**

**Signal sampling**

By means of library or Internet facilities and within the context of signal sampling, determine what is meant by the 'Nyquist Criteria'. Illustrate your answer by making reference to the waveform described in Activity 6.3 – what is the minimum frequency at which it would it be necessary to sample this waveform in order to ensure that it could be faithfully reproduced?

## 6.5 Interaction devices

In the case of early computers (and here we mean computers developed until the early 1970s), users generally interacted very little with the machine. For the majority of users, programs were coded and submitted to a computer operator who would subsequently load each program into the computer and allow it to execute. The results produced by the programs were then returned to the users. This approach was referred to as 'batch programming'. Most commonly, programs were submitted on sets of punched cards, paper tape (often referred to as punched tape) or, in the case of more advanced systems, on magnetic tape.

Consider for a moment a user of early computer systems. In order to perform some computer-based activity, the user would follow the following steps:

- Design and code a program. Store the executable program (together with any necessary data) on an appropriate form of media
- Submit the program to a computer operator for execution
- When time is available on the computer, the computer operator loads the program onto the machine (together with any necessary data). The program is then executed.
- Eventually, the user obtains the results produced by the program.

Unfortunately, all too often the program would fail to run correctly due to coding errors or design flaws. These would then have to be fixed, and another attempt made to run the program. Clearly, this represents a very frustrating and time-consuming approach and contrasts greatly with modern computing, which is underpinned by real-time interaction.

The days of batch processing are (fortunately) long gone, and in modern computing the interaction process is extremely important. Xerox is credited as being the first company to bring together the mouse, keyboard, and bitmapped display in the early 1970s.

## *Bitmapped graphics*

Spend a moment closely examining the image depicted on your computer screen. If you have very good eyesight, you will see that it comprises an enormous number of tiny dots. These dots are grouped in 3s to form pixels (an abbreviation of 'picture elements'). In each group of three, one dot is responsible for the production of green light, one for red, and the third for blue light (the three primary colours). Typically, a computer screen comprises ~1,000 pixels horizontally and ~800 pixels vertically. Each pixel can be set to a different colour (in software) and to a different level of brightness (again in software). Consequently, by changing the colour of the individual pixels (and their intensity) we can create the images on the computer screen.

Each pixel has a corresponding location in memory where its attributes (colour and intensity) are defined. Thus, by writing a binary value to a particular memory location, we cause a particular pixel on the computer screen to be illuminated to a certain level of intensity and colour. The area of memory used for this purpose is called the 'video memory', and is often located on a special card (circuit board) within the computer that is called the 'video card'.

Employing a direct mapping technique between screen pixels and memory locations is referred to as 'bitmapped' (or, more accurately, 'pixmapped') graphics.

The concept of a bitmap (or pixmap) display enabled the development of systems to support the depiction of menus, icons, etc. Interaction tools such as the mouse can be used to move the cursor across the screen and make selections from the menu system. This is the commonly used interaction technique employed in the modern computer and is referred to as the 'event-driven user interface'.

**Activity 6.5**

### The role of the display in both input and output

The computer display provides a window into the digital world enabling us to see the results of the computational process. Explain why the computer display performs a pivotal role in the interaction process.

We next briefly examine several popular interaction devices.

## *The keyboard*

The keyboard continues to provide a vital means for effecting human/computer interaction. The design of the so-called 'QWERTY' keyboard dates back over 100 years, and in fact originally this layout of the letters on the keyboard was intended to slow down typing speeds and thereby reduce the frequency with which mechanical typewriters 'jammed'. Despite today's keyboards being free of mechanical components – we still use this key layout!

A computer keyboard has approximately 100 keys, the great majority of which allow 'alphanumeric' characters to be input to the computer. However, a small number of keys have a different purpose. For example, the 'shift' key serves to modify the action of other keys on the keyboard. The 'control' (CTRL) key serves a similar function.

Signals pass from the keyboard to the computer along a serial interconnect. Within the keyboard there is a 'keyboard scanner' whose function is to identify that a key has been pressed, and identify the particular key. Each key on the keyboard acts as a 'push button', the pressing of which causes an electrical current to flow. Thus the keyboard comprises essentially ~100 buttons (push switches), so the keyboard scanner must identify which one of these buttons has been pressed and provide this information to the computer. In the simplest scenario, each button would be directly connected to the keyboard scanner, but this would necessitate the keyboard scanner having 100 input ports to which the buttons could be connected. This would be an inefficient approach, and so a more cost-effective coding technique is used (see Figure 6.10). As can be seen from the diagram, there is a set of horizontal wires, and a set of vertical wires. These wires do not directly touch but a keyboard button is located at every point where they cross over.

The set of horizontal wires is connected to an output port (meaning that the hardware is able to output signals (binary codes) to these wires), and the set of vertical wires is connected to an input port (i.e. their individual logic states may be read by the hardware).

By using a coding technique we can reduce the number of wires that must be connected to the keyboard scanner. The approach works as follows:

1. The vertical set of wires is usually in a logic-high state

2. The processor outputs a sequence of codes to the horizontal set of wires (via Port 1). These codes take the form – 1111111110, 1111111101, 1111111011, etc. As may be seen, a logic low is output to one horizontal wire at a time (all other wires being at a logic-high state)

3. If a key is pressed, it electrically connects one horizontal wire to one vertical wire. Let us assume the key pressed connects the third horizontal wire (as counted from the top) with the tenth vertical wire (as counted from the left-hand side), see Figure 6.10.

When the processor outputs the code 1111111011, the third horizontal wire will become a logic low, and since this is electrically connected to the tenth vertical wire (because of the key pressed), it follows that the tenth vertical wire will also become a logic low. This logic state is detected via Port 2 and provides identification of the key that has been pressed.

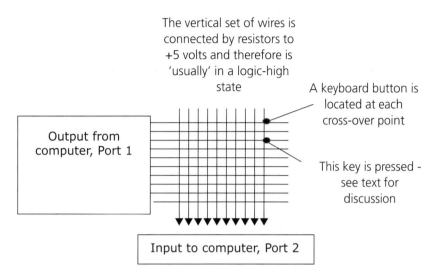

The vertical set of wires is connected by resistors to +5 volts and therefore is 'usually' in a logic-high state

A keyboard button is located at each cross-over point

Output from computer, Port 1

This key is pressed - see text for discussion

Input to computer, Port 2

**Figure 6.10:** Typically a keyboard contains ~100 keys. Rather than connecting each key individually to the keyboard scanner, a coding technique is commonly used. The connections (wires) illustrated in the diagram permit the 100 keys to be connected to the keyboard encoder by means of 10 output wires and 10 input wires. The horizontal and vertical wires drawn in the diagram are not physically in contact, but are connected together by the keyboard keys that are electrically located at the points where the vertical and horizontal wires cross over one another.

In essence, if we have 100 keys, then we can encode these using 10 horizontal wires and 10 vertical wires. Similarly, if we had an imaginary keyboard layout with 256 keys, then we would need to use 16 horizontal wires and 16 vertical wires (we obtain these numbers by taking the square root of the number of keys).

As indicated above, an important function of the keyboard hardware is to detect when a key is pressed and to identify the particular key. Additionally, it is responsible for the generation of the ASCII codes (see Section 4.4) which can be understood by the processor, and which identify the character or control key that has been pressed.

In summary, when a key is pressed, the event is recognised by the keyboard hardware and the particular key is identified. The keyboard hardware then generates the appropriate ASCII code for transmission to the CPU and will typically generate an interrupt. As a result, the processor will enter an interrupt service routine via which it will read the ASCII code.

In the above description we have made a number of simplifications. For example:

- **The 'shift' key:** when the 'shift' key is pressed, its purpose is to modify the functionality of other keys, e.g. switching between lower-case 'a' and upper-case 'A'. This operation is handled by the keyboard hardware without reference to the processor

- **The use of mechanical switches:** the signals generated by mechanical switches do not give rise to 'clean' transitions between logic-low and logic-high states, but typically generate the sort of signal illustrated in Figure 6.11. As a result, and unless precautions are taken, it can appear that a key has been pressed multiple times, when in fact it has only been pressed once. The keyboard hardware must 'clean up' such signals in order to produce smooth transitions between logic states. This may be accomplished by the inclusion of special logic gates known as 'Schmitt triggers'.

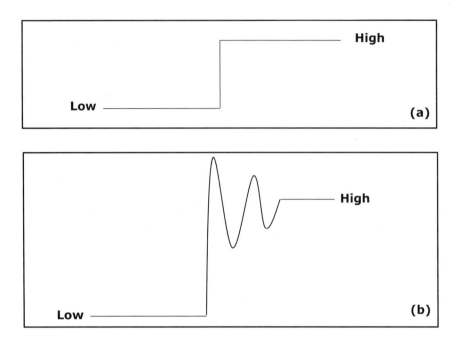

**Figure 6.11:** In (a) we illustrate an idealised digital waveform with a transition from a logic low (approximately 0 volts) to a logic high (approximately 5 volts). In reality, signals do not behave in this manner and when, for example, a mechanical switch or push button is used to cause a transition, the waveform will change in a manner as illustrated in (b). Note: the extent and duration of the overshoot ('bounce') have been exaggerated for clarity. Software simulators are available to simulate the behaviour of electronic circuits. However, these often operate on idealised waveforms and this can result in a difference between the simulated result and the performance of physical hardware.

## The mouse

The mouse has a shorter history than the keyboard and was originally prototyped in 1964 at Stanford University. Being constructed in a wooden box, the original mouse differed somewhat in appearance from the modern version.

Two types of mouse are commonly encountered today:

- The first and most widely used is a **mechanical device.** Movement of the mouse causes a small ball to rotate and this turns two 'wheels' located at right angles to each other within the mouse. The rotation of these wheels is sensed by optical devices. Thus when we move the mouse the ball rotates, and in turn so do the wheels. Their rotation is converted into a series of electrical pulses. If, for example, we move the mouse backwards and forwards then only one of the wheels will rotate (indicating no sideways movements). Similarly, if we move the mouse from side to side, the other wheel will rotate. When, for example, the mouse is moved in a diagonal direction, both wheels will rotate, and for different angles of movement the wheels will rotate at a different relative rate. The simplest way to properly appreciate the operation of the mouse is to remove the ball by removing the plastic surround on the underside of the mouse (this usually requires a rotation of the disk by half a turn). Once you have removed the ball from the mouse you will be able to see the two wheels that the ball causes to rotate.

It is generally simple to remove the ball from a mouse – and from time to time this is necessary as sometimes the wheels need cleaning. If ever you find that your mouse is not working very well, then the problem is probably caused by dirt or hairs adhering to the two wheels

- A second form of mouse that is becoming increasingly popular does not make use of a ball, but is an **all-electronic device.** In this case, the mouse uses a special mouse-pad upon which a matrix of vertical and horizontal lines are printed. The horizontal lines are a different colour from the vertical lines. The mouse is equipped with a light source that shines down onto the grid lines, and two photo detectors that can detect the light reflected from the mouse mat (a photo detector converts light energy into electrical energy). Each of the photo detectors is equipped with a filter so that it can only receive light reflected from either vertical or horizontal lines, but not from both. Thus, one photo detector receives light reflected from the horizontal lines, and the other photo detector receives light reflected from the vertical lines. As the mouse is moved across the mouse-pad, the photo detectors are able to detect its passage across the vertical and horizontal gridlines.

The output signal from the mouse to the computer passes along a serial interconnect.

### Other interaction devices

There are a variety of other devices that can be used to effect interaction with the computer. In connection with (for example) computer games, a joystick is often used. Normally, the joystick supports two-dimensional interaction, but more advanced forms of joystick now support three-dimensional navigation.

Joysticks can operate in either 'absolute mode' or 'rate mode'. In the case of the former, a motion of the joystick (up, down, left, or right) produces a corresponding movement of the cursor. The extent to which the cursor is moved is directly proportional to the amplitude of movement of the joystick.

In contrast, in the case of a joystick operating in absolute mode, the amplitude of movement of the joystick determines the speed at which the cursor moves. Thus, if the joystick is moved to the left, the cursor will move in the same direction and its speed will be determined by how far the joystick has been deflected. Returning the joystick to its central position results in the cessation of cursor motion.

The touch screen, track ball, track pad, and track point devices provide further examples of interaction devices.

## 6.6 The display

The traditional computer display is based upon cathode ray tube (CRT) technology. The cathode ray tube (see Figure 6.12) dates back more than a hundred years and has provided a remarkably flexible means of achieving high-quality image depiction. The basic principle of operation is most readily understood by initially considering the monochrome (black and white) display. This operates as follows:

- An electron gun (see Figure 6.13) is used to generate a beam of electrons. This beam travels from the rear of the CRT to the screen. The screen is coated with a phosphor material and when the electron beam strikes the phosphor, visible light is produced (the kinetic energy of the electrons is imparted to the phosphor material and causes the emission of light.) The overall result is the appearance of a spot of light emanating from the centre of the screen. If the electron beam is turned off, the spot of light will rapidly – almost instantaneously – disappear.

**Figure 6.12:** The type of cathode ray tube encountered in computer monitors and television sets. It is constructed from a thick glass vessel which contains a high vacuum. In fact, a cathode ray tube is potentially a very dangerous device and must be handled with great care (to avoid implosion caused by the difference between atmospheric pressure and the internal vacuum).

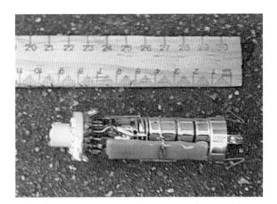

**Figure 6.13:** An electron gun used to generate an electron beam. Electron guns must be handled with care as the electrode responsible for the production of the electron beam (the cathode) is coated with toxic materials. The electron gun operates via a process of thermionic emission whereby a heated cathode is made to emit electrons. These electrons are accelerated by high voltage (typically, in the case of a computer monitor, ~25,000 volts). Note: the high voltages used within a monitor are potentially lethal.

- In order to form a useful display, the electron beam is scanned across the surface of the screen at high speed. To scan the screen, the electron beam starts from the top left-hand side, moves horizontally across the screen to the right-hand side, and then very quickly returns to the left side to a position just below the starting point. The process is repeated some hundreds of times and in this way, the electron beam sweeps out a series of horizontal lines on the screen. Once it reaches the bottom of the screen, it starts again from the top left-hand corner. (Typically, it performs an entire scan 50 to 100 times per second.) This is known as a 'raster scan' display, see Figure 6.14

- The scanning of the beam is achieved using a number of electromagnets (coils of wire through which electricity is passed). These magnets are contained within the type of assembly illustrated in Figure 6.15. The magnetic fields that they produce cause the electron beam to be deflected. These coils are located around the 'neck' of the CRT, as may be seen from Figure 6.12

- As the beam sweeps across the screen it illuminates a set of closely spaced horizontal lines, and by modulating the beam (rapidly adjusting the strength (current) of the beam) under computer control, images may be formed. This process is illustrated in Figure 6.16 where we show the electron beam being turned off at appropriate locations to enable the depiction of a black circle on a white background

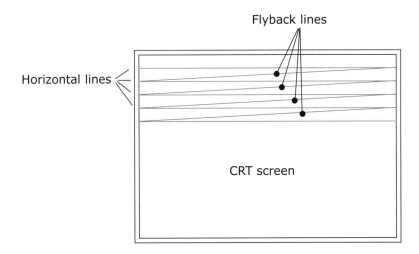

**Figure 6.14:** A raster scan creates a series of visible horizontal lines.

- In order that the electron beam can travel from the electron gun to the screen, air must be removed from within the display tube – a high vacuum must be maintained (with a pressure of the order of $10^{-7}$ Torr).

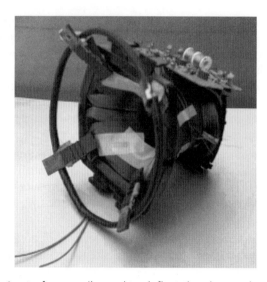

**Figure 6.15:** A set of scan coils used to deflect the electron beam. This assembly contains four coils. These operate in pairs – one pair being responsible for the vertical deflection of the beam and the other pair for horizontal motion. Electron beams can be deflected at extremely high speeds using simple technologies (much faster than, for example, laser beams).

In the case of a CRT able to depict colour images, three electron beams are used and these simultaneously sweep across the screen in the manner described above. The operation of the display is based on the mixing of the three primary colours (red, green, and blue), which when combined in suitable proportions can produce light of any colour. To achieve this goal, the CRT screen is coated with three different phosphors each of which is responsible for the production of a particular primary colour. Two different approaches are in common usage for the distribution of the phosphors on the screen. The simplest layout is illustrated in Figure 6.17. Dots of phosphor are printed onto the screen and these are arranged in groups of three. Each electron beam is responsible for the production of a different primary colour. Thus one beam addresses all the phosphor dots responsible for the emission of blue light, the second beam addresses the dots that emit red light, and the third the dots that emit green light.

Each pixel comprises a set of three phosphor dots ('sub-pixels') and by controlling the individual strengths (currents) of the electron beams, pixels of different colours and different levels of brightness can be formed.

For this approach to work correctly, it is vital that each electron beam excites phosphor dots of only a single colour. Thus, for example, the electron beam responsible for activating the blue sub-pixels must not have any impact on the red and green phosphor dots. To meet this requirement, it is necessary to employ additional hardware in the form of a 'shadow-mask' – see Figure 6.18. Typically, a shadow-mask comprises a thin sheet of metal within which on the order of 800,000 holes are precisely cut (the number of holes equals the number of pixels that may be illuminated on the screen). The shadow-mask is positioned just behind the CRT screen and each hole is precisely aligned with a group of three sub-pixels, see Figure 6.19. The approach imposes geometrical constraints and ensures that each electron beam can only address (excite) its designated set of phosphor dots.

Unfortunately, the shadow-mask technique is not without problems. Firstly, it is difficult to manufacture the mask and ensure its proper alignment with the phosphor dots.

Even more seriously, many electrons collide with the mask (rather than passing through the holes) and so a significant portion of the beam current is lost. This negatively impacts on brightness of images that can be produced for a given beam current.

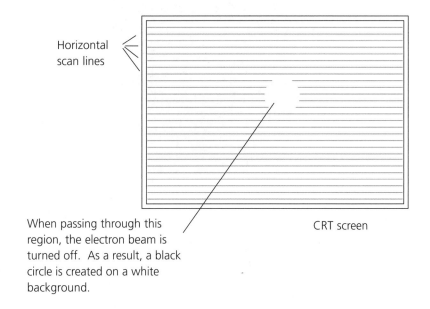

Horizontal scan lines

When passing through this region, the electron beam is turned off. As a result, a black circle is created on a white background.

CRT screen

**Figure 6.16:** The use of a raster scan to create a black circle on a white background

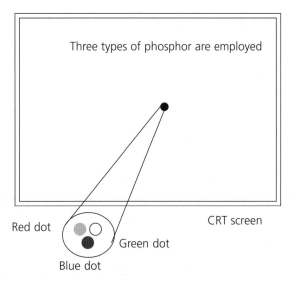

Three types of phosphor are employed

Red dot

Green dot

Blue dot

CRT screen

**Figure 6.17:** A colour CRT – each pixel comprises three 'sub-pixels'. These are arranged as shown and are able to produce red, green, and blue light

**Figure 6.18:** A shadow-mask. This is constructed from a thin metallic plate in which of the order of 800,000 holes are precisely cut. The function of the shadow mask is to ensure that each of the three electron beams is only able to strike a phosphor of a particular colour. Some monitors use alternative forms of shadow-mask.

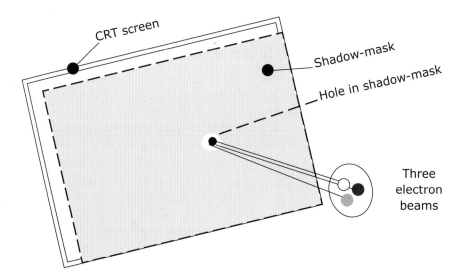

**Figure 6.19:** The shadow-mask imposes geometrical constraints such that each beam can only address (excite) a single set of phosphor dots.

**Activity 6.6**

### Display characteristics

Imagine that you are purchasing a computer display. Describe the characteristics that you consider to be particularly important.

# 6.7 Display metrics

The performance of a computer display is described by means of various 'metrics' (measures). In this section, we briefly examine some of these metrics. You may wish to look at your own computer configuration and see how the display performs in terms of these measures.

- **Display bandwidth:** this refers to the total number of pixels that may be activated on the computer display. The bandwidth is normally quoted as the product of its horizontal and vertical values. For example, a commonly encountered bandwidth is 1,024 x 768 – meaning that the monitor is able to depict 1,024 pixels horizontally and 768 pixels vertically. These numbers are often rounded to 1,000 and 800 respectively, giving a total number of pixels of ~800,000. The greater the number of pixels that are available, the greater the amount of fine detail that can be depicted on the display. Of course, as we increase the size of the display, then we should in theory increase the total number of pixels that can be illuminated. In this way we can maintain the same 'display resolution' (this represents the number of pixels per unit length (e.g. pixels per cm)). However, in order to save cost, displays are often scaled in size without increasing the display bandwidth. (You may have noticed when viewing large-screen projection TVs that images can be seen to comprise discrete elements – the image is said to be 'pixellated'.)

  Recall discussion in Section 6.5 concerning the 'bitmapped' ('pixmapped') graphics approach. Fundamental to this technique is a one-to-one mapping between screen pixels and locations within video memory. Consequently, as the resolution of the display is increased, the extent of the video memory must also be enlarged

- **Colour:** this metric is used to determine the range of colour values that can be assigned to each pixel. Early computer monitors did not support colour depiction, nor did they support a grey-scale (shades of grey). Each pixel could only take on one of two values (corresponding to a pixel being illuminated or otherwise). This represented the true bitmapped display (i.e. one bit per pixel). Today's computer monitors support high-quality colour imaging and typically each pixel is represented within video memory by 16 or 24 bits. (In this case we refer to a 'pixmapped' rather than 'bitmapped' display.) If, for example, we use 24 bits per pixel, then each pixel can take on (in principle) $2^{24}$ different shades of colour and levels of brightness.

  It is instructive to pause for a moment and calculate $2^{24}$ using your calculator. This is an extremely large number, indicating a tremendous 'colour palette', i.e. range of colours and levels of brightness. Even more remarkable is the ability of the human eye to derive benefit from such a range.

- **Refresh rate:** when the electron beam(s) of the cathode ray tube scans across the surface of the screen (as we have previously described), it causes the phosphorescent coating(s) on the screen to emit light. However, once the electron beam has passed over the surface, the amount of light that is emitted gradually diminishes (fades away). This is the same effect that we encounter with the fluorescent light. If you happen to be in a room that uses fluorescent lighting, separate your fingers on one hand, close one eye, and wave your hand rapidly in front of the open eye as you look towards the source of the fluorescent lighting. You will notice that as your hand moves, at moments the light will not appear to be present. In short, the fluorescent tube does not continually emit light, but rapidly cycles between emissive and non-emissive states. Similarly, the cathode ray tube based display does not continuously emit light, and to ensure that the image appears to be continually present the screen must be regularly refreshed (i.e. the electron beam must regularly re-scan the surface of the screen, and so re-excite the phosphors).

If we look towards a source of light that does not continually emit light, but rather cycles between emissive and non-emissive states, at a frequency of less than ~20 times per second, then the light source will appear to flicker. If we increase the frequency whereby the light source cycles between emissive and non-emissive states to a frequency of greater than ~25 times per second, then the light seems to be continually present. This is because the rate of flicker is greater than what is called the 'critical flicker fusion frequency'. For most people, this occurs at around 20Hz, and denotes the frequency at which a flickering light source appears to be continually present (flicker-free).

In short, the computer screen must be refreshed at a frequency greater than the critical flicker fusion frequency, and this suggests that we need to refresh the screen ~20 to 25 times per second. In reality, computer monitors are refreshed at much higher frequencies since although we may not be able to readily detect a flickering light source that is refreshed at this rate, we can still subliminally detect the flicker, i.e. it is detected within the brain. Whilst we may not be aware of subliminal flicker, it can trigger problems such as nausea and headaches. (You may have encountered the concept of subliminal advertising where, during movies, an advertisement is flashed up onto the screen in such a way that it cannot be seen consciously, but can be detected by the brain. Quite a lot of experimentation was done with this in the 1950s and, for example, in cinemas, images of drinks and food would be flashed up onto the screen for such a brief time that the audience did not visually perceive the adverts. However, it was shown that when this type of advertisement was employed, sales of corresponding drinks and food increased. In most countries, subliminal advertising is now banned – in principle…) Quality computer monitors now support refresh rates in excess of 100 hertz and when refreshed at this rate, we can be sure that neither visual flicker nor subliminal flicker are problematic.

**Activity 6.7**

**The raster scan**

Consider a computer display that measures 40cm horizontally and 30cm vertically. Assuming that it has a display bandwidth of 1,000 by 800 and supports a refresh rate of 50Hz, determine the speed that the electron beam sweeps across the screen (you may neglect the time that the electron beam spends performing retraces (flyback) and therefore can assume that all the time is spent in drawing the horizontal scan lines).

## 6.8 Summary

In this chapter we have introduced a range of concepts relating to computer input/output. The techniques used to convert between analogue and digital signals have been outlined and we have discussed the importance of sampling analogue signals at a rate which is sufficient to ensure that no information is lost. In this context the Nyquist Criteria was introduced and this indicates that an analogue signal must be sampled at a rate that is at least twice the frequency of the highest frequency component within the signal.

In Section 6.5 we briefly considered several basic devices by which we are able to interact with the computer and subsequently turned our attention to the display. Although this provides the primary means by which we view the results of the computational process, it is important to remember that it also plays a pivotal role in our interaction with the digital world. Within this context, the display enables us to navigate the cursor (by means of, for example, the mouse) and perform interaction operations using menus, icons, etc.

## 6.9 Review questions

**Question 6.1** Explain what is meant by quantisation error in the context of an analogue-to-digital converter.

**Question 6.2** What do you understand by the expression 'batch processing'?

**Question 6.3** What do we mean by the 'QWERTY' keyboard layout, and why was this particular layout initially adopted (rather than, for example, laying out keys in alphabetical order)?

**Question 6.4** Distinguish between the mechanical and non-mechanical forms of mouse.

**Question 6.5** What is a pixel?

**Question 6.6** Why does a colour cathode ray tube based monitor employ three electron beams?

**Question 6.7** What is the purpose of a shadow-mask within a colour CRT?

**Question 6.8** In the case of an ADC offering a precision of n bits and that employs the 'successive approximation' technique, what is the maximum number of steps needed to perform a conversion?

**Question 6.9** A sinusoidal wave has a frequency of 20Hz.  What is its periodic time?

**Question 6.10** A current of 5 amps is passed through a 20 ohm resistor.  Calculate the voltage that is produced across the resistor (i.e. the 'volts drop' across the resistor)

## 6.10 Feedback on activities

### Activity 61:  Digital-to-analogue conversion accuracy

Twelve bits can take on $2^{12}$ different values – i.e.  4,096 values.  The smallest step in voltage that we can therefore generate is 10 divided by 4,096, which is approximately 0.002 volts.

### Activity 6.2:  An alternative to successive approximation

When considered on the basis of the number of iterations that are on average required to obtain a binary value that most closely represents the analogue input, the successive approximation approach is more efficient.  For example, when we employ the 'ramp technique', the worst-case scenario occurs when the analogue input is closest to the maximum input voltage level.  In this case, we would need to make a large number of steps – in the case of an 8-bit implementation we would need to make (in the worst case) 255 steps.  More generally, in the worst case and assuming a precision of n bits, we would need to make $2^n - 1$ steps.  However, the successive approximation technique ensures that for a precision of n bits the maximum number of steps needed is n.

### Activity 6.3: Waveform parameters

(a) 4 volts
(b) 8 volts
(c) Frequency = 1/periodic time.
The periodic time equals four seconds. Thus the frequency = 0.25Hz.

### Activity 6.4: Signal sampling

Consider a waveform with a frequency f and that is to be sampled and converted into a digital representation. The Nyquist Criteria indicates that in order to reconstruct such a waveform (i.e. ensure no loss of information), it is necessary to sample the signal at a frequency of 2f. For example, consider the simple sinusoidal waveform discussed in Activity 6.3. The frequency of this wave is 0.25Hz. The minimum frequency at which it must be sampled (in order that it can subsequently be faithfully reconstructed) is 2 x 0.25Hz – i.e. 0.5Hz.

### Activity 6.5: The role of the display in both input and output

When we interact with a computer, we make considerable use of the mouse and this allows us to move the cursor to any location on the screen and make selections from the menu system. The computer screen plays a very important role in ensuring that we properly navigate the cursor, i.e. move it to the correct position. Try navigating the cursor with your screen turned off! Without the screen it would be impossible to move the cursor to the correct position necessary to make the required selection. Thus, the screen not only provides a window into the digital world, but also plays a very important role in allowing us to interact with this world.

### Activity 6.6: Display characteristics

Here are some of the criteria that may influence your selection of a display:

1. The size of the display. This is normally measured as the length of the diagonal across the screen. Unfortunately, manufacturers also include in their measurement the part of the display screen that is hidden behind the plastic surround!

2. The resolution of the display. This provides a measure of the number of pixels per unit length (e.g. so many pixels per centimetre or inch). Displays have different resolutions in the vertical and horizontal directions (generally). The higher the resolution, the better.

3. Colour palette. This provides an indication of the range of colours and greyscales that may be assigned to each pixel. Typically, monitors offer a 24-bit colour palette.

4. Refresh rate. This indicates the frequency at which the display can be refreshed. The higher the refresh rate, the better as this avoids any problems that we may experience as a consequence of flicker.

Notice that the characteristics of the display must be supported by the performance of the video card through which the processor is connected to the display.

**Activity 6.7: The raster scan**

If we neglect the time spent in performing flyback, then in a single raster scan of the screen the electron beam moves 40 x 1,000cm = 400m. The electron beam performs 50 scans per second and therefore the total distance travelled (per second) is 400 x 50 =20,000m. Thus the deflection speed is 20km.$s^{-1}$. In fact, the speed is somewhat greater than this as, for example, we have not taken into account the additional distance moved as a result of flyback.

# CHAPTER 7

# The central processing unit

## OVERVIEW

In earlier chapters, the processor has largely been regarded as a 'black box' and we have focused upon signals that are applied to the processor, and its response to these signals. In this chapter, we consider aspects of the processor's internal architecture and provide an insight into the way the processor is able to execute a series of instructions.

**Learning outcomes**   On completion of this chapter you should be able to:

- Discuss the functionality of key elements within a simple processor model

- Describe how key elements in a simple processor model may be interconnected, to form an elementary processor

- Understand the basic utility of a Register Transfer Language (RTL)

- Discuss the purpose and implementation of a 'stack'.

## 7.1 Introduction

In the previous chapters, we have focused on external aspects of the processor and have treated it as a 'black box' (in the sense that we have considered signals generated by the processor and passed back to it). In this context we have described the processor's 'fetch' and 'execute' cycles. As we have seen, a processor fetches op-codes and operands from memory, acts upon them and returns the results of the computation (where appropriate) to memory. This occasionally leads to confusion as it would seem that the processor undertakes three basic cycles – fetching instructions, executing instructions, and returning results to memory. However, it is important to remember that the return to memory activity is an inherent part of the execution process. It is for this reason that we specifically allude to the fetch/execute cycle and not to the fetch/execute/return cycle.

In this chapter we take a brief glimpse into the workings of the processor. Today's processors generally have a fairly complicated architecture, and our purpose is not to discuss such an architecture in depth but rather to provide a more general insight into various exemplar operations performed by the processor. In order to best explain the way in which some basic functions are performed, we employ a simple processor model.

We begin by describing the purpose of various 'sub-units' within our simple processor model. These sub-units are in fact encountered in most modern processors – however, whilst a typical real processor would, for example, contain a plurality of registers that can be used in support of arithmetic and logical operations, for simplicity our processor model will use only one such register. In section 7.3 we briefly introduce the use of a 'Register Transfer Language' (RTL) and provide simple examples of a formal notation to describe various operations within a processor.

In section 7.4 we discuss the purpose of a 'stack' that is used when subroutines are called and when a processor services an interrupt. Within this context we discuss the use of a 'stack pointer' register. Section 7.5 provides an opportunity to bring together some of the concepts introduced in this chapter.

## 7.2 General processor architecture

As just indicated, the architecture of the modern processor is generally quite complex and so, to most readily describe some key aspects of a processor's internal features, we confine our discussion to a simple processor model. In figure 7.1 we illustrate various key elements that comprise this model (and which are found in typical 'real' processor implementations), the functionality of which we briefly outline.

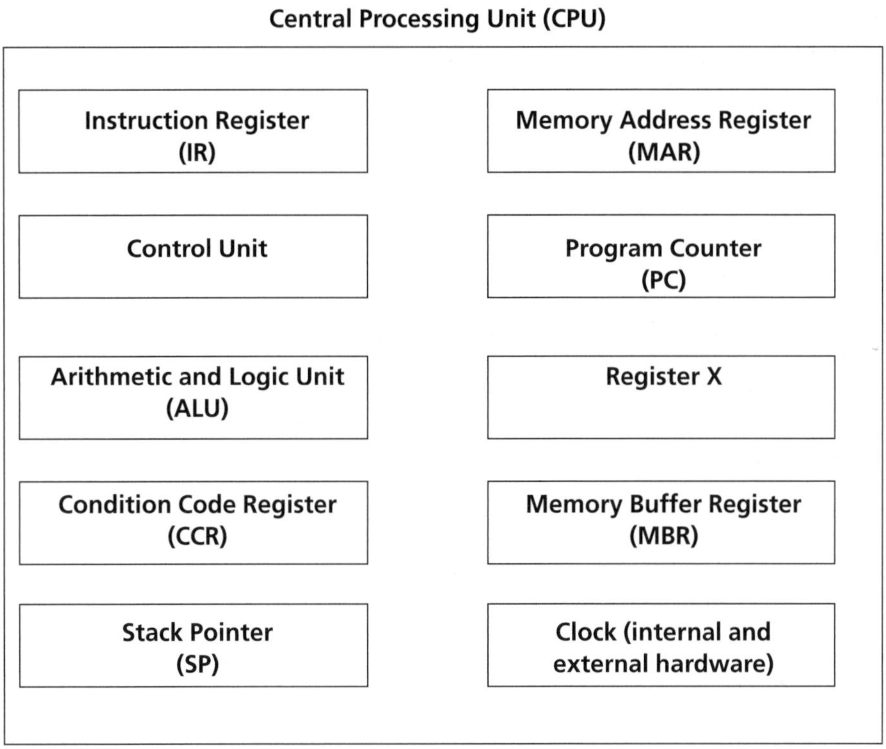

Central Processing Unit (CPU)
Instruction Register (IR)
Memory Address Register (MAR)
Control Unit
Program Counter (PC)
Arithmetic and Logic Unit (ALU)
Register X
Condition Code Register (CCR)
Memory Buffer Register (MBR)
Stack Pointer (SP)
Clock (internal and external hardware)

**Figure 7.1:** Key 'sub-units' within the simple model processor

## *The program counter and memory address register*

In Section 3.6 we briefly discussed the purpose of the program counter (PC) which acts as a pointer to where the processor is up to in the execution of a program. If the contents of the PC are lost (or in some way corrupted), then the processor would have no record of the next memory address that is to be accessed and so program execution would fail. As indicated in Figure 7.2, the PC is connected to the memory address register (MAR) which acts as the interface (or gateway) between the PC and the address bus.

Program Counter (PC)
Memory Address Register (MAR)
Address bus

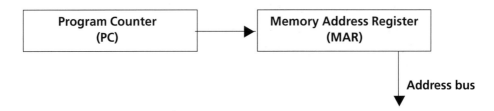

**Figure 7.2:** The memory address register interfaces the program counter with the address bus

Recall from Chapter 1 that a computer is able to execute instructions in sequence, by selection, and by iteration. In the case that instructions are executed sequentially (and if we assume that each instruction (opcode together with any associated operand) occupies a single memory location, see Figure 7.3), then as the processor moves on to execute each subsequent instruction it is only necessary to increment (add one) to the value stored in the PC, see Figure 7.4.

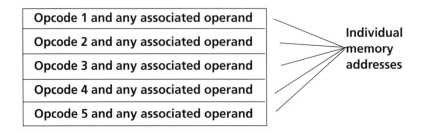

Figure 7.3: For simplicity, we assume that each opcode (together with its associated operand) is stored in a single memory address – i.e. that an opcode (and associated operand) does not span more than a single memory location.

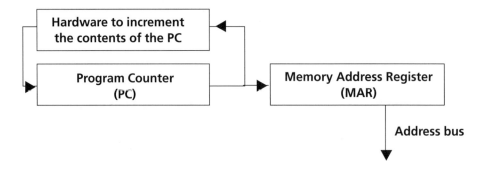

Figure 7.4: If we assume that each instruction (opcode and any associated operand) is contained within a single unique memory location (i.e. that they do not span more than one memory address), then when executing instructions in sequence it is only necessary to increment the value stored in the PC.

In the case that instructions are executed by selection and by iteration, we need to provide hardware that will enable a completely new value to be loaded into the PC. By way of example, consider the repeated execution of a set of instructions (i.e. by repeated iteration) as indicated in Figure 7.5.

In this simple example, the processor executes an instruction at address $0000 (this is a value that we have arbitrarily chosen). The next instruction is at address $0001 – followed by address $0002, etc. This process of sequential instruction execution continues until we reach address $0005. Here, we assume the processor encounters a 'jump' instruction. This instruction is equivalent to the contentious 'GoTo' statement encountered in many high-level programming languages (it is also known as an 'unconditional branch') and we will assume that it instructs the processor that the next instruction to be executed is at address $0000.

Thus, program execution 'loops back', and within the processor this necessitates the loading of a new value into the PC (the address $0000).

In Figure 7.6 we extend Figure 7.4 to indicate the need for additional hardware that will enable the PC to be loaded with a particular binary value. This load operation may occur when, for example:

- A 'jump' instruction is encountered
- A branch instruction is encountered. (Branch instructions enable the processor to execute instructions by selection; the action taken depends on the outcome of some computation. By analogy, the branch instruction may be considered to parallel the 'If… Then…Else…' instruction employed in high-level languages)
- Program execution is initiated
- The processor is to commence execution (enter) an interrupt service routine.

| Address $0000 | Opcode 1 and any associated operand |
|---|---|
| Address $0001 | Opcode 2 and any associated operand |
| Address $0002 | Opcode 3 and any associated operand |
| Address $0003 | Opcode 4 and any associated operand |
| Address $0004 | Opcode 5 and any associated operand |
| Address $0005 | 'Jump' to address $0000 |
| Address $0006 | |

**Figure 7.5:** The use of a 'jump' instruction that results in the repeated execution of a set of instructions (i.e. the execution of instructions by repeated iteration)

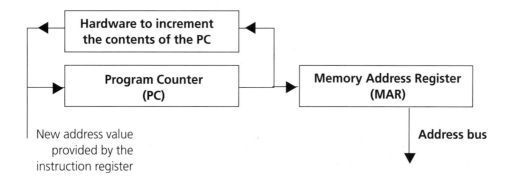

**Figure 7.6:** As indicated in the text, we need to provide a mechanism whereby a new address may be loaded into the program counter. As will be discussed shortly, in the case of 'jump' and 'branch' instructions, this address may be generated by the instruction register.

## The memory buffer register (MBR)

In the previous section, above, we focused on processor 'sub-units' that operate on the generation of addresses and, as we indicated, the MAR acts as the interface between the address bus connections and the PC. The memory buffer register performs a similar function in relation to the flow of opcodes and operands into and out of the CPU. In fact, the MBR interfaces the data bus connections with several sub-units within the CPU that deal with the processing of opcodes and operands. Thus when data is to be written to memory or when a read operation is performed, the MBR serves as a temporary buffer.

## The instruction register (IR)

In the case of our simple processor model, we have assumed that each opcode (together with any associated operand) is stored in a single memory location. In the case of 'real' processors this is often not the case and an opcode/operand combination can span two or even more memory locations – however, for simplicity we overlook this complication. Furthermore, we will assume that an opcode can have a maximum of one operand (i.e. an opcode has no associated operand or one operand).

When an instruction fetch occurs, the opcode and operand are passed through the MBR to the instruction register. Here (as in memory) the opcode and operands are segregated, see Figure 7.7.

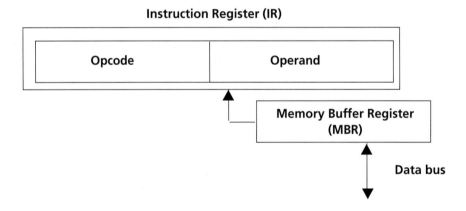

**Figure 7.7:** The instruction register allows hardware within the processor to extract opcode and operand information from the instruction currently in execution

## The arithmetic and logic unit (ALU) and Register X

As its name implies, the arithmetic and logic unit is responsible for the arithmetic (e.g. addition and subtraction) and logic (e.g. shifting a binary number so many places to the left or right). Register X (or simply 'X') is the name that we will use when referring to a register used for the temporary storage of a value during a mathematical operation. For example, a program fragment may contain instructions of the form illustrated in Figure 7.8.

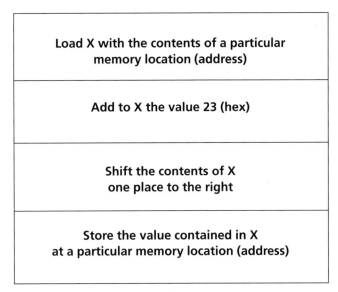

**Figure 7.8:** Indicating the use of Register X as a temporary store during arithmetic and logical operations

As each instruction is executed, appropriate signals are applied to the ALU to indicate the mathematical operation to be performed, together with the source of input data and the destination of the result. In this context, it is important to remember that the source and destination referred to here relate to registers within the CPU. For example, the MBR and Register X are possible source and destination registers, see Figure 7.9.

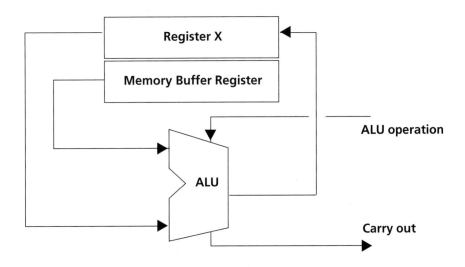

**Figure 7.9:** The ALU is shown taking input from Register X and the MBR and returning the result of an operation to Register X. Note the form of symbol that is frequently used to represent the ALU.

## A full adder

In Section 2.4 we described the operation of a half-adder. One of the pivotal functions performed by the ALU is the addition of two binary numbers. This involves not only the addition of corresponding bits but also the handling of carry bits. This is illustrated in Figure 7.10. In Figure 7.11 we provide a circuit diagram for a full adder. Complete Table 7.1 and hence demonstrate that the circuit behaves as a full adder. Note that to facilitate this process, the table includes entries for intermediate connections within the circuit.

| A | B | $C_{in}$ | L | M | N | O | Sum | $C_{out}$ |
|---|---|---|---|---|---|---|-----|-----------|
| 0 | 0 | 0 | | | | | | |
| 0 | 0 | 1 | | | | | | |
| 0 | 1 | 0 | | | | | | |
| 0 | 1 | 1 | | | | | | |
| 1 | 0 | 0 | | | | | | |
| 1 | 0 | 1 | | | | | | |
| 1 | 1 | 0 | | | | | | |
| 1 | 1 | 1 | | | | | | |

**Table 7.1:** An incomplete truth table for a full adder

## Constructing a full adder using two half-adders

A full adder may be constructed using two half-adders and an OR gate. Using the truth table completed for Activity 7.1, and by reference to Section 2.4 (or otherwise), show how this may be achieved.

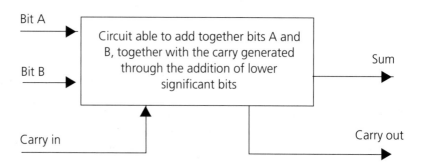

**Figure 7.10:** A full adder – this is able to add together two bits, together with a carry bit. The circuit provides two outputs – the sum and the carry out.

## The addition of binary numbers

In Figure 7.10, a full adder is represented as a rectangle equipped with three inputs and two outputs (i.e. we have represented a full adder as a 'black box'). Using this form of representation for the full adder circuit (able to add together pairs of bits – and deal with carry-in and generate carry-out signals), show how these units could be interconnected to enable the addition of two three-bit numbers.

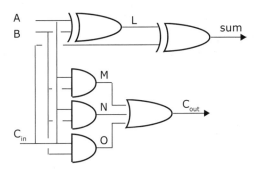

**Figure 7.11:** A circuit diagram for a full adder

## *The condition control register (CCR)*

The individual bits (commonly referred to as 'flags') that comprise the CCR have different meanings and are set or reset according to the outcome of the last operation performed by the ALU. For example, one bit within the CCR is used to indicate whether an arithmetic operation generated a carry. Thus, for example, if the processor were to perform an addition instruction this may or may not generate a carry of 1 (e.g. in the case that the binary value 00000011 is added to 11111111 a carry of 1 would occur). If the next instruction to be executed is a conditional branch (in which the condition for branching depends on whether or not a carry of 1 has occurred), a check would be made to determine the status of the carry bit within the CCR. Other bits in the CCR may be used to indicate that an ALU operation has generated a negative result and to indicate a result of zero. The CCR is sometimes referred to as the 'processor status register' (PSR).

## *The control unit (CU)*

This is responsible for orchestrating and managing all operations performed by the processor (such as register transfers and defining each arithmetic operation to be carried out by the ALU). All timing and synchronisation of signals, register transfers and other activities are derived from a clock signal generated by hardware within, and external to the processor. As we have discussed, the instruction register (IR) holds the opcode and operand of the current instruction that has been fetched from memory. The control unit must decode each opcode to identify the signals that must be generated to permit successful instruction execution. In the case of a conditional instruction (conditional branch) the control unit will also take input from the condition control register (CCR). This interconnectivity is indicated in Figure 7.12.

### The stack pointer (SP)

This is covered in depth in Section 7.4.

In Section 7.5 we briefly consider the use of the above sub-systems for instruction execution.

## 7.3 The Register Transfer Language (RTL)

When describing the internal operation of a processor, special notations generally referred to as 'Register Transfer Languages' (RTLs) are commonly adopted. These are not programming languages but rather provide a concise and (hopefully!) unambiguous way of describing events that take place as transfers are made to and from memory, between registers, etc. In this section we briefly show how such notations may be used to describe simple events that occur within a processor.

- **The contents of a location:** when referring to the contents of a register or memory location we make use of square brackets; [ ]. Thus, we could refer to the value stored by the program counter (PC) as: [PC]. Similarly, the contents of the memory buffer register (MBR) would be referred to as [MBR]

- **Assignments:** if we wish to assign a particular value to a register (or memory location) or to transfer 'something' between locations, we make use of the assignment operator (denoted by '←'). For example, if we wished to load the program counter with a certain value (for example, 37 (hex)) we would write:

    [PC] ← $37

Here, the '$' indicates the use of a base 16 value. Alternatively, we may wish to transfer the contents of the memory buffer register to Register X (as used in the previous section). In this case we would write:

    [Register X] ←[MBR]

Note that the source location is specified on the right-hand side and the destination lies on the left.

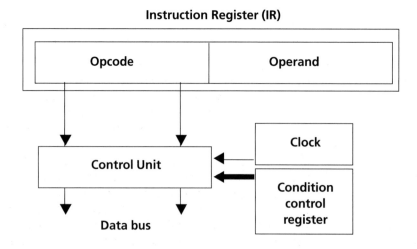

**Instruction Register (IR)**

**Figure 7.12:** The control unit is shown taking input from the IR and CCR

- **Denoting an address:**  to indicate the specification of an address we make use of rounded brackets; ( ).  Additionally a memory location is typically specified using the letter 'M'.
  Thus if we were to write:

  [MBR] ←[M(8000)]

  ... this would indicate that the contents of memory address 8000 are to be copied to the memory buffer register.

- **Arithmetic operations:**  these are readily indicated.  For example, in order to indicate that the contents of the program counter are to be incremented, we would write:

  [PC] ←[PC]+1

- **Concurrent operations:**  if two or more events are to occur at the same time (concurrent events), they are indicated on the same line (being separated by ';').
  For example:

  [PC] ←[PC]+1;  [Register X] ←[MBR]

**Activity 7.4**

**Using RTL**

Explain the meaning of each of the following expressions:

1. [IR] ←[MBR]

2. [MBR] ←[M([MAR])]

3. ALU← [Register X] ; [PC] ←[PC]+1

## 7.4 The stack

In Figure 7.1, we indicated the presence of a 'stack pointer' within the simple model processor, and in this section we briefly review its purpose.  Let us begin by considering two situations in which it is necessary to save the contents of the various registers located within the CPU:

- **On entering an interrupt service routine**
  In Chapter 4 we discussed the events that take place when an interrupt occurs.  Recall the simplest case – a processor is executing code when an interrupt signal is applied to the processor's interrupt port.  In this situation, the processor will complete the execution of the current instruction, save the contents of its various registers, and execute an 'interrupt service routine' (ISR).  Once it has completed the execution of the ISR, the original contents of the register are restored (i.e. the contents that were saved prior to the execution of the ISR), and the processor picks up from where it was previously up to in instruction execution.  This summarises aspects of the description provided in Chapter 4. However, we did not indicate where the register contents were saved.  In fact the registers are saved in a part of memory (RAM) that is designated to be the 'stack'.  We will shortly discuss the operation of this stack, but before doing so it is instructive to consider a second situation in which it is necessary to save (and later restore) register contents.

- **On entering a subroutine**

    Let us suppose that we are creating a program and find that we will need to regularly perform some mathematical calculation. We will assume that this calculation cannot be performed by one or two lines of code, but that it takes perhaps 10, 20, or perhaps even 100 program statements. One approach would be to paste these lines of code into our program whenever they are needed, see Figure 7.13.

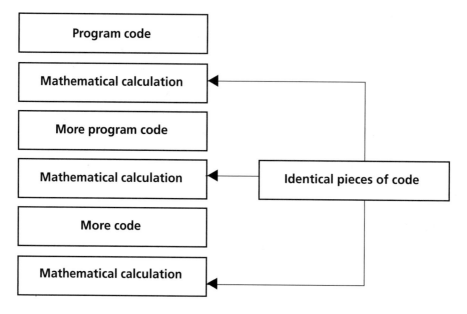

**Figure 7.13:** Identical pieces of code are repeated throughout a program

For a number of reasons, this approach does not represent an optimal solution. For example, as a result of repeatedly inserting the code responsible for the mathematical calculation into the program:

- The overall program length is increased
- The general structure of the program could become more difficult to follow
- It would be necessary, if we needed to make some change to the code responsible for the mathematical calculation, to modify each of the code segments responsible for performing the calculation. Inadvertently missing one out could have serious ramifications (remember that we may be performing this calculation hundreds or even thousands of times at different stages within the body of the program!).

An alternative (and much more elegant) approach is to make use of 'subroutines'. These are often referred to by today's high-level language programmers as functions or procedures. Continuing with the above example of a mathematical calculation frequently employed throughout a program, we code this calculation within a subroutine. This is a program (set of instructions) that can be invoked from any point within another program, see Figure 7.14. In this illustration we have created a subroutine called 'mathematical calculation' (to parallel the example provided in Figure 7.13) and this is invoked three times as the 'main' program executes.

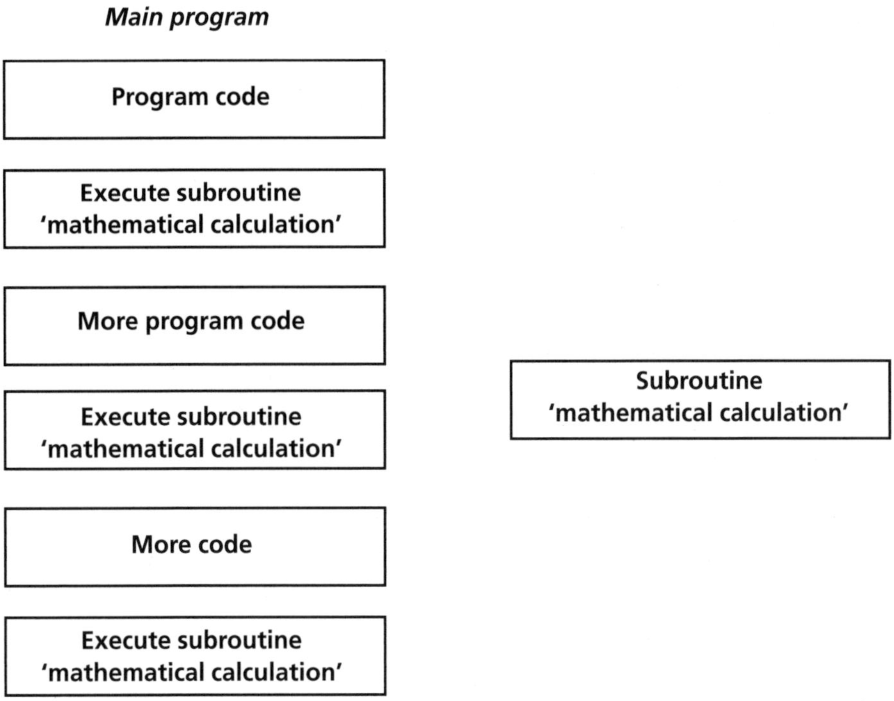

**Main program**

Figure 7.14: The use of a subroutine

When a subroutine has carried out its designated task, program execution continues from the point immediately following the instruction used to invoke the subroutine. Typically, an assembly language instruction of the following form is used to invoke a subroutine:

BSR TEST

... where BSR is the mnemonic for 'branch to subroutine' whose name (in this case) is 'TEST'.

Similarly to return from a subroutine, an assembly language instruction which has a mnemonic of the form RTS ('return from subroutine') is used.

Before the subroutine can be executed, the contents of the registers within the processor must be saved, otherwise it would be impossible for program execution to correctly recommence following the 'return from subroutine' instruction. As when an ISR is invoked, register values are saved in a special part of memory (RAM) known as the 'stack'.

Having identified two situations in which it is necessary to save the contents of the registers within a processor, we can now turn our attention to the operation of the stack.

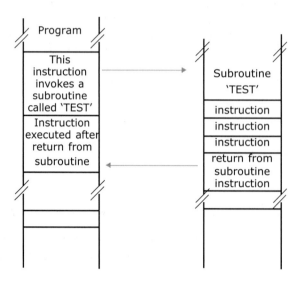

**Figure 7.15:** Invoking and returning from a subroutine

Computers employ various forms of stack – the particular version that we are presently concerned with is known as a 'last-in first-out' stack and can be readily understood by analogy to a 'stack' of plates or dishes, see Figure 7.16. The last plate placed on the stack will be the first one that is removed when needed. In terms of this analogy we can consider the plates as representing binary values that have been stored in the 'stack' – the last value to be stored is the first that can be removed.

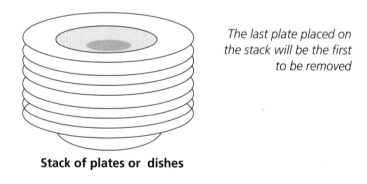

*The last plate placed on the stack will be the first to be removed*

**Stack of plates or dishes**

**Figure 7.16:** The operation of a 'last-in first-out' stack

To set up a 'stack' we employ a special register that is often referred to as the 'stack pointer' (SP), as was shown in figure 7.1. We initialise this to a convenient RAM address – this address will indicate the location of the bottom of the stack. If the contents of a register (we will call this Register A) are saved onto the stack (and here, for simplicity we assume that the register value can be stored in a single memory location (i.e. it does not span multiple locations)), it will be stored at the address pointed to by the SP. The SP will then be automatically decremented (equally, the value of the SP could be incremented – this depends on the processor architecture).

In the case that the SP is decremented, the stack 'grows' downwards in the address space (towards lower value addresses)) to point to the address of the next available location in the stack. If the contents of another register (Register B) are now saved, they will be stored at the next address indicated by the SP. Again the address indicated by the SP will be decremented, enabling it to point to the next free stack location. When register contents are restored from the stack, the last register stored will be the first to be restored (i.e. in the above scenario Register B will be restored prior to Register A).

As more values are stored on the stack, it increases in size and naturally it is important to ensure that the growth in the extent of the stack does not result in it overwriting areas of RAM that contain other data or program instructions.

## 7.5 The overall architecture of a simple processor model

In Section 7.3 we identified various 'sub-units' common to most processors. These may be interconnected to form a simple model processor able to perform the fetch/execute cycle. In the two activities that follow, you are asked to consider the flow of opcodes and operands between these sub-systems.

**Activity 7.5**

### A simple processor model: a load operation

Consider the 'sub-systems' illustrated in Figure 7.17 and employed for the 'simple model processor' described in this chapter. Suppose that memory address $20 contains an instruction of the form:

LDX $84

... where LDX is the assembly language mnemonic for 'load into Register X the following value' (in this case the value is $84). By means of directed lines (lines with arrows), indicate in Figure 7.17 the fetch and execute cycles for this instruction. You should number each line that you draw to indicate the order in which events take place. For simplicity, you may assume that the MAR has been loaded with address $20.

Using the notation that we have introduced in the previous section, describe this sequence of events.

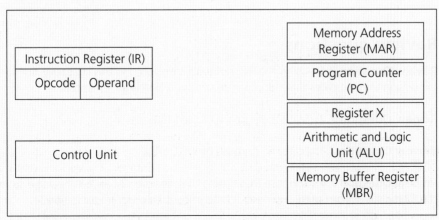

**Figure 7.17:** Some 'sub-systems' within the simple model processor

**Activity 7.6**

**A simple processor model: a store operation**

Repeat Activity 7.5 but for an instruction of the form:

StoreX $20

... where we will assume StoreX is a mnemonic meaning 'store the contents of Register X' – in this case at memory address $20. For simplicity, you may assume that this instruction is already in the IR.

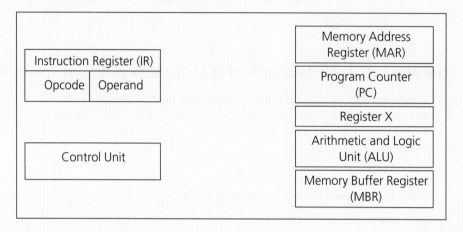

## 7.6 Summary

The purpose of this chapter has been to introduce some of the basic ideas that underpin the operation of the central processing unit (CPU). Rather than focus on one specific processor type, we have employed a simple processor model, and this has enabled us to introduce concepts without being distracted by the complications that arise in real processor architectures. Additionally, we have employed simple instruction mnemonics and have not considered any particular processor's instruction set. You are encouraged to make use of library or Internet facilities and obtain an instruction set for a commercially available processor and thereby gain an insight into the range of instructions supported by processors such as those in the Motorola 68000 family (e.g. the 68000, 68020, 68030, 68040 or 68060).

## 7.7 Review questions

**Review Question 7.1:** Using the RTL notation introduced in this chapter write an expression that indicates that the program counter value is incremented.

**Review Question 7.2:** State the purpose of the MBR.

**Review Question 7.3:** State the purpose of the CCR.

**Review Question 7.4:** Suppose that during the execution of an ISR the value stored in the SP register is corrupted. How would this impact on program execution?

**Review Question 7.5**: Using the RTL notation introduced in this chapter, write an expression that indicates that the contents of Register X should be passed to the ALU.

**Review Question 7.6:** Does the following RTL expression represent a read or write operation?

[M(3)] ←[MBR]

**Review Question 7.7:** Can a full adder be constructed using half-adders?

**Review Question 7.8:** State one event that takes place immediately prior to the execution of a subroutine.

**Review Question 7.9:** What type of stack is used by a processor for saving register contents?

**Review Question 7.10:** Using the form of RTL introduced in this chapter, how would you indicate concurrent events?

## 7.8 Feedback on activities

### Activity 7.1:  A full adder

| A | B | $C_{in}$ | L | M | N | O | Sum | $C_{out}$ |
|---|---|---|---|---|---|---|-----|-----|
| 0 | 0 | 0 | 0 | 0 | 0 | 0 | 0 | 0 |
| 0 | 0 | 1 | 0 | 0 | 0 | 0 | 1 | 0 |
| 0 | 1 | 0 | 1 | 0 | 0 | 0 | 1 | 0 |
| 0 | 1 | 1 | 1 | 0 | 0 | 1 | 0 | 1 |
| 1 | 0 | 0 | 1 | 0 | 0 | 0 | 1 | 0 |
| 1 | 0 | 1 | 1 | 0 | 1 | 0 | 0 | 1 |
| 1 | 1 | 0 | 0 | 1 | 0 | 0 | 0 | 1 |
| 1 | 1 | 1 | 0 | 1 | 1 | 1 | 1 | 1 |

**Table 7.2:** A truth table for a full adder

### Activity 7.2:  Constructing a full adder using two half-adders

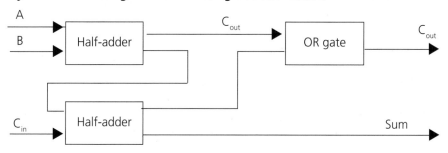

**Figure 7.18:** The implementation of a full adder using two half-adders

### Activity 7.3: The addition of binary numbers

Below we assume that a three-bit number (the bits are denoted K, L and M (where K represents the least significant bit and M the most significant bit)) is to be added to another three-bit number. These bits are denoted X, Y and Z (we assume that X is the least significant bit and Z the most significant bit).

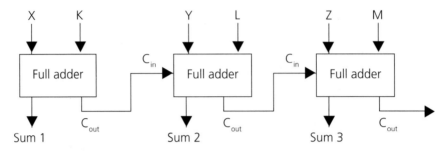

**Figure 7.19:** The addition of two three-bit numbers

### Activity 7.4: Using RTL

1. The contents of the memory buffer register are copied into the instruction register.

2. The contents of the memory address register provide a memory address. The contents of this address are copied into the memory buffer register.

3. The contents of Register X are copied to the arithmetic and logic unit. Simultaneously, the contents of the program counter are incremented.

### Activity 7.5: A simple processor model: a load operation

$[MBR] \leftarrow [M(20)]$          $[IR] \leftarrow [MBR]$

$CU \leftarrow [IR(Opcode)]$          $[Register\ X] \leftarrow [IR(Operand)]$

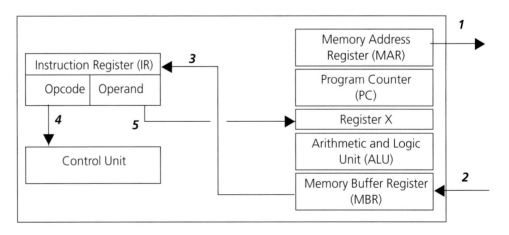

**Figure 7.20:** A simple load operation

**Activity 7.6:  A simple processor model: a store operation**

CU←[IR(Opcode)]              [MAR] ←[IR(Operand)]

[MBR] ←[Register X]          [M(20)] ←[MBR]

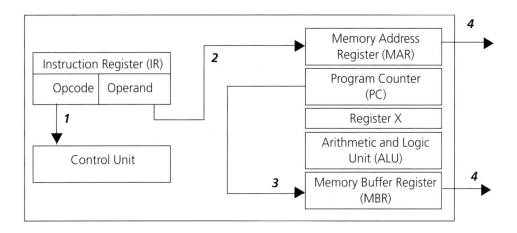

**Figure 7.21:** A simple store operation

# CHAPTER 8

# Aspects of the operating system

## OVERVIEW

The operation of computer hardware is controlled by software. The operating system provides a broad range of functions which control and support the operation of the hardware, and provides an environment in which applications programs can execute. The operating system enables, for example, multiple users to simultaneously access a computer and/or enables multiple programs to simultaneously execute. In this context, it is critical that the operating system imposes controls so that, for example, a program that is being run by one user cannot corrupt the data or programs being executed by another user.

**Learning outcomes** On completion of this chapter you should be able to:

- Explain the need and function of ROM-based basic input/output system (BIOS)

- Identify and describe the functions of an operating system (O/S)

- Describe the role of device drivers

- Describe the operation of a multi-tasking technique

- Outline the operation of virtual memory.

## 8.1 Introduction

In previous chapters we have occasionally referred to the 'operating system', and have simply assumed that it takes the form of a collection of software routines that play a pivotal role in the operation of the computer and in interfacing with a computer's hardware systems. We now consider the function of the operating system (O/S) and other associated software in a little more detail

In the next section, we review events that occur when a computer is turned on (or reset). Here, we consider the function of the 'bootstrap routine' (which in the case of the PC is referred to as the BIOS). This loads critical portions of the O/S into RAM and then passes control to them. This leads on to related discussion in Section 8.3 of the purpose of the 'reset vector'. Subsequently we review some of the many tasks performed by the modern O/S, and in section 8.5 we consider several general types of operating system.

Virtual memory plays an important role in the operation of the modern computer, enabling the main memory to appear (from a software perspective) to be essentially unlimited in its extent. In Section 8.6 we outline aspects of this memory management technique, and in Section 8.7 we consider multi-tasking (this enables multiple users or multiple programs to effectively run concurrently (in parallel) on a single processor computer).

## 8.2 Basic input/output system (BIOS)

When a computer is turned on (or reset), one of the initial tasks that must be performed is the loading of key portions of the operating system (we will discuss the role of the operating system shortly) (which are stored on the hard disk) into main memory. Once placed in main memory, these routines (programs) can be directly accessed and executed by the processor. This task is performed by a 'bootstrap' program stored within non-volatile memory (ROM). In the case of a PC, the BIOS ('basic input/output system') is responsible for the bootstrap process. The BIOS is a collection of software that is used to perform various tasks, and it is used when a computer is turned on (or following a reset) to bring the machine to a state in which it is ready to run higher-level programs. To do this, it loads critical parts of the operating system from secondary storage (usually hard disk) into primary storage (RAM). During the operation of the computer, the BIOS also provides a software interface to I/O systems. Figure 8.1 shows the location of the BIOS in relation to hardware and software components.

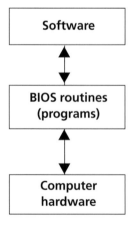

**Figure 8.1:** BIOS in relation to the computer software and hardware

As indicated in the diagram, the BIOS provides software systems with a simple interface to the hardware and often acts as the intermediary between the hardware and the operating system. The BIOS is typically stored in PROM (programmable read-only memory) (recall – PROM is a non-volatile form of memory).

**Activity 8.1**

### The function of the BIOS software

Explain why the BIOS is needed. Your explanation should include a description of one essential role fulfilled by the BIOS software.

## 8.3 The reset vector

When a computer is turned on (or following the reset button having been pressed (a system reset)), the processor must know the address of the first instruction that it should execute. In short, the processor must know the address that it should output onto the address bus in order to access the first instruction.

This is achieved by means of a 'reset vector'. When a processor is powered on, or following a system reset, it performs a read operation from a special memory location which stores the 'reset vector'. The address of this location is defined within the processor and the data contained therein is interpreted as representing the address of the first instruction that should be executed. Consequently, the vector acts as a pointer to the first instruction that the processor should execute. This approach is illustrated in Figure 8.2.

The use of a reset vector enables the code that is to be executed at power-on (or following a system reset) to be located at any position within the processor's address space. If we change the address of the first instruction that the processor should execute when, for example, it is reset, then we simply need to alter the reset vector to point to the new address. Naturally, the reset vector is stored in non-volatile memory and is typically located at the highest address(es) within the processor's address space. (In fact, the reset vector may span more than one memory location.)

**Activity 8.2**

### The reset vector

The reset vector may span more than one memory location. Suggest a reason for this.

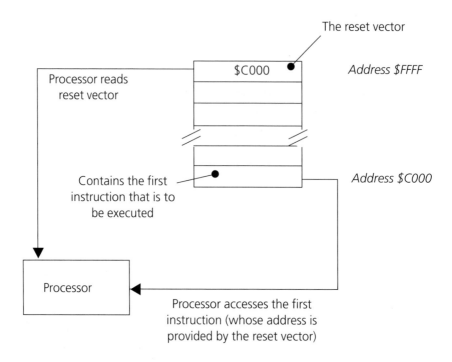

**Figure 8.2:** Here we illustrate the use of the reset vector. By way of example, we have assumed that the reset vector is located at address $FFFF and the entry point to the code which is to be executed when the processor is either reset or powered on is located at address $C000; recall the use of the '$' symbol indicates the numbers that follow are in hexadecimal (base 16). Hence, the processor accesses the reset vector (which has been set to $C000) and uses this to access the first instruction that it must execute.

## 8.4 Operating system

The term 'operating system' is applied to a collection of programs that perform a variety of tasks. These include the management of computer resources, support for communications (with both the computer user and peripheral hardware), and the creation of an environment in which applications programs run and in which they are able to share resources in an orderly manner. For example, in the case of your PC, the operating system is responsible for performing read and write operation to secondary storage media, provides the interface via which you are able to interact with the PC, and provides the environment in which applications programs such as Microsoft Word and Adobe Photoshop execute.

In fact, the operating system plays a pivotal role in practically all aspects of computer operation. Some of the main tasks of an operating system are:

- To receive input from the user (e.g. commands and data)
- To act on commands provided by the user
- To provide output to the user

- To create environments in which a user program can execute
- To manage the file system (including the directory structure)
- To enable programs to share resources and thereby support 'multi-tasking'
- To provide resources for a user program via special instructions – often referred to as 'system calls'
- To interface with hardware such as the keyboard, display screen, printers, hard disk drives. Often such interfaces are implemented using programs called 'device drivers'
- To provide security (e.g. password protection, the protection of files belonging to each user, etc.)
- To provide network communications and thereby allow computers to communicate
- To provide a convenient user interface (using, for example menus, icons, etc)
- The provision of text editing facilities
- The provision of various utilities that may be accessed by a user such as system tools, calculator, calendar
- The provision of back-up facilities.

This list is by no means exhaustive and you may wish to consider adding to it. In Figure 8.3 we illustrate the operating system within the layered model that was previously indicated in Figure 8.1.

## Applications software

The upper-most layer shown in Figure 8.3 represents the programs that you choose to run on your computer – such as a word-processing activity or computer game. These are referred to as applications programs. The lower layers provide an environment that can (at least in principle) be hardware independent, and this allows an applications program to operate without knowledge of precise hardware configurations. In principle this facilitates 'software portability' – the same program should operate on different computer platforms. Unfortunately, this objective is not always achieved and the developer of applications programs often needs a sound knowledge of a computer's architecture.

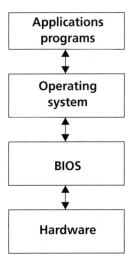

**Figure 8.3:** The operating system provides resources to a user's program

## *The process*

The term 'process' is widely used in relation to operating systems. Unfortunately, depending on the O/S under discussion, the term can take on different precise meanings. For our purposes, we will use a relatively straightforward definition:

- **A process is an environment in which a program can execute.**

In the case of a 'multi-tasking operating system' (i.e. one that permits more than one program to appear to run 'simultaneously' – we'll deal with how this is achieved later in the chapter), each program has an associated process. The use of processes plays a pivotal role in the architecture of such operating systems. Each program may be considered to be 'encapsulated' within a process and when, for example, an applications program wishes to communicate with a computer resource it does so via the process, see Figure 8.4.

The general role of the process can be readily understood by means of a simple analogy:

Consider your local bank. This has a number of resources – money, computers, Internet banking facilities, etc. Suppose that these resources were not managed, and that anybody were able to go into the bank and directly manipulate the resources. For example, anybody could help themselves to as much money as they wanted – and it was left to the individual to record how much money they had taken. Obviously there would be a great deal of chaos, and it is fairly certain that after a few hours there would be very little money left in the bank! The resources offered by the bank are therefore managed and, for example, this prevents one person from taking money from another person's account. Here, management is achieved by encapsulating the resources rather than the individual, and in this respect the scenario is not quite accurate in describing the use of processes within a computer.

Whenever resources are shared, we need to put controls in place to ensure that they are shared properly and equitably. The same applies to the computer in which the hardware is shared between a number of programs. Without controls, chaos would ensue. For example, in the 'free-for-all' scenario, one program could overwrite areas of main memory containing the code and data belonging to another program! Each process 'encapsulates' a program and ensures that resources are not used inappropriately. (Even in the case of a computer which does not permit multi-tasking, we still have to put controls in place. For example, we would want to ensure that an applications program could not overwrite areas of main memory in which operating system code (or data) resides).

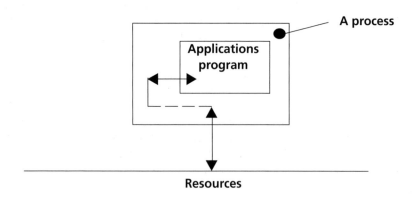

**Figure 8.4:** In this model, the process encapsulates a program and manages all communication

## *Operating system*

As we have seen, the O/S performs many functions.  These include memory management, file management, user interface implementation, I/O interface, resource allocation and security (protection), which we briefly now consider:

- **Memory management**

  As indicated previously, when a computer is turned on (or following a system reset), the O/S – or necessary portions of the O/S – are loaded into main memory (RAM).  A portion of the operating system always occupies some of this memory.  In fact, more recent operating systems often require larger amounts of memory and therefore a substantial increase in the RAM.

  The O/S manages the remaining memory and shares it between itself and the processes that have been started.  This allocation is based on the memory management scheme adopted by the operating system.

- **File management**

  A disk stores data and information and has no inherent mechanisms for organising data or information into files and files into directories.  The O/S provides a level of disk organisation, in that it establishes the disk structure that allows users to create partitions, directories, volumes and other disk subdivisions.

  The file management system maintains the directory structure and stores directory and file information such as the date and time at which files and directories were last modified along with details of file ownership and access rights.

- **Input/output interfaces**

  As discussed in Chapter 5, the hard disk employs cylinders (a set of tracks) that are arranged into sectors.  When you access a disk file, there is a 'flurry' of activity.  Between making the request and the retrieval of the desired file the operating system plays a major role.  The operating system employs a file management system to translate the request into an address that the disk controller can act upon.  Once the file location is identified, low-level O/S commands cause the read/write heads to move to the proper cylinder and select the appropriate sectors from which data is read (or to which it is written).  Once the data is read into memory, the O/S delivers it to the requesting program (process).

- **Resource allocation**

  Most operating systems allow multiple tasks (processes) to run concurrently (multi-tasking).  Although it might appear to the user that the computer is actively executing tasks in parallel, in reality, a computer with a single CPU can only actively execute one task at any instant.  As we discuss shortly, when multi-tasking, the processor alternates between the tasks – allocating 'time slices' to each.

  Fundamental to the implementation of multi-tasking is the equitable sharing of resources.  Thus, for example, no one process should be able to access a critical resource for an unlimited time and so prevent the resource from being available to other processes.  The operating system must therefore manage resource allocation in such a way as to maximise efficiency of usage.  Some operating systems enable processes to be allocated a priority (priorities are usually indicated numerically).  Thus, higher priorities are given to processes that are of greater importance to either the operation of the computer or the needs of the user.

- **Security**

  We are all aware of the importance of protecting our computers and personal data.  The operating system provides several mechanisms by which security is established.  The O/S system can act to protect the system from internal and external intrusions.

Internal intrusions include the possibility that one process may overwrite memory occupied by another processes data. Also in the case of systems that are shared between a number of users the operating system provides the security that controls file access permissions. Typically, associated with each file is information that indicates user privileges (i.e. who may read, write or delete the file).

**Activity 8.3**

**Tasks performed by an operating system**

In this section we have listed fourteen tasks performed by an operating system.

State two additional tasks.

# 8.5 Types of operating system

In the early days of computing, operating systems were largely 'non-interactive' and a user had little if any opportunities for interacting with the computer during the execution of a program. In contrast, in the case of today's 'interactive' operating systems the user/programmer comes into direct (and almost continuous) contact with the computer. In this section we briefly discuss various operating system paradigms:

- **The simple batch system**
- **Multi-programmed batch systems**
- **Time-sharing systems**
- **The personal computer**
- **Parallel systems**
- **Real-time systems**
- **Distributed systems**
- **The device driver.**

## *The simple batch system*

This approach to computer operation dates back to the early days of computing (from the 1950s to the early 1970s) and provides us with an example of the 'non-interactive' operating system paradigm. As we have previously discussed, a user would design, code, and store a program (together with associated data) and pass it to a computer operator. At a convenient time the operator would load the program (commonly referred to as a 'job') into the computer's main memory and initiate its execution. Some time later, the results generated by the program (job) would be returned to the user.

In the case of this type of approach, the user has no direct access to the computer and the turnaround time would invariably be quite long. On the other hand, the operating system (often referred to as a 'monitor program') needed to support this type of computing model is very simple. The key actions of the monitor program are:

- To read in programs (jobs) one at a time from input devices such as punched-card readers or magnetic tape drives
- As the job is read, it is placed in the user program area as shown in Figure 8.5 and control is passed to it

- As the job is completed, it returns control to the monitor program (which has remained 'resident' in main memory)
- The monitor program proceeds to read the next job.

**Figure 8.5:** Memory layout for a simple batch system

## *Multi-programmed batch systems*

Unfortunately, in the case of the simple 'batch system', the processor relies on the operator to continuously supply new 'jobs'. Logistically, this can be difficult to arrange on a 24/7 basis (especially as it is often difficult to predict in advance the exact time for which a program will run prior to its completion). As a result the machine could be idle for significant periods of time. The multi-programmed batch technique was intended to overcome this inefficiency. Here, several jobs simultaneously reside in main memory, and the CPU is 'multiplexed' (shared) among them.

Consider four jobs that when separately executed using the simple batch technique will exhibit the following execution times:

    Job 1: 5 minutes
    Job 2: 20 minutes
    Job 3: 15 minutes
    Job 4: 10 minutes.

If these are submitted in this order to a computer that employs the simple batch technique, then Job 1 will be completed after 5 minutes and at this time Job 2 will begin execution. Thus it will be completed 25 minutes after the start of Job 1. Job 3 will then begin execution and will be completed 40 minutes after the start of Job 1. At this point, Job 4 will begin execution and the time to complete all four jobs will be 50 minutes. Of course, this assumes that one job begins execution immediately following its predecessor – and this relies on the efficiency of the computer operator(s). In practice, delays between loading the jobs are likely to result in a somewhat longer overall execution time.

Let us now consider the case of the four jobs running on a computer that employs the multi-programmed approach. In this case, all four jobs are loaded into main memory (see Figure 8.6) and can share CPU access. Thus, for example, the CPU may execute Job 1 for a time period t, followed by Job 2, then Job 3 and then Job 4 (all for the same time period).

In this scenario, it will then return to its execution of Job 1 and so the process will continue until jobs are completed and results are returned to the operator. Here, the computer time is being used very efficiently – the machine is always busy!

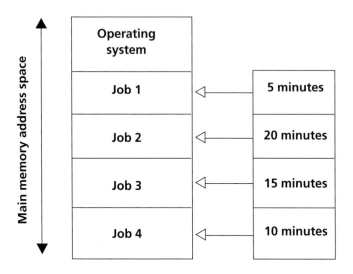

**Figure 8.6:** The simple multi-programming approach

The operating system needed to support this approach is somewhat more complex than that used for the simple batch program technique. For example, the O/S must ensure that all jobs are kept in main memory, that one job cannot write to areas of memory designated to the other jobs and that CPU access is correctly scheduled.

## Time-sharing systems

The 1960s and early 1970s saw the growth of large computer installations. Such computing facilities were made available to large numbers of users on a time-sharing basis. Each individual user would access the computer by means of a terminal (the name given to a display and keyboard through which a user could interact with a computer via a serial interconnect. Most commonly, terminals were able to support the depiction of text (ASCII characters) and had only very basic graphics facilities. Perhaps the most well-known of all terminals is the VT220 (which was very popular in the 1970s) through which they could enter commands, edit their programs, etc, and view the results of the computational process. As time went by, these installations became ever larger and their design was greatly influenced by 'economy of scale'. This meant that doubling the money spent on the implementation of a large computer installation would result in a significant increase in performance (for example, doubling the money spent on an installation could result in, for example, a fourfold increase in performance.)

As a result, installations rapidly grew in size, and operating systems became ever more complex. The increasing operating system complexity strongly related to the complexity of the algorithms needed to ensure that computer facilities were equitably shared between users, and that the work of one user could not be corrupted by a program being executed by another user. Furthermore, as the computer installations became ever larger, their construction took longer. Given the rate at which computer technologies were developing, this meant that a computer installation could on the day of its commissioning be already out of date.

An additional problem related to computer performance.  Although these centralised machines allowed users to interact with the computer, it was impossible for a user to obtain guaranteed performance.  The performance experienced by a user would be strongly influenced by:

- The **number of users** currently accessing the machine
- The **type of applications** being run by other users.

For these and other reasons, the use of centralised computing resources gradually lost favour, and, as hardware costs decreased, smaller computers began to become more cost-effective.

## The personal computer

During the 1970s, pioneering work was carried out by Xerox on the development of small computer systems with the idea of placing each computer on the user's desktop.  The computer was therefore 'personal' to the user and since the machines were not shared, they offered guaranteed performance.

At this time, Xerox implemented many revolutionary changes.  Their overriding concept was that users were not interested in the computer, but rather in getting computer-based tasks accomplished in a simple and straightforward manner.  The mouse, which was prototyped in the mid-1960s, became an integral part of the personal computer, and so too did the bit-mapped display discussed in Chapter 6.

Xerox recognised that users would not want to work in isolation.  They therefore advanced networking techniques and developed the Ethernet networking standard, which we will discuss in future chapters.  This provides a low-cost approach to the interconnection of computers and computer-related hardware, and so not only did the personal computer offer guaranteed performance but it was also able to allow users to share data and other material between machines.

Xerox also played a pivotal role in developing the event-driven user interface.  This is the interface paradigm almost universally used today which employs icons, menus, etc, through which selections can be made by means of the mouse.

The personal computer began to gain widespread acceptance in the early 1980s.  Although Xerox failed to commercially exploit the developments they had made in the 1970s in respect of the personal computer, other companies such as IBM and Macintosh ensured that the personal computer concept became a major success.  Since that time, the personal computer paradigm has played the dominant role in computing.

## Parallel systems

The demand for ever more processing power continues to increase and in order to handle computationally expensive problems, computer architects have, for many years, investigated parallel computing paradigms.  In this scenario, one computer is equipped with a plurality of processors.

Parallel systems offer the advantages of increased throughput, increased reliability, and economy.  Making use of parallel processing facilities is difficult – some problems do not lend themselves to parallel computation.  Furthermore, equitably dividing tasks between processors is difficult.

## Real-time systems

A real-time system is one that has to process and respond to externally generated input stimuli within a finite and specified period. Note that the correctness of operation depends on:

- The computed value(s)
- The time in which the value(s) is delivered.

In the case of real-time systems, the failure to respond to an event within a certain time is as bad as computing the incorrect response. Such systems are often used in situations where incorrect operation may have life-and-death implications (e.g. in aircraft, nuclear power stations, and cancer treatment).

## Distributed systems

In essence, a distributed system enables autonomous machines to co-operate with each other in undertaking some common task. Distributed systems can be defined as a collection of autonomous heterogeneous machines that are connected to each other, and to the outside world, via a network running distributed software (this may not necessarily be homogeneous). Such systems are developed to enable autonomous machines to multi-task processes across a network, both co-operatively and simultaneously.

## The device driver

Suppose that a manufacturer were to produce a new peripheral device for use with the personal computer. Naturally, from a hardware perspective, this device would be designed to connect to some existing interface within the PC – for example, it might connect to the serial port, the parallel port, or use the USB (universal serial bus). Once the hardware is connected to the machine, it is necessary for the operating system to establish communication with it. However, since this is a new piece of hardware it is quite likely that the operating system will have no knowledge of its architecture/functionality and will therefore not be able to make use of the facilities that it offers.

By making use of 'device drivers' this problem may be easily resolved. Continuing with the example used in the previous paragraph, the manufacturer of the hardware would also produce a device driver. This is software which acts as the intermediary between the O/S and the hardware that is connected to the computer. (See Figure 8.7.)

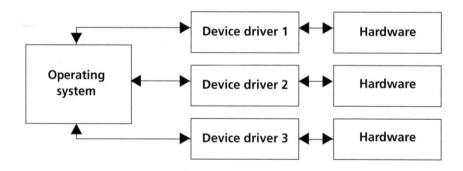

**Figure 8.7:** The use of a 'device driver' to communicate and interact with hardware systems

An operating system such as Microsoft Windows is usually supplied with a range of device drivers. These may, for example, enable the O/S to function with a variety of hard disks supplied by different manufacturers. On the other hand, when new hardware is to be installed on a computer, there is no guarantee that the O/S will be equipped with an appropriate device driver. Hardware suppliers therefore usually include the required software (or provide Internet-based download facilities).

**Activity 8.4**

**The importance of the device driver**

When you buy a peripheral for a computer, you may also require additional software. Explain why this is sometimes (but not always) the case.

# 8.6 Virtual memory

As discussed in the previous section, the early 1980s was a period when the PC began to gain widespread acceptance. In parallel with this development, manufacturers produced workstation computers. These represented professional computer facilities offering many of the advantages of mainframe computing, but without the need to share resources. A particularly important feature of the workstation was its incorporation of the 'virtual memory' technique (which had previously been employed in larger computer systems). This memory management paradigm is briefly reviewed in this section.

Virtual memory was pioneered at the University of Manchester in the 1960s and plays a pivotal role in the operation of the modern computer. Let us consider an early personal computer in which the processor is equipped with a 16-bit address bus. A 16-bit address bus can access just over 64,000 memory locations. For simplicity we will assume that all of this address space is occupied by main memory (RAM) and that only ~14,000 locations are required by the O/S. Consequently, some 50,000 locations are available for use by any programs we may wish to run.

For many applications this may well represent an adequate memory space, but problems occur if we attempt to execute an applications program that is larger than the available address space, i.e. a program that cannot fit into the address space offered by the processor. Since those early days, applications programs have continued to grow in size and a processor's address space (although much larger than that offered by the early processors) is shared between many programs (processes) and by the operating system itself. The issue investigated in the 1960s at the University of Manchester was how to make the processor appear to have an essentially unrestricted address space (specifically, how to make main memory appear to be unrestricted in its extent). The solution was found in the 'virtual memory' approach. This can be understood as follows:

- Consider the hard disk and main memory. Rather than moving individual bytes (or words) between the two, we move *groups* of bytes – these groups are called 'pages'. We can imagine individual memory locations as being represented by the lines printed on a sheet of A4 paper; many lines make up a page. It is within this context that the term 'pages' was adopted – we do not transfer individual 'lines' between the hard disk and memory, but rather the groups of lines contained in a page

- Memory is divided into pages and each page represents the minimum number of bytes that we are able to transfer between the main memory and the hard disk. Suppose that we want to run a program. The first page of the program (the executable file) is read from hard disk into memory. This page begins execution. Soon we will find that we have either executed all the instructions contained on the page, or that we need to bring in some form of data from the hard disk to main memory. As we require more program instructions or more data, we continue to read pages from the disk into main memory.

Here again, we can imagine by way of analogy that we are reading physical pages and perhaps laying these out on a table (the table would represent the physical size of the main memory). To make this analogy work, you have to consider that you cannot place one page on top of another – they must all be laid out side by side on the table. Eventually, the surface of the table is filled and there is no more space for additional pages. So it is with memory; eventually the memory is filled with pages. We now need to make space for additional pages. To do this we 'return' pages to the hard disk. Which pages do we return? If your table was covered with pages from which you were studying, then you would remove from the table the pages that you have not used for the longest time. So it is with virtual memory; we return to the hard disk the pages that have been modified and that are the least recently used. In this way, we can make space for additional pages in memory. We are never bound by the limitations of main memory – there is always room for additional material – and we simply make space for it.

There are, of course, various complications to the implementation of virtual memory. For example, the operating system must keep track of exactly which pages are currently in main memory. In fact, when you shut down your personal computer, one of the tasks carried out automatically during this procedure is the return of all pages that are currently in main memory (and that have been modified) to the hard disk. If you simply turn off the power to your PC without shutting it down, then the next time that you turn it on you will receive a message indicating that it was improperly shut down. Potentially this could have caused corruption to files, and therefore the computer follows a procedure that checks for and attempts to correct such problems.

The workstation offered support for virtual memory, but early PCs did not accommodate this technique. Eventually this situation changed and virtual memory plays a pivotal role in the operation of today's PC.

As for the workstation, the 1980s was a period in which a range of workstations became available and these employed a variety of operating systems. As the PC was produced in ever-larger numbers its cost decreased, performance increased and an abundance of low-cost applications programs were developed specifically for the extensive PC market. Despite the tremendous opportunities offered by high-quality workstations, they were unable to compete with the PC in terms of cost, and suitable applications programs were often expensive (due to the relatively small customer base). Ultimately, the PC took the dominant role and today it offers largely the same functionality as the workstations of twenty years ago.

Activity 8.5

**Virtual memory**

Describe in your own words why virtual memory is vital to the operation of the modern computer.

# 8.7 Multi-tasking

As we have discussed, multi-tasking was first developed in order to enable a number of users to share a single centralised computing resource (e.g. a mainframe). The classic PC represents a single-user machine and therefore there is usually no requirement for a multi-tasking system able to support multiple concurrent users. On the other hand, the absence of this technique meant that only a single program could run at any one time. Clearly, concurrent program execution is desirable (e.g. the ability to print a file whilst undertaking a word processing activity) and so, over time, multi-tasking techniques were incorporated into the PC.

A standard PC usually has only one processor and is therefore unable to execute more than a single process (or, more specifically, a single instruction) at any moment of time. However, concurrent program (process) operation can be achieved by sharing (multiplexing) the processor between programs (processes). In short, the processor spends an amount of time executing one program, an amount of time executing a second program, an amount of time executing a third program, etc, and then returns to processing the first program again. This approach is referred to as pre-emptive multi-tasking and is one of several paradigms that may be adopted in order to achieve the goal of concurrent program execution.

The interval that the processor allocates to a program (before moving on to the next) is called the 'timeslice' – this time is defined by the operating system. Let us suppose that we wish to execute two programs concurrently. We will call these programs A and B (to be more exact, we should refer to these as processes). The processor begins executing program A, and at the end of the timeslice interval turns its attention to executing program B. In turn, at the end of this timeslice it will return to executing program A. It will continue to switch between these two programs until one of the programs runs to completion or until a program requires access to other resources (or input). In this simple model, a process may exist in three states. These are as follows:

- **Ready:** a process which is ready is – quite simply – ready to execute. It is waiting for its turn within the processor. Typically, there will be a number of processes that will be ready to run, i.e. ready to be executed by the processor. These are all placed within a 'ready queue'
- **Wait:** a process which is in the wait state is waiting for access to some resource. It may be waiting for access to the hard disk, or may simply be waiting for keyboard input from the user. The processor in a wait state is not ready for execution within the processor, and therefore it is not held in the ready queue. Once it gets the input it is requiring, then it will again become 'ready to run', in which case it will be put into the ready queue and await its turn in the processor
- **Active:** a process in this state is currently being executed by the processor. It will continue to be executed by the processor until the end of the current timeslice. If there are any other processes in the ready queue awaiting execution, then at the end of the timeslice this process will be returned to the ready queue and another process will be run by the processor. On the other hand, if there are no other processes ready to run (i.e. in the ready queue) then the process currently executing will continue to do so for subsequent timeslices.

Some operating systems support process priority. The priority of a process is a numerical value that indicates its relative importance. In the multi-tasking model that we have just described, the process priority is used to determine which process in the ready queue is to run next. Different operating systems handle process priorities in different ways and it is sufficient to note that high-priority processes should not be allowed to prevent processes with a lower priority from gaining CPU access.

The multi-tasking model described above is summarised in Figure 8.8. Here, process 6 is currently active and processes 1, 3 and 4 are in the ready queue. Since process 1 has the highest priority, at the end of the current timeslice it will be the next to gain access to the CPU. The timeslice duration is defined by a timer which generates an interrupt at the end of each timeslice. Processes 2 and 5 are in a wait state – both are requiring some form of input before they can continue execution. Once they have this content, they will be returned to the ready queue.

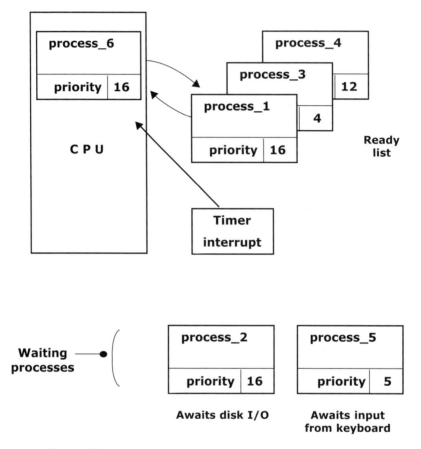

**Figure 8.8:** An approach to multi-tasking. Here, processes may exist in three states: ready, waiting, and active. This multi-tasking model is generally referred to as the 'round robin' approach (© B G Blundell 2005).

Multi-tasking does have associated penalties. At the end of a timeslice the processor must save the context of the program it is currently executing, and restore the context of the program that it is to execute for the next timeslice. This overhead is similar to the one we saw earlier in connection with interrupt handling. The storing and retrieval of program contexts occupies a finite time. The designer of the multi-tasking system must take this overhead into account when deciding upon the appropriate timeslice interval. Typically, timeslices may be in the order of 1 to 5 milliseconds. Making the timeslice interval too short means that the overheads, such as the ones we have just mentioned, begin to dominate. Making the timeslice interval too long means that processes which are in the ready queue will have a longer time to wait before they get access to the processor.

The design of multi-tasking systems is complicated and there are many different paradigms that can be adopted. Unfortunately, the best paradigm to be used is strongly influenced by the nature of the programs that are being run on the computer. In fact, a number of operating systems that have been developed over the years have made use of more than one ready queue. The usefulness of this approach can easily be seen by thinking for a moment of queuing in your local supermarket. It can be extremely frustrating to have to join a long queue when only wanting to purchase a single item. (It can be equally frustrating when you choose the shortest queue but in actual fact this has the longest wait time because in the event it takes fifteen minutes for the person in front of you to actually pay!) The idea of a fast checkout can certainly help people who are only wanting to make a small number of purchases. Similarly, we can use a double queuing system to allow processes to gain rapid access to the CPU.

**Activity 8.6**

**Pre-emptive multi-tasking**

What do you consider would be the main disadvantage of reducing the extent of the timeslice used in the 'round-robin' multi-tasking paradigm described above?

## 8.9 Summary

In this chapter we have described various aspects of the operating system. As you have seen, many of the underlying principles employed by the modern operating system are based on techniques which have been in place for more than thirty years. Operating systems are growing, both in terms of size and complexity. (For example it is interesting to compare the size of an early version of Microsoft Windows to current releases.) As operating systems become larger and increasingly complex, so too do they place greater demands upon computer resources. In fact, today's operating systems represent a major computational overhead, and consume a significant portion of processor power and main memory capacity.

We have briefly outlined the principle of virtual memory by which a processor appears to have an unlimited main memory address space and multi-tasking. Additionally, we have emphasised the importance of the 'process' and described this as an environment in which a program is able to execute.

## 8.10 Review questions

**Question 8.1** What is the BIOS? Explain one major function that it performs.

**Question 8.2** State three functions of an operating system used in a personal computer.

**Question 8.3** Define the term 'distributed system'.

**Question 8.4** Is it possible to run a program on a computer that does not have an operating system? Explain your answer.

**Question 8.5** What is a device driver in a computer system?

**Question 8.6** Within the context of multi-tasking, what is a 'timeslice'?

**Question 8.7** State two critical aspects of a computer's operation within a real-time system.

**Question 8.8** In the case of the traditional time-sharing computer installation, state two variables that would influence the level of performance experienced by individual users.

**Question 8.9** During the 'shutdown procedure' carried out by a PC, state one task that is performed by the O/S.

**Question 8.10** Describe one reason that may cause a process that is currently 'active' to enter a 'wait state'.

## 8.11 Feedback on activities

### Activity 8.1: The function of the BIOS software

When a personal computer is turned on, the operating system will not automatically run as it is stored on the hard disk. Consequently, we need a way of bringing a portion of the operating system into the main memory. This is one of the essential tasks carried out by the BIOS software. Usually, entry to the BIOS is gained by means of the reset vector, and the BIOS software executes. This is contained within a non-volatile memory device on the motherboard. The BIOS is able to access the hard disk and bring a portion of the operating system into the main memory area. The BIOS then passes control to the operating system.

### Activity 8.2: The reset vector

The number of memory locations occupied by the reset vector is determined by the address bus width and the extent of each memory location. For example, consider the case of a 32-bit address bus and 16-bit memory locations. Here, we would need to store the reset vector across two memory locations (each holding 16 bits and so in total storing a 32-bit address).

### Activity 8.3: Tasks performed by an operating system

Various answers can be given to this question: for example, multi-tasking, i.e. enabling more than one program to appear to execute concurrently, and access to the system clock which enables, for example, a program to determine the current date and time.

### Activity 8.4: The importance of the device driver

When a peripheral is connected to the computer, the operating system needs to know how to interface with it. This communication is achieved via a device driver. Windows, for example, includes many device drivers. Sometimes therefore, Windows is able to recognise the peripheral (for example, the hard disk), and no additional software needs to be loaded (the device driver often being found on the Windows CD). On the other hand, some peripherals will not be recognised by Windows, i.e. it will not contain an appropriate device driver. In this case, you will need to make use of software provided with the peripheral device.

**Activity 8.5:  Virtual memory**

Even when a computer is equipped with only a relatively small amount of main memory, the virtual memory approach enables this memory to appear to have an almost unlimited extent. If, for example, a computer was equipped with 16 megabytes of main memory, half of which was needed by the operating system, applications programs would usually be restricted to the remaining eight megabytes.  However, if the virtual memory approach is adopted the extent of the main memory would (from a software perspective) be essentially unlimited.

**Activity 8.6:  Pre-emptive multi-tasking**

When the processor switches between processes at the end of each timeslice, an overhead is incurred.  This overhead relates to saving the context of one process, and restoring the context of another.  As the extent of the timeslice is reduced, this overhead becomes more significant.  A balance must therefore be struck between the size of the timeslice, and the scale of the overhead cost which is incurred during multi-tasking.

# CHAPTER 9

# Networking computers

## OVERVIEW

The modern computer is seldom used in isolation – computers are networked in such a way that they can, for example, share data and resources. In this chapter, we introduce some basic concepts in relation to the networking of computers and introduce the IEEE 802 and OSI models.

**Learning outcomes**     On completion of this chapter you should be able to:

- Discuss important communication parameters: bandwidth, bit-rate and latency

- Describe feature of a communications protocol

- Discuss the use of a layered structure in the implementation of communications protocols

- Discuss the importance of adopting standards for computer communications

- Outline the organisation of the OSI model and TCP/IP.

## 9.1 Introduction

Today's computers are seldom used in isolation but are interconnected so that they can communicate and therefore share both digital material and remote resources. This communication is achieved via computer networking technologies that, for example, enable the transfer of data via electrical cables, fibre optic cables, and wireless links. In the remaining chapters of this book, we focus on issues relating to the networking of computers.

In the next section, we discuss three basic metrics that are used in the characterisation of certain aspects of the network – specifically, bandwidth, bit-rate, and latency. Subsequently, in Section 9.3 we consider three different general forms of network: the 'local area network (LAN), the 'metropolitan network (MAN), and the 'wide area network' (WAN). Essential differences between these networks include the network's geographical extent. Section 9.4 deals with network topologies and here we consider various interconnection schemes that can be used to connect together a number of computers. (Note: when dealing with computer networking, computers and other network devices are usually referred to as 'nodes'.)

The development of software systems via which computers can communicate in a reliable manner is a complex process, and a 'layered' software structure is generally adopted. This matter is discussed in Section 9.5 and in Section 9.6 where we describe some of the advantages and disadvantages associated with the establishment of communication standards.

Finally, in Sections 9.7 and 9.8 we consider protocols used in the implementation of computer communications. We begin this discussion by describing the 'Open System Interconnection' (OSI) model which (if fully implemented) enables computers produced by different manufacturers to communicate via different forms of interconnect. In Section 9.8 we discuss aspects of the 'Transmission Control Protocol/Internet Protocol' (TCP/IP). This underpins Internet communications and was first proposed in the early 1970s.

## 9.2 Bandwidth bit-rate and latency

When discussing computer networks, we generally refer to the individual computers as 'nodes'. Consider two such nodes that are directly connected together via some form of transmission medium (e.g. an electrical cable), see Figure 9.1.

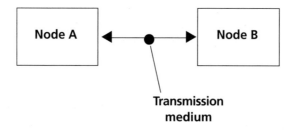

**Figure 9.1:** Two nodes (computers) connected via some form of transmission medium

Let us suppose that we were to transmit a sinusoidal signal from Node A to Node B, and that we gradually increase the frequency of this signal. As the frequency becomes greater, we would find that the amplitude of the signal received at Node B would begin to diminish. In Figure 9.2(a) we depict the transmission of a low-frequency signal and as may be seen, the amplitude of the transmitted and received signal are approximately the same (we assume that the transmission link is quite short). The situation depicted in Figure 9.2(b) is somewhat different. Here, the frequency of the transmitted wave has been increased and the signal received by Node B is considerably attenuated.

Different types of transmission medium are able to support the passage of signals within a certain frequency range, and the 'bandwidth' provides us with a measure of this range. For example, a telephone system traditionally supports the passage of signals (without unacceptable attenuation) in the range ~300Hz to ~3,300Hz (Hz: cycles per second). This gives a bandwidth of 3,000Hz (3kHz).

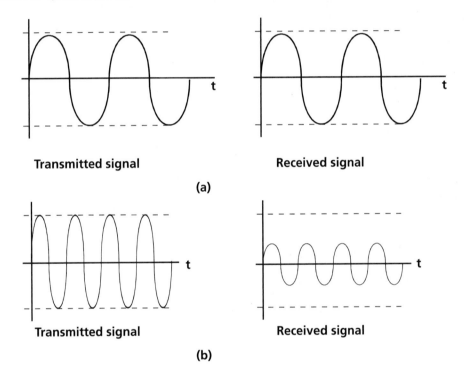

**Transmitted signal**          **Received signal**

**(a)**

**Transmitted signal**          **Received signal**

**(b)**

**Figure 9.2:** In (a) the amplitude of the transmitted and the received signals are approximately the same. In (b) the transmitted signal has been increased in frequency and the signal that emerges from the interconnect is significantly attenuated.

The sinusoidal signal referred to above is a continuous (analog) signal of constant frequency. When we consider the transmission of digital signals through an interconnect, matters become more complicated. Some 200 years ago the remarkable French mathematician, Jean Baptiste Joseph Fourier, discovered that periodic complex waves (i.e. complex in shape) can be produced by adding together a set of sinusoidal waves (of appropriate frequency, amplitude, and phase). Specifically, a periodic wave which we will refer to as f(t) can be generated according to the following expression (here, we indicate that the wave is a function of time (t) – hence the inclusion of t within the bracket.

This should not be confused with our use of the symbol 'f' (i.e. a stand-alone symbol), which represents frequency):

$$f(t) = \frac{c}{2} + \sum_{n=1}^{\infty} a_n \sin 2\pi n f t + \sum_{n=1}^{\infty} b_n \cos 2\pi n f t$$

The first term is simply a constant and need not concern us. The other two terms represent the sum of a number of sine and cosine waves and '$a_n$' and '$b_n$' denote their amplitudes (the symbol $\Sigma$ denotes the sum of a series of terms). For example, this equation can give rise to a series of sine terms:

$$a_1 \sin 2\pi f t + a_2 \sin 4\pi f t + a_3 \sin 6\pi f t + ...$$

The series of terms generated by this equation is referred to as the 'Fourier Series'. Given that a periodic waveform can be constructed through the addition of a number of waves that are sinusoidal in form, it follows that we can consider any wave to comprise a number of 'frequency components'. For example, consider a digital binary waveform such as the clock signal used within a computer. This waveform may be generated (synthesised) by adding together a number of sinusoidal signals (for more detail see Stallings, W., *Data and Computer Communications*, 5th Ed., Prentice-Hall, (1997)):

$$\frac{44}{\pi} \left[ \cos 2\pi f t - \frac{1}{3} \cos 6\pi f t + \frac{1}{5} \cos 10\pi f t - \frac{1}{7} \cos 14\pi f t + ... \right]$$

As may be seen from this expression, the terms form a series in which individual terms differ in both frequency and amplitude. In short, if we add together terms that have the appropriate amplitudes and the appropriate frequencies we can construct (synthesise) the periodic clock waveform. Looking at this from the other point of view, we can say that the clock waveform comprises a set of sinusoidal waves. As mentioned above, any transmission medium has a finite bandwidth which means, for example, that sinusoidal waves of higher frequencies will be attenuated more than sinusoidal waves of lower (intermediate) frequencies. As a result, higher-frequency components within the clock waveform will be more strongly attenuated, and this leads to the distortion of our clock waveform as it passes along a transmission medium. In fact, if we were to inject into the transmission medium an ideal (perfectly shaped) clock waveform, we could not necessary assume that the waveform that will emerge from the medium will not have been distorted. The distortion may be caused by several factors, one of which is the attenuation of the higher-frequency components that comprise the wave.

As we increase the frequency of the clock waveform that is injected into the transmission medium, distortion problems are likely to increase. Here, it is particularly important to note that as we increase the frequency of the clock waveform, there is a corresponding increase in the frequency of the components that comprise the wave. Therefore, these components are more likely to be attenuated as a consequence of the bandwidth limitations of the transmission medium, and in turn this results in greater signal distortion.

When describing the characteristics of a transmission medium or transmission link, we generally refer to the 'bit-rate'. The bit-rate provides us with a measure of the rate at which bits are transmitted through the medium (for example, a conventional modem is usually said to have a bit-rate of '56K', i.e. ~56,000 bits per second).

Unfortunately, the term 'bandwidth' is sometimes used to refer to bit-rate. Whilst bandwidth and bit-rate are related, from a technical point of view they are not the same thing. Consider an interconnect that has a bandwidth f into which a signal that has L signal levels is injected (e.g. if this signal were to be generated by an 8-bit DAC, a signal comprising 256 possible levels would be produced). The relationship between bandwidth (f) and bit-rate (b) is given by:

$$b = 2f \log_2 L$$

For example, assuming the use of an 8-bit DAC, L equals 256. If the bandwidth of the channel is 2,000Hz, then the maximum bit-rate is:

$$b = 2x2000x\log_2 256 = 32,000 bits/\sec ond$$

(note the use of log to the base 2. Here 256=$2^8$ and $\log_2 2^8$=8. Similarly, if we were to use a 10-bit DAC, $\log_2 1024$=$\log_2 2^{10}$=10)

Clearly, we have two opportunities to increase the bit-rate. The first is to increase the bandwidth of the channel, and the second is to increase the number of signal levels. However, if we assume that the channel (interconnect) is already in place, then there is little we can do to increase its bandwidth. Increasing the number of signal levels provides a practical solution – up to a certain point. Here, it is important to note that any electrical or wireless link is subject to noise (extraneous signal). Such noise may be generated within the interconnect itself or may be induced by external agencies (for example, during an electrical storm, noise (unwanted signals) is induced into metallic conductors). As we increase the number of levels within the signal that is injected into the transmission medium then, unless we increase the overall signal amplitude, the voltage difference between adjacent levels will decrease. In turn, the presence of noise will make it increasingly difficult to distinguish between levels, and ultimately differences in signals levels will be swamped by noise. In short, for a given interconnect, we can only go so far in increasing L. In the late 1940s, Claude Shannon investigated the theoretical transmission capacity (b) of a channel and obtained the following theoretical result (he assumed the presence of 'white' noise):

$$b = f.\log_2 \left[1+\frac{S}{N}\right]$$

S denotes the signal strength (power) and N the noise power (the ratio of S and N (S/N) is referred to as the signal-to-noise ratio). This equation indicates that in order to increase the bit-rate we must either:

- **Increase the bandwidth of the interconnect**
- **Increase the signal power**
- **Decrease the noise power.**

Once we have exhausted these options we have attained the maximum bit-rate for the interconnect. However, we can further increase the capacity of the interconnect for information transfer by use of encoding techniques. For example, we can employ file compression techniques to reduce the amount of binary data that needs to be transmitted. By way of a very simple illustration, suppose that we have an image file that we wish to transfer between computers. For simplicity we will assume that this comprises 5 by 5 pixels and that each pixel is either white or black and can therefore be represented by a single bit (recall that when each pixel is represented by a single bit we refer to this as a 'bitmapped image').

The image is illustrated in Figure 9.3(a) where we indicate each white pixel by 'w' and each black pixel by 'b'. In Figure 9.3(b) we indicate the image using binary values and here a white pixel is denoted by a binary '0' and each black pixel by a binary '1'. If we were to transmit each individual pixel value, we would need to send 25 bits to the remote computer. On the other hand, we can use an approach that is known as 'run-length encoding' and so reduce the number of bits that must be transferred. Referring to Figure 9.3(b), let us suppose that we start at the upper left-hand corner and work across the image (i.e. along the top row of pixels). We note that all pixels are white. We now move to the next row – again all pixels are white. The third row also consists of white pixels – in fact the first seventeen pixels that we encounter are white. Subsequently, we have three black pixels followed by five white pixels.

Thus we can represent the image as comprising 17 white pixels followed by three black pixels and then five white pixels (this assumes that we work across each row from left to right and begin with the top row). This information is recorded in Table 9.1.

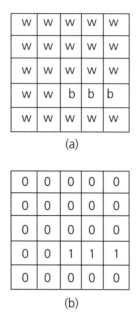

(a)

(b)

**Figure 9.3:** The use of a simple compression technique

| Pixel value (code) | Number of identical pixels (run length) | Binary value for the number of pixels (run length) |
|---|---|---|
| 0 | 17 | 10001 |
| 1 | 3 | 11 |
| 0 | 5 | 101 |

**Table 9.1:** A simple encoding technique

To transfer this file we need only transmit the pixel codes and the binary run length values. In principle this requires the transmission of only thirteen bits, and from this information the recipient node can reconstruct the image (this process is known as file decompression). Thus instead of transmitting the twenty-five individual pixels, we need only transfer thirteen pixels (although in reality, to ensure that the recipient can decode the transmission, we would need to adopt a slightly more complex coding scheme).

## Data compression – in brief

There are two general methods of data compression. One is known as 'lossless' data compression and the other one as 'lossy' compression:

- **Lossless compression:** In the case of this approach the data compression and decompression techniques are simply the inverse of each other. After decompression the original data is recovered without any information loss. Huffman encoding provides an example of this technique

- **Lossy compression:** here the decompressed data is not an exact representation of that which was transmitted – some loss occurs. Typically, the original uncompressed data and the final decompressed data are very similar, although in the case of, for example, video images, the overall image quality suffers.

## *Latency*

A parameter that we need to take into account when discussing the transmission of signals between nodes concerns 'latency'. This provides us with an indication of the delay that ensues between signals being injected into an interconnect and their emergence from it. For example, suppose that we were using a conventional modem to provide us with an Internet connection between our computer in the UK and a remote computer in the US. Typically, our modem will operate at a bit-rate of 56,000 bits per second. This is the maximum speed at which the modem is able to transmit bits onto the telephone connection through which we are gaining Internet access. This bit rate tells us nothing of the time it will take for the bits to arrive at the computer in the US – i.e. the transit time of each bit. This time delay (latency) will depend upon a number of things. For example:

- The time it takes for the bits to propagate along the cables and other links that connect our computer to the remote computer in the US. Signals travelling through metallic conductors (wires) and fibre optic cable travel at a speed that is somewhat slower than the speed of light. Signals transmitted using wireless links will travel at approximately the speed of light. (The propagation of such signals is slowed down slightly by the presence of the atmosphere. However, for all intents and purposes we can consider such signals to travel at the speed of light, which is approximately $3 \times 10^8 \text{ms}^{-1}$)

- Delays that might be caused when the signals pass through intermediate computers and other network devices.

**Activity 9.1**

**Transmission latency**

Suppose that a computer on the Earth is used to communicate with a computer on the Moon. Approximately how long would it take for a signal transmitted from the Earth-based computer to arrive at the computer on the Moon? You should assume that the signal travels at the speed of light ($\sim 3 \times 10^8 \text{ms}^{-1}$) and that the distance between the Earth and the Moon is ~384,400km.

## 9.3 Types of network

The way devices are connected to each other in a network depends on the 'line configuration'. This denotes the physical transmission pathway used to transmit data from one node to another. There are a number of ways to connect the network devices – for example, point-to-point and multipoint line configurations:

- **Point-to-point:** this line configuration provides a direct dedicated line between two devices. The entire capacity of the line is dedicated to these two devices
- **Multipoint:** this line configuration allows a number of devices to be attached with a single line (interconnect). In this configuration more than two devices can share the interconnect and are able to communicate with each other.

The implementation of a point-to-point configuration is not always practical because, for example, devices may be far apart. Furthermore, a large set of devices would require an impractical number of connections. As a result, we employ a shared communication network, as illustrated in Figure 9.4.

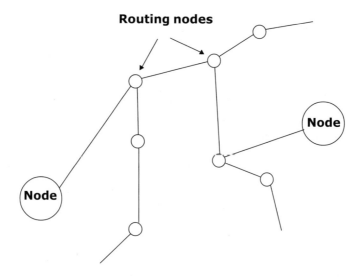

**Figure 9.4:** Nodes connected by a shared network topology

Traditionally, networks are categorised using three classifications:

- **Local area network (LAN)**
- **Metropolitan area network (MAN)**
- **Wide area network (WAN)**.

These differ in terms of:

- **Size** of the network
- **Ownership** of the network
- Physical **extent** of the network
- Physical **architecture**.

Below, we briefly discuss these classes of network.

## Local area networks (LANs)

These operate within a limited geographical area, such as a building, hospital or a university campus, and connect physically adjacent devices. Due to the close proximity of the nodes, an organisation can install its own transmission media (such as cables) without relying on common carriers, such as those provided by British Telecommunications (BT). A LAN is usually privately owned and its extent is limited to a few kilometres. Traditionally, LANs often use a single type of interconnect throughout the transmission system. A LAN allows resources (such as hardware devices, software, and data) to be shared between personal computers. The most common topologies for a LAN are bus, ring and star and mesh, depicted in Figure 9.5.

## Metropolitan area networks (MANs)

The physical size of a MAN is greater than that of a LAN and as its name implies, a MAN may be used to support communication between devices dispersed across an entire city (e.g. a cable television network). MANs are often used to connect a number of LANs into a larger network so that resources can be share (e.g. a company with offices throughout a city). A MAN can connect together different topologies of LAN.

## Wide area networks (WANs)

These networks are used to connect devices located in widely dispersed geographical areas, such as cities and countries. Unlike LANs, which utilise their own hardware and transmission systems, WANs usually depend on the services provided by common carriers, leased lines, and private communication devices to communicate between devices (nodes) in the network. A WAN consists of interconnected routing (switching) nodes that direct data from one node to another so that it can reach the desired destination. These series of interconnecting switches consist of hardware and software that establish a temporary connection between devices. A WAN uses different technologies to transfer data through these switches. Two of these are:

- **Circuit switching:** here, a dedicated transmission path is established between the communicating nodes (traditionally the telephone network employed this approach – the establishment of a single dedicated connection between two phones for the duration of the telephone call)

- **Packet switching:** rather than establishing a dedicated communication path, packet switching divides data to be transmitted into chunks (packets) and these are sent across shared interconnects. Packets (commonly referred to as frames) contain not only the data chunks but also the information needed to allow them to be routed across the network and so reach their intended destination. In one scenario, packets do not necessarily have to follow the same route across the network and so can arrive at their destination out of order (this is called the 'datagram' approach). However, as we will discuss shortly, each packet contains the information needed to enable the recipient to correctly reassemble them.

# 9.4 Network topologies

The way in which nodes within a network are interconnected is called the 'network topology'. Topologies are either physical or logical:

- **Physical topology:** this refers to the actual layout of the network, i.e. the way the nodes are actually connected together by the media (e.g. cables) that transmit the data signals

- **Logical topology:** this refers to the way that data signals pass through the network from one node to the next, regardless of the physical interconnection of the nodes.

## *Physical topologies*

Physical topologies are arranged in different configurations; the most commonly used are bus, ring, star and mesh. These topologies are illustrated in Figure 9.5.

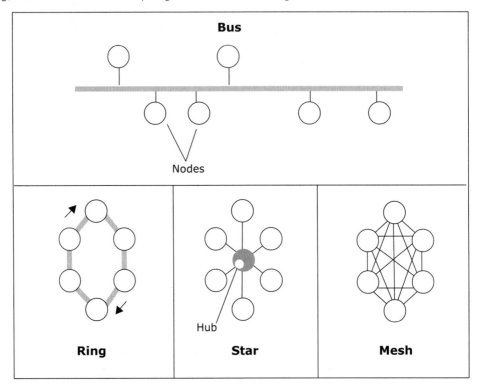

**Figure 9.5:** Various network topologies

- **Bus:** in this case the nodes are connected to a single length of a common cable referred to as a 'backbone'. Nodes may be connected to the bus by 'droplines'; these being connections linking each device to the main cable (i.e. bus). The bus is terminated at both ends to prevent signals from being reflected back along the bus cable. The terminator takes the form of a resistor

- **Ring:** here, the nodes are connected to one another in a closed loop configuration, where each device is linked to the two adjacent ones, forming a physical ring of cable. Unlike the bus arrangement, the ring topology provides a dedicated point-to-point connection path between the individual devices. A dedicated path refers to the condition whereby the line moves signals only between the two devices it connects

- **Star:** unlike the bus and ring topologies, the devices are not directly connected to each other. Instead, every device has a dedicated point-to-point connection to a central control unit called the 'hub', which dispatches data signals to and from the devices

- **Mesh:** in a fully connected mesh topology every device is linked directly to every other device by a dedicated point-to-point path. This is used to ensure no break in communication in, for example, control systems. In the event that a link fails to work, data signals can travel via a number of other links to reach their destination. This topology requires many interconnects – the number increases rapidly as more nodes are included in the network. In fact for a network comprising n nodes, the number of connections (N) needed to implement a fully connected topology is given by:

$$N = \frac{n}{2}(n-1)$$

### The fully connected topology

Consider a network that employs a fully connected topology and that (as indicated in Table 9.2) comprises 5, 10, 20 or 50 nodes. For each case, complete the table by indicating the number of network interconnects that would be needed.

| Number of nodes | Required number of interconnects |
|---|---|
| 5 | |
| 10 | |
| 20 | |
| 50 | |

**Table 9.2:** A fully connected network topology

## Logical network topologies

As indicated previously, the logical topology refers to the way in which data travels, and how access to shared transmission media is decided. Two of the most common topologies used to date for network access are known as broadcast and token passing techniques. However, and perhaps unfortunately, token passing is now seldom used, and the broadcast technique typified by the Ethernet CSMA/CD is most frequently employed. These two approaches are briefly summarised below:

### Broadcast

- Each device sends its data to all other devices on the network
- No specific order is followed by the networked devices using the network
- The access criteria is first-come, first-served.

The most widely used access mechanism is called 'Carrier Sense Multiple Access with Collision Detection' (CSMA/CD) and is defined in the IEEE 802.3 standard. This technique coordinates traffic to maximise the rate of successful delivery.

### Token passing

- This involves passing a special short electronic message called a 'token', in sequence, to each device on the network (e.g. typically a ring topology is used)
- A device wishing to transmit waits for the token to arrive before it can send data, transmits the data, and then sends out the token to the next device
- When no devices have data to transmit, the token cycles around the ring.

These two approaches are considered in greater detail in Chapter 10.

## *Comparing physical network topologies*

When selecting a particular topology, a primary consideration is the chosen mode of communication between the networked devices. These can be divided into two categories:

- **Peer-to-peer,** where the devices share and have equal access to the medium; examples of related topologies include ring, mesh and bus
- **Primary-secondary,** where a central device controls communication traffic and the remaining devices can only transmit through the central device. An example of a related topology is the star configuration.

There are many factors to be considered when selecting a topology. For example:

- Network **cost**
- The degree of **reliability** that is required
- Total **number of users**
- **Network management** issues – support for centralised management
- The ability to **prioritise communications**.

## 9.5 The layered approach to computer communications

In order to enable two or more computers to communicate in a meaningful manner, we must define with great care all aspects of the communication process (i.e. we must define a 'communications protocol'). By way of a useful analogy, let us consider the situation in which the director of a company in the UK wishes to communicate with a person in another company located in China. The director may ask a secretary to put the call through and will provide sufficient information for the secretary to identify the person who is to be phoned. Here, the director may not give the actual phone number – it may be left to the secretary to obtain this information. From this point, the director has no further involvement until the phone connection is in place. The secretary will locate and dial the number and this will initiate various electronic/software activities. Neither the director nor secretary have any interest in knowing the details of how the electronic and software systems will route the call. It may be carried by electronic cables, fibre optic cables, or be routed via a satellite. Additionally, it may use communications systems that route the call across the Atlantic through the US and then across the Pacific Ocean, or it may be routed in an easterly direction. These low-level issues are of little interest to the secretary – a number is dialled and processes occur that result in a phone ringing in an office somewhere in China. Hopefully, the intended recipient is available and the secretary notifies the director. Both parties must now adopt/agree on a common language and must exercise a degree of hand-shaking (in this sense we mean that only one person should talk at any one time). Finally, at the end of the conversation, an acceptable convention is used to bring the call to a conclusion. All these issues form part of the 'communications protocol' that is needed to enable a useful dialogue, and it is important to note that the elements that underpin the communication do not need to have any knowledge of the overall purpose that they will serve. For example:

- The secretary does not necessarily know why the call is to be placed – the information exchange may be confidential to the company director and the recipient of the phone call
- The keypad via which the secretary enters the phone number converts the key presses into electrical signals. These signals are dispatched and initiate various routing actions. However, the keypad is not involved in these actions – it serves a single function

- The director has no knowledge of the path taken by the 'voice signals' as they are routed to China.  Perhaps they pass via trans-oceanic cables or are beamed to an orbiting satellite

- Any cables used during the conversation have no 'knowledge' of the meaning that will be placed on the digital signals that they transmit.

The establishment of a communications protocol that enables computers (and other digital systems) to communicate is, in many ways, similar to the protocols used to support the sort of phone conversation referred to in the above analogy (although computer communications are perhaps more complex).  To handle the design implementation and maintenance of such systems, a 'layered' approach is adopted.  In Figure 9.6, we indicate two computers that need to communicate.  Perhaps, for example, an applications program running on Node A wishes to send a data file to a similar program running on Node B (just as in the same way the company director mentioned above wishes to talk to a person in a remote location).  In order to transmit the data a number of tasks must be performed, and these are carried out by layers of software located on both nodes.

Each layer carries out a number of specific tasks and directly communicates with the immediately adjacent software layers.  However, from a logical point of view each layer communicates with a corresponding layer on the remote computer – i.e. corresponding software layers located on the two nodes have similar/equivalent functionality.  The lowest layer on either node is responsible for interfacing with the physical interconnect.

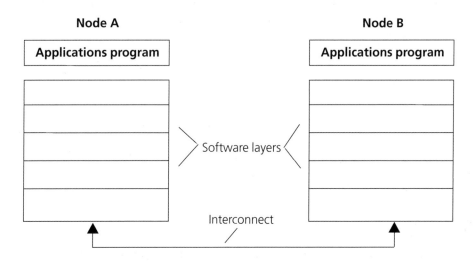

**Figure 9.6:** An applications program on Node A wishes to send data to an equivalent program on Node B

In order for Node A to transmit a data file to Node B, various events must take place.

For example:

- Node A must inform the communications network of the identity of the destination system (Node B)

- Node A must ensure that Node B is prepared to receive the data

- The file transfer applications program on Node A must ensure that the file management program on the destination system is ready to accept and store the file

- If the file formats used on the two systems are incompatible, one or other system must perform a format translation function

- File transfer must be carried out in an orderly manner and in such a way that the two communicating machines do not block other network traffic. This will involve splitting the data file into packets (chunks) and appending various information to each packet
- Node B provides acknowledgement of receipt
- Node B reassembles the packets in order to reconstruct the original data file
- Node B must attempt to detect any errors in the data it has received. In some cases Node B may be able to correct errors
- In the case that secure transmission is required, the data may be encrypted by Node A prior to transmission. Node B must then perform the reverse process.

To achieve this high degree of cooperation between computers, the tasks are broken into subtasks that are implemented individually using a layered approach. These layers form the data communication protocol architecture. Examples of such layered architectures are: the Open System Interconnection (OSI) model, and the Transmission Control Protocol/Internet Protocol (TCP/IP). Key advantages of a layered structure include:

- The complex communications protocol is divided into subtasks and these are implemented within a layered structure. Each layer has limited functionality and this 'divide and conquer' approach facilitates the design and implementation of the system
- Higher-level layers need have no knowledge of tasks performed by the lower layers. Thus, for example, a higher-level layer needs no knowledge of the type of interconnect that is in use. Again, this facilitates the design process
- When changes are made to the communications protocol, only certain relevant layers need to be modified/replaced. This makes it easier to upgrade software and undertake software testing.

Structuring software using a layered approach tends to result in *larger programs* which run *more slowly* than if a non-layered approach were to be adopted. However, these two weaknesses are outweighed by the benefits that are associated with the layered approach – especially in terms of providing a structured framework within which the complex issues associated with computer communications may be resolved.

## 9.6 Standards

Standards play an important role in our everyday lives and facilitate the operation of products produced by different manufacturers. For example:

- Countries adopt a standard type of mains plug and socket. Without such a standard, we would find that we had to continually rewire mains plugs or employ some form of adaptor. This provides an example of a national standard
- Car manufacturers adopt a standard for the relative placement of the clutch, brake and accelerator pedals. This provides an example of a global standard
- Computers are equipped with standard interface sockets (e.g. serial, parallel and USB) via which they are able to connect to peripheral devices. This provides an example of a global standard.

Standards may come into being in various ways. For example:

- A standard may be established (imposed) by the company that plays the most dominant role in any particular area. For example, the serial and parallel ports employed by today's PC were implemented on the earliest PCs introduced by IBM.  They soon became standard for desktop computing

- A standard may gradually evolve
- A standard may be developed/defined by a committee of experts.

Although standardisation can facilitate our use of technologies and products, standards seldom reflect an optimal solution.  For example, the VHS videotape format became a standard, while other superior and equally cost-effective formats fell by the wayside.  Furthermore, in the case of standards developed by committees, these often reflect many technological compromises and take long periods to develop.  Such standards are often out of date even before they are released!

From a computer user's perspective, standards are extremely important because they allow a combination of products from different manufacturers to be used together.  Standards ensure greater compatibility and interoperability between various types of equipment and technologies.

In data communications, standards provide guidelines to manufacturers and service providers to ensure compatibility, connectivity, and interoperability of technologies – an essential requirement in today's global market.  Key advantages of standards are:

- To ensure a large market for hardware or software products – thus encouraging mass production
- To allow products from different vendors to communicate, thus giving customers more flexibility in the selection and use of equipment.

On the other hand, standards do have limitations:

- They tend to slow down technological change.  This is due to the fact that, in some cases, by the time a standard is developed, subjected to scrutiny, reviewed, compromised and endorsed by all concerned parties – and then disseminated, more efficient technologies could have developed
- Many standards may exist for the same thing.  It is often difficult to decide which standard will provide better compatibility and remain in place for the greatest amount of time.

Many official computer-related standards are defined by the following organisations:

- **ANSI** (American National Standards Institute)
- **ITU** (International Telecommunication Union)
- **IEEE** (Institute of Electrical and Electronic Engineers)
- **ISO** (International Organization for Standardization)
- **VESA** (Video Electronics Standards Association).

Car drivers generally use agreed signals when turning left or right.  Aeroplane pilots follow specific standardised rules for communicating throughout the world.  Similarly, for any computer-based systems to communicate successfully, they need to 'use the same language'.  This means that what is communicated, how it is communicated, and when it is communicated must conform to some mutually acceptable conventions agreed between the parties involved.  These conventions are known as a 'protocol', which can be defined as a set of rules governing the exchange of data between two or more devices.

Typical tasks performed by protocols are as follows:

- To make sure that the source device activates the data communication line
- To inform the transmission system about the destination system
- To make sure that the source device communicates with the destination device before sending data
- To make sure the destination device is ready to accept the data
- To make sure that the destination file management system is ready to store incoming files
- To ensure compatibility between source and destination, and to perform format translation.

In the 1980s, many companies entered the desktop computing market and this led to a rich diversity of products. Unfortunately, these systems would often not operate together, nor could software developed for use on one particular type of machine necessarily be used on another. In short, although the lack of standards enabled product diversity, it hampered computer usage. Quickly, standards were developed (and/or evolved) and these impacted on many areas of computing. For example:

- **Compatibility improved.** By conformance to standards, hardware and software systems developed by different manufactures could be used together (although there were often unforeseen problems)
- **The diversity of available products decreased**
- **Backwards compatibility became an important issue.** For example, a new model of computer, or a new release of an operating system should support the function of older products. This has greatly increased hardware and software complexity and retarded the development of radically new computer products.

## 9.7 The OSI model

The Open System Interconnection (OSI) reference model was developed by the International Standards Organization (ISO) and provides a framework for protocol development. By implementing a communication protocol that adheres to the OSI model, systems developed by different manufacturers are able to communicate. The tasks that must be performed to enable machines to communicate in an effective and efficient manner are incorporated within a seven-layer hierarchy, as indicated in Figure 9.7 Although the protocols detailed within this reference model are seldom used, the model provides us with an excellent conceptual framework for understanding the tasks performed by the various software layers. Below we briefly summarise aspects of the functionality of the various layers.

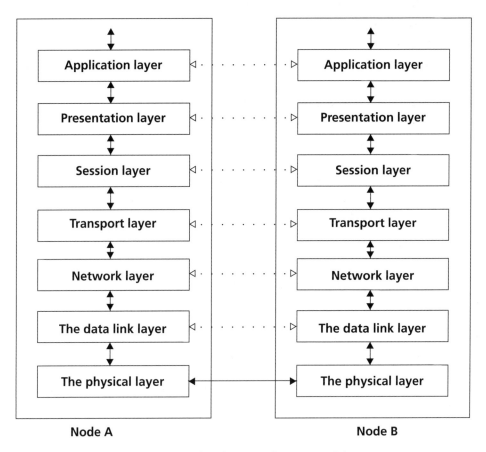

**Figure 9.7:** The layers within the OSI reference model

## Application layer

This should not be confused with the applications programs that may be running on a computer. The application layer provides network access to the user and to applications programs. This layer passes data to (and receives data from) the presentation layer, and logically communicates directly to the application layer on the remote computer. This is indicated in Figure 9.7 where the horizontal lines indicate the logical communication of each layer with its remote counterpart. The application layer needs know nothing of the tasks carried out by the lower layers – it needs only interface with the user (and applications programs) and with the presentation layer.

## Presentation layer

Different computers may employ different character set formats. A user is not interested in such differences and one of the tasks undertaken by the presentation layer is to translate between different formats that may be used to represent numbers, characters and other symbols. Additionally, the presentation layer is also involved in ensuring secure data transmission (consequently, when data is being transmitted the presentation layer undertakes encryption, and when data is being received it performs decryption).

## Session layer

A user or applications program may need to open a 'session' with a remote machine. For example, a user may wish to log on to a remote computer and carry out various tasks and this will involve the transmission and reception of data over a period of time. This necessitates synchronisation whereby each node knows when it can transmit and when it is to receive data (i.e. when it must 'listen'). The session layer deals with this synchronisation and additionally is involved in error recovery. Consider the case that a file is being transmitted between two nodes, and during this process the network fails. Without the support of the session layer it would be necessary to start the transmission process again from the beginning. However, the session layer inserts checkpoints into the transmitted data stream and these are used to efficiently recover from such failures. Following a failure, transmission can be recommenced from the point at which the last checkpoint was successfully delivered to the destination node. The session layer carries out various other activities, such as bracketing a set of related and non-independent activities. For example, there may be a need to carry out a task on a remote machine, which involves the execution of a series of commands. Perhaps if only some of these commands are executed (i.e. they are not carried out in their entirety) problems will ensue. If the individual commands are executed as each arrives at the remote machine then, in the case that the network connection fails, there is the likelihood of incomplete execution. One task performed by the session layer relates to the buffering of such commands – as each arrives it is temporarily stored and not passed to higher layers until all commands (and any associated data) have been received. The series of commands may then execute in full.

## Transport layer

This acts as the intermediary between the lower layers (whose implementation is dependent on the underlying network architecture) and the three upper layers which provide user services and whose architecture is (at least in principle) independent of the detailed network characteristics. The type of transport service that is provided to the session layer is determined by the transport layer. Suppose a node wished to send an extremely large file to a remote machine via a shared network (or set of interconnected networks). Without judicious design (in relation to the type of transport service used), there is the possibility that such a transmission could block the network(s) in such a way that whilst the transmission is in progress no other machines could communicate. The approach commonly used to prevent such a situation is to split the data into chunks ('packets') which are individually encapsulated within a frame containing all the necessary data needed to enable a packets delivery to the intended destination. The splitting of the data into smaller units is carried out by the transport layer. These packets may traverse a set of networks by different routes and so arrive at their destination out of order. The transport layer reorders packets and so enables them to be correctly reassembled.

## Network layer

This layer decides on routing issues, determining the path that should be followed by packets when they traverse networks. In fact, in such a situation the path taken is not defined solely by the source node but by all the nodes (network devices) through which packets pass on their way to the destination. Consider the situation illustrated in Figure 9.8.

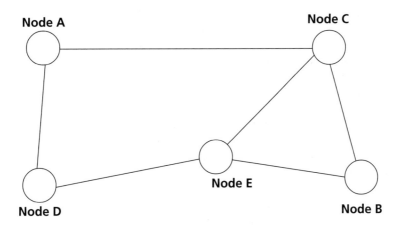

**Figure 9.8:** A simple network in which a packet may be sent from Node A to Node B via different routes. The circles represent nodes, and the lines network interconnects.

**Network routing**

Activity 9.3

Consider the network topology illustrated in Figure 9.8.

How many different routes may be taken by a packet sent from Node A to Node B?

State any assumption that you make.

Identify at least two factors that would influence/define routing decisions.

Suppose that a packet is to be sent from Node A to Node B. The packet will have to pass through at least one intermediate node (network device). These nodes may simply forward the packet, or may decide on the direction of the next step in its voyage. Thus, for example, Node D simply performs a forwarding function, whereas Nodes C and E are able to make routing decisions. The transport layer plays a critical role in determining the time it will take for packets to reach their destination and in this sense the actions of the transport layer impact on transmission latency.

## The data link layer

This layer is responsible for various low-level network specific tasks and plays a crucial part in the detection and correction of errors that may occur during the transmission process. Correction may be achieved by means of additional information inserted into messages prior to their transmission that can be used to modify bits corrupted during the transmission process. Alternatively, correction may involve requesting re-transmission. Additionally, the data link layer plays a pivotal role in managing network access and ensuring that network 'collisions' (which occur when two or more nodes attempt to transmit onto the same LAN at the same time) are handled correctly (we discuss this matter further in the next chapter). Devices connected together via networks do not necessarily demonstrate the same transmission/reception characteristics.

Thus a device able to transmit at high speed (i.e. that has a high bit-rate) could readily swamp a slower recipient. Buffering techniques are used to circumvent this problem and this necessitates a protocol that ensures that the capacity of the buffer is not exceeded. This is referred to as flow control.

## The physical layer

This layer deals with the transmission of the bit stream through the transmission medium, and the connection strategy used to enable the transfer of bits from one node to another. Thus the physical layer defines the signal levels, the type of transmission medium employed (e.g. twisted pair cable, coaxial cable, fibre optic cable), and also the techniques that will be used to permit the passage of data, such as circuit switching (in which a dedicated path is set up between two communicating nodes), packet switching, etc. Different forms of transmission media are discussed in the next chapter.

**Activity 9.4**

### The OSI model architecture

Select the terms, from the list that follows, which are appropriate to each question. Note that terms may be used more than once – or not used at all.

1. OSI and ISO: how they are related?

2. Which layer ensures the end-to-end delivery of the entire message?

3. Which layer transmits a data frame?

4. Which layer ensures encryption and decryption in the OSI model?

5. Which layer controls the dialogue between two devices?

6. Which layer is closest to the transmission medium?

7. Which layer is just above the network layer?

8. Which layer lies between the network layer and the session layer?

9. Which layer is responsible for changing the data bit into an electromagnetic signal?

10. How does the protocol travel through the OSI model?

*Answer list:*

| | |
|---|---|
| Standard agency | Open System Interconnection |
| Physical layer | Data link layer |
| Network layer | Transport layer |
| Session layer | Presentation layer |
| Application layer | Bottom up and top down |

## 9.8 The TCP/IP protocol

In the late 1960s the US Department of Defence's Advance Research Project Agency (ARPA) initiated a project that centred upon the interconnection of geographically dispersed computing systems. Gradually a large-scale network of university and government computing facilities evolved (this network was named ARPANET), which used packet switching techniques and initially employed leased phone lines. Early networking protocols were slow and unreliable and in 1974 a new set of protocols were proposed. These formed the basis for TCP/IP (Transmission Control Protocol/Internet Protocol (TCP/IP) which today underpins the operation of the Internet.

A protocol such as TCP/IP must support a number of essential requirements such as:

- **Reliability:** in terms of both data integrity and timely delivery
- **Fault tolerance:** the failure of a network segment should not seriously disrupt overall network operation; it must be possible to route packets along different paths so that they can still reach their destination
- **Transparent communications:** different computer systems and LANs should be able to communicate transparently.

It is convenient to employ a layered model in order to most readily conceptualise TCP/IP. We can therefore consider TCP/IP within a four-layer framework (a five-layer model is sometimes preferred). In Figure 9.9 these layers are depicted, and are placed alongside the layers that comprise the OSI model. Below we briefly summarise aspects of their role:

## Application layer

This layer provides communication services to the user and to applications programs. It can be viewed as corresponding to the application, presentation and session layers found in the OSI model. The application layer contains all the high-level protocols (such as those that we commonly encounter when accessing the Internet – such as DNS (Domain Name System) and HTTP).

## Transport layer

Two different protocols are defined in this layer (TCP and UDP (User Datagram Protocol)). These differ in a number of important respects. For example:

- **Reliability:** in the case of UDP, error correction is not implemented – the onus for this activity is placed on the applications program. This contrasts with TCP in which error detection and correction form an integral part. Free from error correction overheads, UDP can (under some circumstances) demonstrate high performance
- **Flow control:** in the case of TCP, flow control is implemented and this prevents a faster machine from swamping a recipient that operates more slowly.

**Activity 9.5**

**User datagram protocol**

Identify two possible applications in which it may be preferable to employ UDP rather than TCP.

OSI layers      TCP/IP layers

| | OSI layers | TCP/IP layers |
|---|---|---|
| 7 | Application layer | Application layer |
| 6 | Presentation layer | |
| 5 | Session layer | |
| 4 | Transport layer | Host-to-host transport |
| 3 | Network layer | Internet |
| 2 | The data link layer | Network interface |
| 1 | The physical layer | |

**Figure 9.9:** A conceptual model of TCP/IP set alongside the layers that comprise the OSI model

A stream of data that is to be transmitted is fragmented into chunks and the transport layer appends various information, before passing these to the Internet layer. At the receiving node, the transport layer reassembles these data chunks. In the case of TCP, the transport layer encapsulates the data chunks into a TCP segment (in the case of UDP, the encapsulated data is usually referred to as a packet. There are differences between the information contained in the UDP and TCP headers.) Here the data is provided with a 'header' containing various important information; see Figure 9.10. It is instructive to consider the purpose of several pieces of information contained in the header:

- **Source and destination ports:** many well known (widely used) application protocols are designated by unique identification numbers provided by the 'Internet Assigned Numbers Authority'. For example, the File Transfer Protocol (FTP) is identified as 'port 21', and the Simple Mail Transfer Protocol (SMTP) as 'port 25'. TCP inserts this information into the header and thereby provides information on the source and destination applications protocol associated with the data to be transferred. The source port and destination port fields are each two bytes long, and values below 256 are used to reference 'well-known' ports.

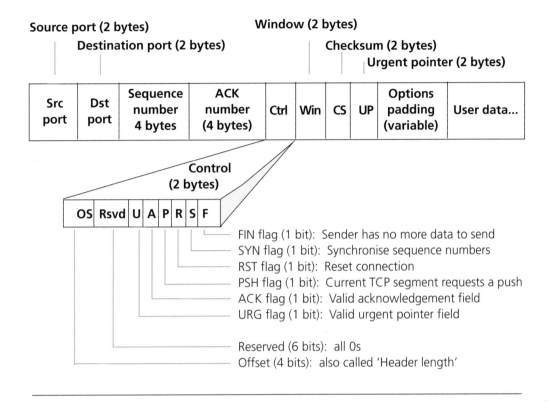

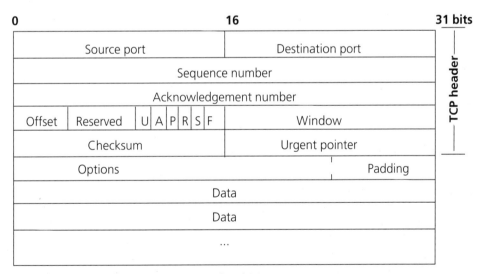

**Figure 9.10:** Information contained within a TCP segment

- **Sequence number:** TCP numbers each byte of data that is transmitted between two nodes during the transfer process. The sequence number references the first byte of data encapsulated within a frame. This is most readily understood by means of an example. Suppose that a set of frames are transmitted between node A and Node B, and that each contains 256 bytes of data. Then the sequence numbers contained in the first four frames transmitted by Node A could be 1, 257, 513, 769 (the process is slightly more complex since the sequence number of the first frame need not be 1). Node B uses these sequence numbers to reconstruct the data chunks and correct for frames being received out of their transmitted order

- **Header length:** this enables the receiving node to determine the point at which the header ends and the data starts. It is necessary to specify this length as headers are not of fixed size
- **Checksum:** this enables the transport layer to perform error detection
- **Options:** various options can be included. For example, one option enables the recipient to inform the source node about the maximum segment size that it is able to accept. This is indicated during the establishment of a connection and ensures that the recipient's buffer will not be swamped by a high-speed transfer.

## Internet layer

At the sending node, the Internet layer takes packets or segments generated by the transport layer, and further encapsulates these to produce datagrams. The additional information appended by the internet layer (the 'IP header') is intended to enable the datagrams to be injected onto any network and travel (via intermediate networks) to the intended destination. During their transit, intermediate network devices will use this information to determine the direction they should take. Since the routing of packets is fundamental to the Internet layer, it may be considered to be equivalent to the network layer used in the OSI model.

## Network interface layer

In terms of its functionality, this layer is equivalent to the lowest two layers used in the OSI model. It further encapsulates a datagram received from the Internet layer producing a 'frame'. This layer makes the connection to the transmission medium and employs the appropriate protocol for launching and receiving frames.

The process of encapsulation referred to above is summarised in Figure 9.11, and in Figure 9.12 an overview of the functionality of the layers that have been conceptualised in connection with TCP/IP is presented.

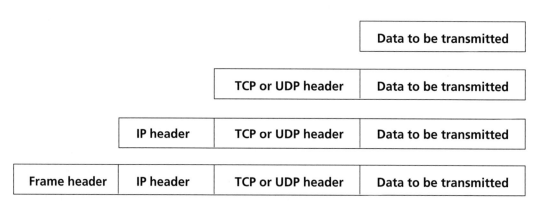

**Figure 9.11:** The process of encapsulation used by TCP/IP. This is depicted for the source (sending) node. At the receiving node, the process operates in the reverse: bottom up.

**Application (4)**
- Similar to OSI application layer
- Serves as communication interface by providing specific application services
- Examples include email, virtual terminal, file transfer, WWW

**Transport (3)**
- Defined by two protocols:

  **User Datagram Protocol (UDP)**
  - a connectionless protocol
  - provides unreliable datagram service (no end-to-end error detection or correction)
  - does not retransmit any unreceived data
  - requires little overhead
  - application protocols include Trivial File Transfer Protocol (TFTP), Network File System (NFS), Simple Network Management Protocol (SNMP), Bootstrap Protocol (BOOTP), and Domain Name Service (DNS)

  **Transmission Control Protocol (TCP)**
  - (the TCP of TCP/IP)
  - connection-oriented protocol
  - provides reliable data transmission via end-to-end detection and correction
  - guarantees data is transferred across a network accurately and in correct order
  - retransmits any data not received by destination node
  - guarantees against data duplication between sending and receiving nodes
  - application protocols include Telnet, FTP, SMTP and POP

**Internet (2)**
- (The IP of TCP/IP)
- Transfers user messages from source host to destination host
- Connectionless datagram service
- Route selection is based on a metric
- Uses Internet or IUP addresses to locate a host within the Internet
- Relies on routers or switches
- Integral part is Internet Control Message Protocol (ICMP); this uses an IP datagram to carry messages about state of communications environment

**Network Interface (1)**
- Connects host to the local network hardware
- Makes a connection to the physical medium
- Uses a specific protocol for accessing the medium
- Places data into frames
- Effectively performs all functions of the first two layers of the OSI model

**Table 9.3:** A summary of some aspects of the functionality of the conceptualised four-layer TCP/IP model

**Activity 9.6**

### The functionality of the OSI and TCP/IP paradigms

Complete the table below by indicating the layers of the conceptualised TCP/IP model that correspond to the OSI layers.

| OSI Model | TCP/IP |
|---|---|
| Application layer | |
| Presentation layer | |
| Session layer | |
| Transport layer | |
| Network layer | |
| Data link layer | |
| Physical layer | |

**Table 9.4:** Layers in the OSI and conceptualised TCP/IP models

## 9.9 Summary

In this chapter we have introduced a range of terminology and techniques used in relation to the networking of computers. Discussion opened with consideration of three important network metrics: bandwidth, bit-rate and latency. As we indicated, bandwidth and bit-rate are often incorrectly assumed to have the same meaning. However, although the two quantities are directly related they actually refer to two different technical aspects of the transmission media, and care should be taken in the usage of these expressions.

In later parts of the chapter we contrasted the use of a dedicated connection to the approach, in which data that is to be transmitted is split into chunks (which are encapsulated) and routed across shared network segments. The use of a dedicated connection is generally referred to as a 'connection-oriented service' and is exemplified by the traditional telephone service. Although today when we make a phone call it is routed across a shared interconnect, in older times a dedicated connection was established between two parties.

This approach has both strengths and weaknesses. Strengths include a guaranteed bit-rate for signal transmission and weaknesses include poor utilisation of the channel (interconnects) signal transmission capacity (during times when there is a pause in the conversation, little use is being made of the transmission media). By sharing a channel between a number of transmissions, we can always (in principle) make sure that we make maximum use of its signal transfer characteristics.

The alternative approach, in which channels are shared and data (encapsulated into frames) is routed across shared transmission media, is referred to as a 'connectionless service' and this approach underpins the operation of today's Internet.

# 9.10 Review questions

**Question 9.1** Fill each blank with a word from each list.

1. Data communication refers to the electronic collection and distribution of _____ between two or more points via a transmission medium.

    a. medium            b. rules

    c. information       d. all of the above

2. A data communication is _____ if it occurs within a building or within a restricted geographical area.

    a. remote           b. local

    c. guided           d. unguided

3. Devices are required to be _____ by a transmission medium to exchange messages from one device to another.

    a. separated        b. distributed

    c. connected        d. all of the above

4. A transmission system is a _____ which connects source and destination.

    a. device           b. receiver

    c. medium          d. gateway

5. A protocol is a _____ or convention that governs data communication. It ensures a cooperative action between the devices for effective data communication.

    a. medium            b. electromagnetic wave

    c. signal             d. set of rules

6. Messages travel through a _____

    a. protocol          b. medium

    c. devices          d. all of the above

7. A _____ ensures cooperative action between the devices for effective data communication.

    a. transmitter       b. source

    c. destination      d. protocol

8. An effective data communication must have three fundamental characteristics. These are:

   a. Delivery, accuracy and timeliness    b. Source, destination and message

   c. Transmitter, receiver and decoder    d. Device, medium and protocol

**Question 9.2**  Choose one item from the list to complete the following sentences:

1. A _____ connection provides a dedicated link between two devices.

   a. multipoint    b. point-to-point

   c. hub           d. all the above

2. In a _____ connection, more than two devices can share a single link.

   a. multipoint    b. point-to-point

   c. hub           d. all the above

3. An organisation wants to share a printer with three computers.  They have _____ line configuration.

   a. multipoint    b. point-to-point

   c. hub           d. all the above

4. An organisation has its headquarter at London and branches all over Asia and Europe.  The branches are connected with headquarters by a _____ network.

   a. LAN           b. WAN

   c. MAN           d. all the above

5. An organisation has five computers and a printer situated in different rooms. The computers and printer are connected in _____ topology.

   a. LAN           b. WAN

   c. MAN           d. all the above

**Question 9.3**  Briefly answer the following:

a) What is meant by point-to-point communication?

b) What are the three main categories for networks?

c) What are the two main technologies used by a WAN to transfer data?

**Question 9.4** Match the most appropriate response or word from the list following each question, to the question itself.

1. Why do we need standards?

    a. To make devices compatible and interconnectable with each other

    b. To make the devices send signals to other devices

    c. To ensure that the media works properly

    d. All the above

2. Standards slow down technological advances.  How accurate is this statement?

    a. False                    b. True

    c. Partially true

3. Many standards may exist for a single entity/product.  How accurate is this statement?

    a. False            b. True

    c. Partially true

4. Which of the following does not set standards for data communication?

    a. ANSI            b. IEEE

    c. NATO            d. ITU-T

5. Which organisation mostly creates standards for programming languages, ie. COBOL, C, etc.

    a. IEEE            b. ITU

    c. ANSI            d. All the above

**Question 9.5**  Briefly answer the following:

a) What is a protocol?

b) What are the main elements of a protocol?

**Question 9.6**  Briefly answer the following:

a) What does OSI stand for and what do we use it for?

b) How many layers does the OSI model have?  List them.

c) What does TCP/IP stand for and what is it?

## 9.11 Feedback on activities

### Activity 9.1:  Transmission latency

Transmission speed (v) is determined by dividing distance travelled (s) by the time taken (t). Thus:

$$v = \frac{s}{t}$$

Therefore:

$$t = \frac{s}{v} = \frac{384,400x10^3}{3x10^8}$$

(Here the distance has been converted to metres.) Thus the transmission time is ~1.3 seconds.

### Activity 9.2:  The fully connected topology

| Number of nodes | Required number of interconnects |
|:---:|:---:|
| 5 | 10 |
| 10 | 45 |
| 20 | 190 |
| 50 | 1,225 |

**Table 9.5:** The fully connected topology

### Activity 9.3:  Network routing

If we assume that the packet does not pass through the same node twice, then there are four possible routes.  Routing decisions can be based on:

(a) Traffic densities across one or more network interconnects (i.e.  avoidance of traffic 'hotspots'.

(b) The failure of one or more intermediate node or network interconnect (often referred to as a network segment).

(c) The financial cost associated with the use of a particular intermediate network/ transmission system.

## Activity 9.4:  The OSI model architecture

*Answer list:*

| | |
|---|---|
| Standard agency   **Q1** | Open System Interconnection   **Q1** |
| Physical layer   **Q6, 9** | Data link layer   **Q3** |
| Network layer  - | Transport layer   **Q2, 7, 8** |
| Session layer   **Q5** | Presentation layer   **Q4** |
| Application layer  - | Bottom up and top down   **Q10** |

## Activity 9.5:  User datagram protocol

Possible applications include the transmission of audio and video streams.  In such cases, and in order to support real-time play out, fast delivery is essential.  Absolute transmission integrity is not usually a requirement for such applications – the human senses of hearing and sight are sufficiently complex and powerful that we can extrapolate across missing data and extract information contained within a very noisy background.

## Activity 9.6:  The functionality of the OSI and TCP/IP paradigms

One noticeable departure from the OSI model is the absence of the session layer in the TCP/IP conceptual model.  This is due to the fact that devoting an entire layer to session protocols has become less important as computer systems have changed with time from large, timesharing systems to private devices.  The top three layers of OSI, (application, presentation and session) are replaced by a single layer, the application layer in the TCP/IP conceptual model.

The transport layer and Internet layers define the TCP and IP protocols respectively.  The former ensures the provision of reliable data transfer, while the latter is used to provide a 'routing' function across multiple networks.

# CHAPTER 10

# Transmission media and data communications

## OVERVIEW

In this chapter, we continue with our discussion on the networking of computers, and focus upon lower-level issues such as transmission media, signals and signal propagation. We also introduce two general techniques that are used to support the sharing of a common network transmission link – specifically, token passing and the contention-based approach.

### Learning outcomes

On completion of this chapter you should be able to:

- Discuss various signal characteristics

- Describe the form and properties of different types of transmission media

- Describe the operation of a contention-based network access protocol

- Explain characteristics of Ethernet and the IEEE 802.3 standard

- Contrast contention-based protocol with the token passing approach.

## 10.1 Introduction

In this chapter we focus on the transmission media that are used in the implementation of networks, and on the protocols via which nodes are able to gain access to a local area network (LAN). In the next section, we briefly review previous discussion in relation to signal characterisation and quickly move on to briefly describe forms of signal impairment. Here, we describe the issues of signal attenuation, noise, channel capacity and delay distortion. In Section 10.3 we discuss three different forms of transmission medium – specifically twisted pair cable, coaxial (coax) cable, and fibre optic cable.

In Section 10.4 we turn our attention to a communications protocol in which nodes contend for network access. This technique underpins the operation of the 'Ethernet' network technology described in Section 10.5, which was used as a basis in developing the IEEE 802.3 communications standard. The format of an Ethernet frame is outlined in Section 10.6, and finally in Section 10.7 we consider a protocol that supports orderly network access (i.e. is non-contention-based).

## 10.2 Concerning signals

In this section we briefly summarise and build on previous discussion in connection with signals and signal transfer.

The transmission of different types of information (i.e. data, text, voice, still pictures, graphics and video) between nodes is made possible by the transfer of electromagnetic signals which are carried by a transmission medium. Signals representing data can be either analog or digital in form (see Figure 10.1).

- An analog signal is continuous (e.g. sinusoidal wave), where the amplitude varies in a smooth manner over time, i.e. there are no breaks or discontinuities in the signal. The human voice provides an example of a source of an analog signal

- As we have seen in previous chapters, a digital signal is discrete and may only take on certain values. For example, a computer employs digital signals. Here only two levels are used – providing the binary number representation. Note: a digital signal is not confined to binary (base 2).

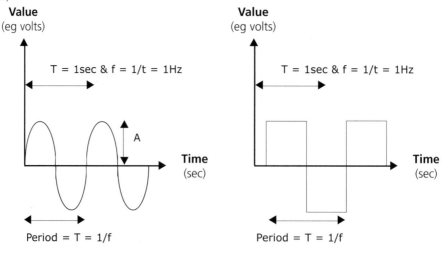

**a: Analog signal**　　　　　　**b: Digital signal**

**Figure 10.1:** Analog and digital signals

Signals can be described by means of a number of quantities:

- **Amplitude (A):** the maximum value of the signal over time; for an electrical signal this is usually measured in volts
- **Period (periodic time) (T):** the time taken to complete one whole cycle; usually measured in seconds (or fractions of a second)
- **Frequency (f):** the number of completed cycles per second; usually measured in Hertz (Hz). Frequency is calculated as the reciprocal of the periodic time
- **Throughput:** the amount of data that can be passed through a connection per unit of time. Typically (for a digital signal) measured in bits per second (bps), kilobits per second, megabits per second (Mbps), and gigabits per second (Gbps). This measures the bit-rate discussed in the previous chapter
- **Bandwidth:** the range of frequencies contained within a signal. For example, a sinusoidal wave contains a single frequency. More complex waveforms may be constructed by bringing together a set of sinusoidal waves (see previous chapter).

**Activity 10.1**

**Waveform characteristics**

Consider the sinusoidal wave illustrated in Figure 10.2. Determine the amplitude, the peak-to-peak amplitude, and the frequency of the wave.

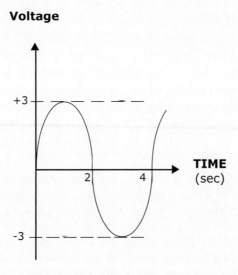

**Figure 10.2:** A sinusoidal waveform

At present most telecommunication systems employ digital signal transmission techniques. Such signals have a greater immunity to noise than do their analog equivalent. Furthermore, they can be processed directly by computer hardware without the need to convert between the analog and digital domains.

The transmission of data across a network segment is achieved via the use of some form of electromagnetic signal. The electromagnetic spectrum is illustrated in Figure 10.3, and as can be seen from this diagram, at one end of this spectrum we find radio waves and at the other extreme, gamma rays. Of particular importance to us when considering communication networks are radiowaves, microwaves and those parts of the spectrum that can be passed along optic fibre cables (e.g. visible light). As we will discuss shortly, radio frequency signals may be transmitted either in free space (e.g. between radio stations) or along special forms of cable.

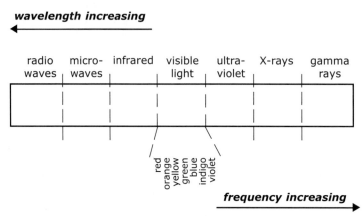

**Figure 10.3:** A part of the electromagnetic spectrum

The different types of radiation indicated in the electromagnetic spectrum differ in terms of frequency and wavelength. The relationship between frequency (*f*) and wavelength (λ) is given by the equation presented below:

$$c=f\lambda$$

where c represents the speed of light, which is approximately $3\times10^8$ m/s. In fact the speed of light limits the fastest transmission of signal that is achievable. However, it is important to note that when signals pass through media other than a vacuum, they propagate at a speed that is less than the velocity of light. Thus, when signals are transmitted through the air, or via cables (either electrical or optical), the speed at which they travel is lower than the speed of light.

Ground-based stations often employ 'line-of-sight' communication techniques. In this way, a signal transmitted from one station propagates in an essentially linear manner to another station (hence, the use of the term 'line-of-sight'). Fortunately, we are not limited to line-of-sight communications; traditionally, long-distance radio communication was achieved using a 'non-line-of-sight' method. It was found that when radio waves of certain wavelengths are beamed upwards, they are reflected by the upper atmosphere, and returned to the Earth's surface; see Figure 10.4. This has provided a very useful technique via which long-range radio communications can be achieved. However, this approach is not commonly used for network communications (and in Chapter 12 we briefly discuss long-distance radio transmission by means of satellites).

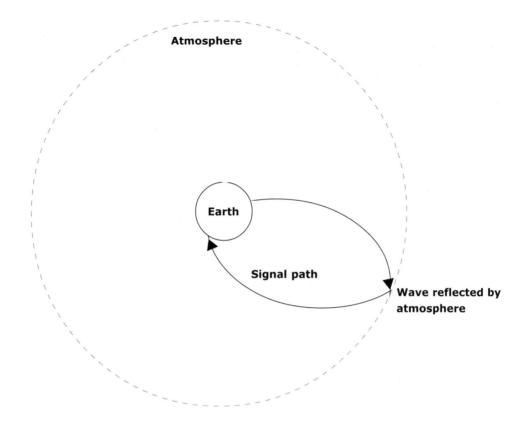

**Figure 10.4:** The reflection of radio waves by the atmosphere (diagram is not to scale)

During their transit, signals may be subjected to various forms of impairment. These impairments degrade the signal quality and quite often lead to error in data transmission. For example, a signal may be contaminated such that one or more 'bit errors' are introduced (a binary 1 is changed into a binary 0 and vice versa). The most common types of signal impairment are:

- **Attenuation:** here the signal strength is reduced as it travels through a transmission medium. As a result it is necessary to insert devices able to amplify (re-generate the signal at intervals). Network devices that regenerate the signal are referred to as 'repeaters'

- **Noise:** this takes the form of an unwanted signal that is (for various reasons) imposed upon the main signal. Sources of this extraneous signal include 'crosstalk' between electrical cables, atmospheric static electricity (particularly prevalent during storms), thermal noise generated within electrical conductors. One major advantage of fibre optic cable is that it offers high noise immunity, but as with electrical cables, signals are gradually attenuated and need re-amplification

- **Channel capacity:** denotes the upper limit to a channel's (transmission medium's) capacity to transfer data (a road has a maximum rate of utilisation – and so does a network interconnect). In the late 1940s, Claude Shannon determined the theoretical maximum data transfer capacity of a communications channel; see Section 9.2

- **Delay distortion:** this is symptomatic of guided media and causes a signal to change in form or shape due to the fact that the velocity of propagation of a signal varies with frequency and, as we noted previously, a complex waveform is comprised of a number of sinusoidal components. These components travel at slightly different speeds in the medium (this is called dispersion). Ultimately this effect may result in signal degeneration.

**Activity 10.2**

**Frequency and wavelength**

Consider an electromagnetic wave that has a frequency of 108Hz.
Assuming that the speed of light is ~$3 \times 10^8 ms^{-1}$, calculate the wavelength of the wave.

## 10.3 Data transmission media

Transmission media are generally classified as either 'guided' or 'unguided'. A physical medium provides a path between the transmitting and receiving nodes through which 'guided' signals pass.

- In the case of guided media, electrical signals are moved between devices using metallic conductors (such as copper). Such cables may be in the form of 'twisted pairs' and coaxial cables. Alternatively, fibre-optic cables may be used to support the passage of light

- In the case of unguided media, electromagnetic waves propagate without needing physical medium; instead, they are broadcast by an antenna. This form of wave propagation is referred to as wireless transmission. At lower frequencies, signals commonly propagate in all directions, whilst at higher frequencies a more directed beam may be formed. Unguided transmissions are especially vulnerable to atmospheric conditions (particularly electrical storms).

We now briefly consider aspects of different types of guided media, which include:

- **Twisted pair cables**
- **Unshielded twisted pair (UTP) cables**
- **Shielded twisted pair (STP) cables**
- **Coaxial (coax) cables**
- **Fibre optic cables**
- **Unguided media: wireless transmission media.**

### *Twisted pair cables*

For 'short haul' lower-bandwidth applications, twisted pair cables are extensively used. A 'twisted pair' comprises two insulated metallic wires that are twisted around each other. As discussed in Section 5.3, a magnetic field whose field strength varies with time will induce a current into a conductor (a time-varying electric field will also have the same effect). Consequently, an interconnect formed using one or more conductors is susceptible to external electromagnetic fields. Changes in the electric or magnetic field strength surrounding a conductor(s) will induce currents and this will give rise to extraneous signal - electrical 'noise'. Such time-varying fields may occur for various reasons. For example:

- They may be produced by equipment that employs high-frequency currents (such as a TV set or radio)

- They may be produced by equipment such as electric motors that generate 'sparks' during operation

- They may be produced by electrical discharges that occur around high-voltage electrical transmission lines

- They may be produced by nearby wires within which currents are flowing.  Changes in these currents will cause the magnetic field around the wire to change in strength and this will induce currents in adjacent wires.  This is referred to as 'cross-talk'.

One approach to alleviating this problem is to transmit differential signals along a pair of wires placed in close proximity.  Rather than measure the voltage that is delivered by a single wire, the receiver measures the differential voltage produced between the pair of wires.  This may be understood by means of a simple example.  Consider the configuration illustrated in Figure 10.5.

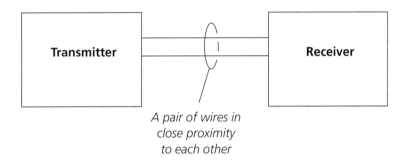

*A pair of wires in
close proximity
to each other*

**Figure 10.5:** The transmission of a differential signal

Let us refer to these two wires as 'Wire A' and 'Wire B' respectively.  In Figure 10.6(a) we illustrate the transmission of a simple digital signal along Wire A, and the transmission of the complementary waveform along Wire B.

The receiver (illustrated in Figure 10.5) measures the magnitude of the difference in these two signals, see Figure 10.6(c).  Let us now suppose that a source of electrical interference induces a voltage into the transmission wires.  Since the wires are in close proximity (as is the case with the 'twisted pair') a similar voltage will be induced into the two wires.  Since the receiver measures (and responds to) the difference in voltage between the wires, the induced noise will (in principle) have little impact (i.e. if the amplitude of the induced voltage appearing in both wires is 2 volts, then the differential voltage will be zero volts).

Usually, large numbers of twisted pair wires are bundled within a single cable;  typical uses include:

- Voice traffic, using an analog telephone network
- Transmitting data within, for example, buildings
- Transmitting both analog and digital signals
- Local area networks (LANs), with data rates of between a few Mbps and 100Mbps (over very short distances).

Typical characteristics of twisted pairs include:

- Low cost and easy to install

- Short range usage, typically 2-3km with repeaters needed at intervals
- Susceptible to interference and noise. Although, as indicated above, susceptibility is reduced by the transmission of differential signals. Additionally, shielding the wires with a metallic braid will further reduce susceptibility to electromagnetic interference.

If the two wires forming the pair are twisted around each other (see Figure 10.7), then each wire is nearer to the noise source and furthest from it at alternate intervals. The result is different voltage levels being induced within the same wire at different intervals, depending on how near or far it is from the noise source. This means that the overall effect of the noise is nearly the same for both wires. The result is, generally, a substantial reduction in the noise level within the twisted pair (as compared to the situation in which the two wires run parallel to each other).

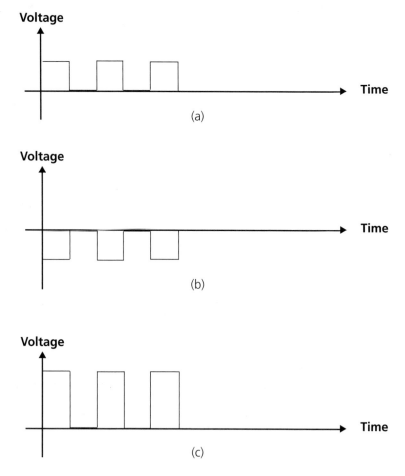

**Figure 10.6:** In (a) and (b) we illustrate the transmission of a signal along 'Wire A', and its complement along 'Wire B'. In (c) we illustrate the differential voltage between Wires A and B.

A twisted pair offers approximately uniform transmission characteristics (e.g. uniform capacitance) and this favours signal propagation. Also in the case that multiple twisted pairs are placed within a single cable, the 'twist length' of all pairs is not the same. By arranging for the pairs to have different 'twist lengths', cross-talk may be further reduced.

## Unshielded twisted pair (UTP) cables

Generally, a group of UTPs are bunched together into a larger cable by casing them in a robust protective outer insulation as in Figure 10.8(a). Their typical characteristics include:

- Used as ordinary telephone wires
- Low cost
- Easiest to install as the cable is lightweight, thin, and flexible
- Suffer from external noise interference – see above discussion
- Data transfer rate, 10-100Mbps.

Industry has developed several categories for grading UTP interconnect. This classifies them according to their quality for handling data transmission, with 1 being the lowest and 5 as the highest. Categories 3, 4, and 5 (Cat 3, 4, 5 for short) are considered 'datagrade UTP', have an ascending number of twists per unit length, and are the most widely used (an important difference between these categories is the 'twist length'. Cat 3 employs 3 to 4 twists per foot, whereas Cat 5 uses 3 to 4 twists per inch):

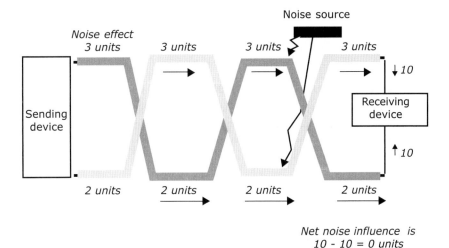

**Figure 10.7:** The influence of an external noise source on a twisted pair of wires. Note: this illustration is intended to be indicative – the overall signal induced in the two wires will certainly not be exactly equal.

## Cat 3

- Voice-grade used by most telephone systems
- Data transmission up to 16MHz

## Cat 4

- Data transmission up to 20MHz

### Cat 5

- Data transmission of up to 100MHz
- Commonly pre-installed in new office buildings.

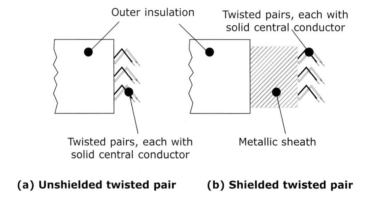

**(a) Unshielded twisted pair**          **(b) Shielded twisted pair**

**Figure 10.8:** In (a) an unshielded twisted pair cable is depicted and in (b) a metallic sheath is used to decrease noise susceptibility

## Shielded twisted pair (STP) cables

This type of interconnect brings together the methods of shielding and the twisting of wires, producing an overall increase in noise immunity. Shielding is provided by a metallic sheath (see Figure 10.8(b)) that covers and encloses the insulated pairs. The shield reduces susceptibility to electric fields. Typical features include:

- Better interference protection as compared to UTP
- More expensive than UTP
- Thicker and heavier than UTP, therefore a little harder to handle and install
- Data transfer rate, 10-100Mbps.

## Coaxial (coax) cables

Coaxial (coax) cable consists of two conductors and offers greater bandwidth than does the UTP approach. It consists of an inner central conductor surrounded by an insulating core (the dielectric). This inner insulation is encased in a conducting layer of metal foil or braid which has a twofold utility (as a noise shield and as a second conductor). The whole assembly is surrounded by an outer insulating jacket (see Figure 10.9).

Coax cables are:

- Used extensively for radio frequency transmission in applications such as the connection between a television and its antenna
- Used for long-distance telephone systems (using frequency-division multiplexing techniques, a coax cable can simultaneously carry more than 10,000 conversations)
- Used for local area networks (LANs)
- Exhibit data transfer rates in excess of 100Mbps

- For high data rate application, repeaters are needed at distances of between 500m and 1,000m.

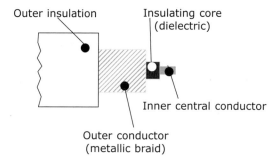

**Figure 10.9:** The construction of a coaxial (coax) cable

## Fibre optic cables

Unlike conventional metallic interconnects which transmit data in the form of electric currents, fibre optic cables are non-metallic and transmit light energy. To achieve this, electrical data signals (individual bits) are converted into light by means of, for example, a light-emitting diode (LED) or laser and this light is injected into the fibre optic cable. The cable comprises an inner core of either glass or plastic (the latter is less expensive and usually used for short-range links as it has lower performance characteristics). An optical fibre is illustrated schematically in Figure 10.10.

The cable consists of three main concentric components:

- The glass/plastic inner core
- A glass or plastic outer layer surrounding the inner core. This has a different refractive index to the inner core. The refractive index of the inner core is higher than that of the outer layer. Consequently, as light propagates along the fibre, it is unable to escape from the inner core (it continually experiences 'total internal reflection'). In an alternative embodiment, the refractive index of the inner core continually varies (in the radial direction). This is known as 'graded index fibre' and in this case the outer layer is not required
- A plastic outer jacket to give protection and robustness to the core and cladding.

The basic principle of fibre optic cable is shown in Figure 10.10. Light from the source enters the core, and rays are reflected and propagated along the length of the fibre. The emerging light rays are then detected and converted back into an electrical signal.

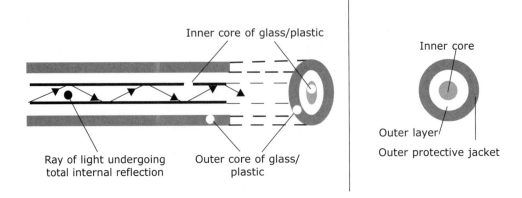

Inner core of glass/plastic

Inner core

Ray of light undergoing total internal reflection

Outer core of glass/plastic

Outer layer

Outer protective jacket

**Figure 10.10:** The composition of an optic fibre, side and end views. (The diagram is not drawn to scale.)

Typical features of fibre optic cables include:

- Higher bit-rates than UTP, STP and coaxial cables (gigabits per second)
- Smaller size and weight than coaxial cable
- Electromagnetic isolation in comparison with metallic cables (i.e. greater noise immunity).

### *Unguided media: wireless transmission media*

In the case of 'unguided media', electromagnetic signals are radiated from an antenna. Wireless transmission can be divided into two categories:

- Directional: whereby the radiated signal wave is collimated into a narrow beam. Consequently, the transmitting and receiving antenna have to be carefully aligned (a typical example is a microwave telephone link). This supports point-to-point line-of-sight communication typically in the range 2GHz to 40GHz
- Omni-directional: the signal waves radiate in all directions and can be picked up by any device capable of receiving them. Television and radio broadcasting provide typical examples of this approach.

## 10.4 Contention-based access (CSMA/CD)

In this section we consider a widely used technique that enables nodes to communicate via a shared transmission media. In general terms, devices may contend for access to the transmission medium or may communicate in an orderly manner. Here we focus on the former approach and in Section 10.6 consider a non-contention-based technique that involves the passage of 'tokens' between nodes. Contention-based networks are associated with today's widely used 'Ethernet' networking technologies, and before we consider this technique in any detail it is instructive to consider a simple analogy which highlights aspects of the contention- and non-contention-based approaches.

Suppose that a number of people attend a meeting and wish to express their views on some topic. One way of organising such a meeting (and ensuring that everybody gets the opportunity to make their views known) is to place somebody in charge, i.e. make one person responsible for deciding who should talk. In this way, when people wish to talk they can make this known by, for example, raising a hand, and they can then be given the opportunity to speak. In this way we avoid the situation where more than one person is speaking at any one time, as that would certainly lead to chaos! Designating a coordinator to determine the person who is given the opportunity to speak provides an orderly approach to communication.

### The use of time slots

As an alternative approach to the implementation of a non-contention (orderly) communications protocol, we could assign to each participant a time slot. Thus, for example, each person may be given a two-minute time slot during which time they have the opportunity to speak (communicate). Once all participants have spoken, the process is repeated and again each person has a further two-minute opportunity to talk. This continues until the discussion (meeting) ends.

Indicate two major advantages and two major disadvantages of this approach.

This approach can also be adopted for computer communications. One computer can be placed in overall charge, and when other computers wish to communicate they notify the controlling machine. The controlling computer ensures that no two computers are transmitting data along the shared medium at any one time. Unfortunately, in this scenario, should the controlling computer fail – so too would the network!

Without the imposition of some order within a meeting, many people may attempt to talk simultaneously. Naturally this is undesirable as it would be very difficult to understand what is being said! Let us now extend our analogy to a situation in which a number of people are participating in a telephone conference-call. Again we have the possibility of more than one person trying to talk at any one time, and in this scenario it is slightly more difficult to place one person in control of who should speak – in the case of a phone call, it is not possible for the participants to give a visual cue such as raising their hand when they wish to speak. However, in the case that two or more people do start to speak simultaneously, a simple protocol is normally followed whereby people stop talking, pause and try again (in fact this part of the analogy is not quite accurate. Often when several people start talking at the same time, or when one speaker attempts to interrupt another, the most dominant/vociferous person continues) – because they are aware that other people are already talking. In this case, those wishing to speak would naturally wait until the current speaker paused. In short, in this simple analogy we have introduced a degree of contention – participants contend for an opportunity to speak.

This type of approach was developed at the University of Hawaii in the early 1970s for use with a packet radio communications system. Here, computer terminals were able to communicate with a central facility by sending 'packets' in the form of radio transmissions. For hardware simplicity, all radios transmitted at the same frequency – thus if two or more transmitters attempted to transmit at the same time their transmissions would be corrupted (rather like many people in a room speaking at once). The technique that was developed to solve this problem is commonly referred to as 'Pure Aloha' and is summarised in Figure 10.11.

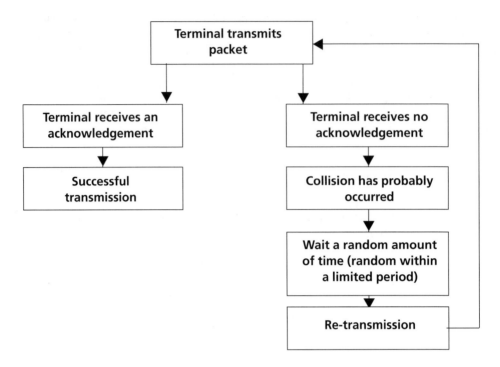

**Figure 10.11:** The 'Pure Aloha' approach

As may be seen from this illustration, the successful receipt of packets results in an acknowledgement. If no acknowledgement is received, the sending node (terminal) waits for a randomised period and then tries again.

**Activity 10.4**

**Slotted Aloha**

'Slotted Aloha' is the name given to a technique that evolved from the 'Pure Aloha' discussed above. In the case of 'Pure Aloha', nodes (terminals) can transmit at any time. However, in the case of 'Slotted Aloha', we divide the time into a number of 'slots' and transmissions can only commence at the beginning of a time slot. (Another way of putting this is to say that a common clock is used and transmitters can only begin to transmit a packet on, for example, a rising clock edge.)

Identify one *advantage* and one *disadvantage* of such a scheme.

In devising a protocol by means of which nodes are able to contend for access to a common communications medium we seek to:

- Ensure that all nodes equitably share the medium (i.e. stop a single node from dominating the medium and thereby preventing other nodes from communicating)
- Maximise the success rate (i.e. maximise the number of frames that are successfully transmitted and minimise collisions).

One widely used approach is referred to by the abbreviation CSMA/CD (Carrier Sense Multiple Access with Collision Detection). An overview of this technique is provided in Figure 10.12. This protocol works as follows:

- All devices (nodes) are connected to a common bus
- Each node may transmit whenever it wishes
- This could result in two (or more) devices transmitting at the same time, thus leading to collisions
- Whilst outputting a frame, the transmitting node listens for a collision. If a collision is detected, the node stops outputting the frame and broadcasts a brief 'jamming signal' – this provides an indication to all nodes that a collision has occurred
- The nodes wishing to transmit wait for a 'random' period and then try again. The random period for which a node waits is determined by the node itself (i.e. independently of other nodes).

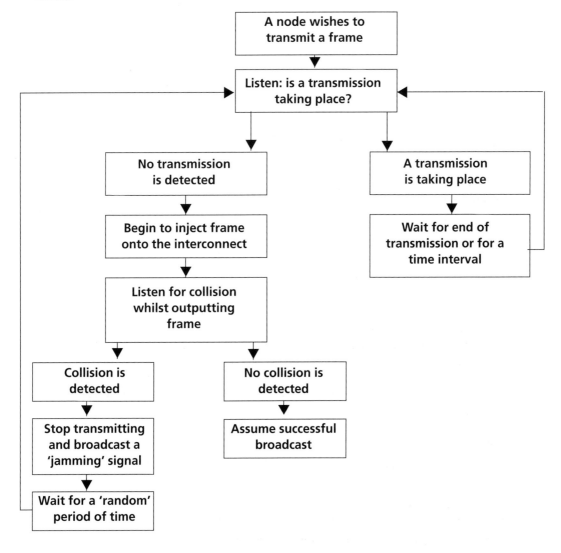

**Figure 10.12:** The CSMA/CD approach

In practice, this approach becomes a little more complex. Here, it is important to remember that signals do not pass along an interconnect instantaneously – they propagate at a finite speed. Consider, for example, the scenario illustrated in Figure 10.13. Here, two nodes are shown; these are connected to a common interconnect and are separated by a distance D along the cable.

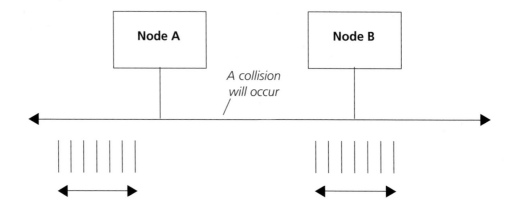

**Figure 10.13:** Two nodes broadcast and the frames propagate at speed **v** along the interconnect

Let us suppose that at an arbitrary time T, Node A starts to transmit a frame. This will propagate along the LAN and it will reach Node B at a time T+D/v (D denotes the separation of the two nodes along the interconnect and v the speed at which the signals travel in the cable) (here, we use speed=distance divided by time). Thus if in the time interval T through to T+D/v, Node B listens for a transmission (and discounting the possibility of transmissions by other nodes connected to the LAN) it will gain the mistaken impression that the interconnect is available.

For the CSMA/CD approach to work correctly, it is important that nodes outputting frames onto the interconnect become aware of the occurrence of a collision *prior* to their having output the entire frame (i.e. they should know that a collision has occurred before the entire frame has been injected onto the LAN). For example, with reference to Figure 10.13, suppose that Node A outputs an entire frame onto the interconnect and, as a consequence of Node B beginning a transmission, a collision occurs. We assume that this is detected by Node B. This node would immediately stop transmitting and would broadcast a 'jamming signal'. Node A would certainly detect this signal and would therefore learn of a collision – however, it would not know whether this collision involved the frame that it had previously output, or frames output by other nodes. This information can only be obtained by ensuring that a node will learn of a collision prior to outputting an entire frame. This depends on several factors:

- The greatest distance that a frame must travel between nodes (i.e. the greatest separation of two nodes on an interconnect)
- The speed of propagation of a frame along the interconnect
- The size of a frame (in terms of the number of bits that it comprises)
- The transmission bit-rate.

The worst-case scenario (longest time interval) occurs when we are dealing with the two nodes (we will refer to them as Nodes A and B) that are separated (along the interconnect) by the greatest distance.  Let us suppose that Node A starts to broadcast and Node B wishes to transmit.  It begins transmission just prior to the signal from Node A reaching Node B.  Since the signal from Node A has not yet arrived, Node B believes that the medium is free and begins transmission.  Almost immediately, Node B detects the collision, stops transmitting and broadcasts the 'jamming signal'.  This then propagates along the interconnect and eventually reaches Node A.  As indicated above, we want to ensure that in this worst-case scenario, Node A has not completed the insertion of the frame onto the interconnect.  Thus, if it takes time $T_{longest}$ for a frame to begin to reach Node B from Node A, it will take this same time for the 'jamming signal' to get back to Node A.  Since we need to make sure that Node A is still outputting the frame, it follows that:

$$T_{frame} \geq 2T_{longest}$$

**Equation 10.1**

... where $T_{frame}$ denotes the time taken by a node to inject a frame onto the interconnect.

However, $T_{longest}$ may be expressed as:

$$T_{longest} = \frac{D_{max}}{v}$$

**Equation 10.2**

... where $D_{max}$ represents the maximum separation of two nodes on the LAN and $v$ the speed at which signals propagate.

$T_{frame}$ is given by:

$$T_{frame} = \frac{N}{B}$$

**Equation 10.3**

Thus (using Equation 10.1) we wish to ensure that:

$$\frac{N}{B} \geq \frac{2D_{max}}{v}$$

**Equation 10.4**

**Activity 10.5**

### Node separation

Consider a LAN in which signals propagate at 200 metres per microsecond and that employs frames that have a length of 30 bytes.  Given a bit-rate of 10Mb.s$^{-1}$, calculate the maximum separation of a pair of network nodes (as discussed above, we assume that collision must be detected prior to a frame having been fully output onto the interconnect).

Returning for a moment to Equation 10.4, it is apparent that for a given bit-rate, size of frame and form of interconnect (which determines the signal propagation speed), there is an upper limit to the maximum separation of two nodes.  Conversely, given a certain maximum node separation, form of interconnect and bit-rate, we must ensure that frames are of a sufficient size.  Recall that a frame comprises the data that is to be transmitted (payload), together with various data that is required to ensure that it can reach its destination.

Here, we can see that frames are likely to vary in size according to the number of bits of payload that are to be transmitted. If there is insufficient payload, then there is the possibility of a frame being overly small and thereby not satisfying the criteria indicated in Equation 10.4. The solution normally adopted is to specify a minimum data payload, and if the real data to be transmitted is less than this, additional 'padding' bits are added (see Section 10.6). These bits serve only one purpose, which is to ensure that the frame is of a sufficient extent so that Equation 10.4 is satisfied.

## 10.5 Ethernet

Today, the most widely used LAN communications protocol is a CSMA/CD approach commonly known as 'Ethernet'. This was pioneered in the 1970s at Xerox PARC (recall earlier discussion in connection with the pioneering work undertaken at Xerox PARC at this time in connection with workstation development). The name 'Ethernet' is derived from the word 'ether', which was the name given to the mysterious all-pervading and invisible medium that was thought to exist and which, for example, was supposed to enable light (and other forms of electromagnetic radiation) to pass through the void of space. (By the end of the 19th century, the existence of an 'ether' had been largely disproved. However, there were some who continued to believe in its existence through until the 1920s. Perhaps today's discussions concerning the existence of 'dark matter' parallel aspects of this earlier debate.) The 'Ethernet' approach is defined in a standard produced by the IEEE (Institute of Electrical and Electronic Engineers) and is referred to as the 'IEEE 802.3 Standard'.

The IEEE 802 family of standards deal with physical elements of a network – for example, the network adapter (via which a computer is connected to the interconnect (this is commonly referred to as the 'Network Interface Card')), cabling, signalling techniques, media access controls, etc. Basically, the IEEE 802 family describes how network interfaces may access and transfer data across media. They also relate to attaching and managing networked nodes. Figure 10.14 relates the IEEE 802 and OSI reference models.

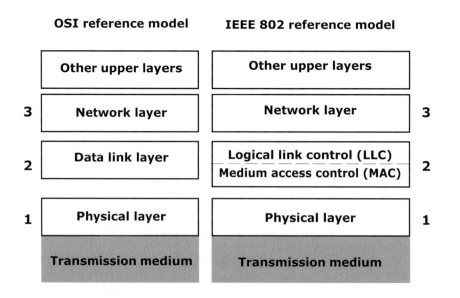

**Figure 10.14:** The OSI and IEEE 802 reference models

The lowest layer of the IEEE 802 standard matches the OSI physical layer with functions that include:

- The encoding and decoding of signals
- The transmission and reception of bits
- The generation and removal of preamble (i.e. a bit pattern) for transmission synchronisation
- Specifying the transmission media and the network topology.

Layer 2 corresponds to the OSI data link layer (DLL). However, the DLL is now divided into two sub-layers – the logical link control (LLC) and the medium access control (MAC) layers. The former performs various tasks. For example:

- It ensures that the network layer (with which it interfaces) need not know of differences in the types of IEEE 802 network that may be in use. Thus, whatever the actual IEEE 802 network implementation is in use, the network layer perceives a common interface
- It provides different service options that impact on reliability of transmission. The Ethernet approach operates on a best-efforts basis – there is no guarantee of the reliability of delivery. However, the LLC layer provides a protocol by which service options ('unreliable datagram service', 'acknowledged datagram service', and 'reliable connection-oriented service') are supported. This is achieved by appending various information to each packet that is passed to the LLC by the network layer.

The LLC layer forms 'protocol data units' (PDUs) and passes these to the MAC layer. This presents an interface to the physical layer and contains information essential for transferring data from one device to another. Once the LLC protocol data unit is formed, it is forwarded to the MAC sub-layer, which attaches control data to both ends as shown in Figure 10.15. The receiving node undertakes a reverse 'unwrapping' process.

Below we briefly review some aspects of Ethernet:

- Ethernet LANs are constructed as logical buses, although they may be physically arranged in other topologies such as the 'star'. Consequently, each frame is transmitted to every network node; however, a frame is accepted only by the node to which it is addressed
- The initial structure of the Ethernet LAN involved a single coaxial cable, in a bus topology format. The maximum data transmission rate was 10Mbps
- Subsequent 'Fast Ethernet' systems evolved, operating at 100Mbps over both twisted pair and fibre optic media
- 'Gigabit Ethernet' works at 1,000Mbps (1 Gigabit per second (Gbps))
- As traffic densities increase, collisions occur more frequently and at high levels of utilisation, this causes Ethernet performance to rapidly decrease.

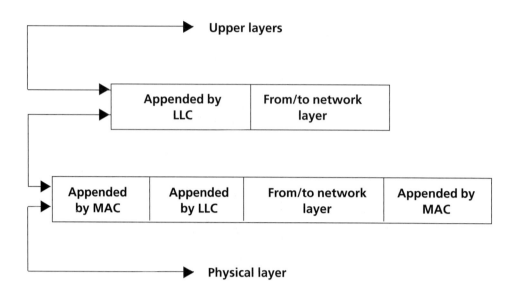

**Figure 10.15:** Content appended by the LLC and MAC layers

Three of the transmission media most commonly used in the implementation of an Ethernet LAN are:

- **Twisted pair cables:** a voice-grade twisted pair is sometimes employed to provide an inexpensive, easily installed network.  The data rate capabilities are quite low
- **Baseband coaxial cables:** these have higher data rate capabilities than do twisted pairs
- **Fibre optic cables:** these provide much higher data transmission than either twisted pair or coaxial cables.  They are more difficult to install and the necessary peripheral hardware (such as bridges and repeaters (see Chapter 11)) is more expensive.

### Twisted pair Ethernet

This is referred to as 10base-T (see Figure 10.16) and employs unshielded twisted pair (UTP) cables.  Some characteristics are:

- It employs a star-topology configuration
- The data transmission rate is typically ~10Mbps
- Networking operations are controlled by an intelligent 'hub', with a port for each device (see Figure 10.16)
- Each device is connected to the hub by a 4-pair UTP cable, with a maximum length of 100 metres
- Although the hub propagates transmitted frames to all devices, network interface cards (NICs) are logically configured so that only the addressed device can receive the frame
- It is very easy to install and less expensive than other embodiments.

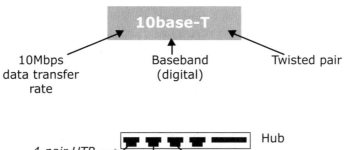

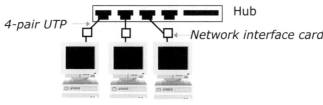

**Figure 10.16:** UTP 10base-T 'Star' topology LAN. The 'network interface cards' (NICs) indicated in this diagram act as the interface between each computer and the network interconnects

## *Thick Ethernet*

This is also referred to as Thicknet or 10base5 (see Figure 10.17) and employs coaxial cable. It was named 'Thicknet' due to its diameter (~10mm) making it difficult to bend and route the cable. Some characteristics are:

- It is used in a bus-topology configuration
- Signals introduced at any point on the bus, travel in both directions to the ends where they are absorbed by a terminator (this prevents the signal being re-reflected back along the cable)
- Typically employs a signal transmission rate of 10Mbps
- Maximum cable segment length is about 500 metres, after which a 'repeater' is required to boost the voltage levels of the signal; see Figure 10.17. (Recall: as signals passing along a cable are gradually attenuated, voltage amplitudes are reduced). A 'repeater' is a network device that reconstitutes the signal (so restoring the signal strength and reducing noise)
- The use of repeaters to restore signal strength introduces a delay in the propagation of signals. As a consequence, a maximum of only four repeaters may be used in a LAN. Ultimately, this limits the overall extent of the LAN.

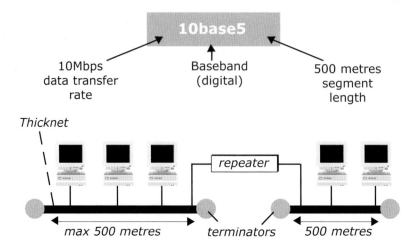

**Figure 10.17:** The 10base5 Thick Ethernet bus topology. Here, a repeater is used to connect two Ethernet segments

### Thin Ethernet

This is commonly referred to as Thinnet or 10base2 (see Figure 10.18) and employs coaxial cable. It was named 'Thinnet' due to the diameter of the cable, which is half that of 10base5. Some characteristics are:

- It utilises a much more flexible cable than 10base5. This makes it easier to install and route around buildings
- As with 10base5, this approach employs a bus topology
- Typical signal transmission rate of 10Mbps
- Maximum cable segment length is ~185 metres, after which a repeater is required to boost the attenuated signal
- 10base5 can support up to 100 nodes per segment. In the case of 10base2 the limit is 30.

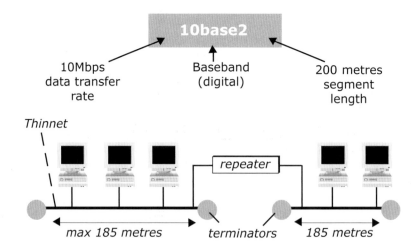

**Figure 10.18:** The 10base2 Thin Ethernet bus topology

## Fast Ethernet

The LAN media discussed so far have a data transfer rate of around 10Mbps. However, many current applications demand higher data transfer rates (e.g. real-time video). Consequently, there has been a need to develop faster Ethernet technologies. In 1995 the IEEE 802.3 Standards Committee introduced a higher speed specification – the IEEE802.3u standard – to define Ethernet operating at 100Mbps. Some characteristics are:

- This broad standard defines various configurations for use with different transmission media
- The media used include different combinations of unshielded twisted pair (UTPs), shielded twisted pair (STPs) and fibre optic cables
- This approach often employs a number of satellite hubs, each of which is connected to a parent hub
- This is also generally referred to as 100base-X. In the case of Cat5 UTP, 'X' is replaced with 'TX' and in the case of optical fibre, with 'FX'.

## Gigabit Ethernet

Current applications require even faster Ethernet networks with data transfer capabilities in excess of the 100Mbps provided by Fast Ethernet. 'Gigabit Ethernet' supports data transfer rates of 1 Gigabit (1,000 megabits per second) (see Figure 10.19). The IEE 802.3 Committee approved the first Gigabit Ethernet in 1998 and this is designated IEEE 802.3z.

- The increased shift to 100base-T fast Ethernet led to more demand for the faster Gigabit technology.
- The media used are mainly fibre optic cables; however, both UTPs and STPs can also be employed
- Maximum cable segment length varies between 550 and 5,000 metres for fibre optic cables, while that for UTPs (4 pairs) is ~100 metres.

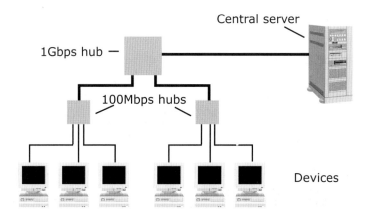

**Figure 10.19:** The Gigabit Ethernet technology

## 10.6 The Ethernet frame

The format of the frame devised in connection with the pioneering work at Xerox PARC – referred to as 'DIX Ethernet', as three major companies were involved with this at an early stage: DEC, Intel and Xerox – and that specified in the IEEE 803 standard are slightly different. However, at this stage of learning, these differences are not critically important and in Figure 10.20 we provide a breakdown of the format of the IEEE802.3 specification.

| Preamble | Start of frame | Destination address | Source address | Length of data field | Data | Pad | Check sum |
|----------|----------------|---------------------|----------------|----------------------|------|-----|-----------|
| 7 | 1 | 2 or 6 | 2 or 6 | 2 | 0-1,500 | 0-46 | 4 |

number of bytes

**Figure 10.20:** The IEEE 802.3 frame format

It is instructive to briefly review the form and function of theses data fields:

- **Preamble:** this provides synchronisation/timing information and enables nodes to determine signal sampling rates. It consists of seven identical bit patterns – 10101010 (alternating 1s and 0s)
- **Start of frame:** this indicates the point at which the actual content (data) of the frame begins. It is a bit pattern of the form 10101011
- **Destination address:** usually 48 bits. The value of the first bit indicates whether the frame is destined for a particular node or for a group of nodes
- **Source address:** address of the node responsible for sending the frame
- **Length of data field:** specifies the combined length of the data and pad fields
- **Pad:** recall that a frame must be of a certain minimum size. As a consequence the data field must hold at least 46 bytes. In the case that the amount of data is less than this value, the pad field is used to extend the length of the frame (and so compensate for the lack of data)
- **Check sum:** used for error checking.

The source and destination Ethernet addresses referred to above (also called MAC addresses) are defined on the 'network interface cards' (NICs) that are used to connect each computer to a LAN. Each NIC contains an address that is stored in ROM. When an NIC detects a frame on the LAN, it compares the intended destination address to that contained in its ROM and hence determines if it is the intended recipient. However, this issue is slightly more complex as 'unicast', 'multicast' and 'broadcast' addressing are supported:

- **Unicast address:** this is used when a frame is destined for a single specified node
- **Multicast address:** this enables a frame to be sent to a specified group of nodes
- **Broadcast address:** this enables a frame to be sent to all nodes connected to a LAN.

An Ethernet address comprises 48 bits and is usually represented as a set of hexadecimal values that (for convenience) are grouped in pairs; for example, 08:00:07:02:04:D4. Note: the left-hand six digits are used to reference the manufacturer of the Ethernet hardware device. In the example that we have just given, 08:00:07 references Apple.

## 10.7 Token passing

In the case of the CSMA/CD approach described above, nodes contend for network access. An alternative technique that is generally referred to as 'token passing' provides us with an example of a protocol in which network access occurs in an orderly manner (i.e. a non-contention-based technique). During the 1980s the Ethernet and 'token passing' (also called 'token ring' since this system most commonly employed a ring topology) were in direct competition. Neither of these approaches is without weaknesses and overall, when considered from a purely technical perspective, they are on a par. The Ethernet-based approach ultimately gained dominance – not as a consequence of its marked technical superiority but because of commercial forces and the mass production of Ethernet hardware which yielded lower costs.

The operation of a token ring relies on the passage of a 'token' between nodes (the continual movement of the token is called 'token passing'. Only the node that has possession of the token may transmit a frame onto the LAN. A token is a small bit pattern (typically 3 bytes) that circulates around the physical ring and is passed from one network interface card (NIC) to another – until it encounters a node wishing to transmit information.

Figure 10.21 illustrates one embodiment of the token passing approach. In this example, we assume that Node A wishes to transmit a frame to Node D:

- Node A waits for the token to arrive. It then 'seizes' the token and modifies it so that it becomes a start-of-frame sequence
- Node A attaches the data that is to be transmitted to the token, adds its address and the address of the intended recipient (Node D) together with other information (such as error checking), and launches the frame onto the ring
- Other devices on the ring cannot transmit, and must wait for the token to become free
- The frame proceeds around the ring. Each intermediate device examines the destination address and (if it is not the intended recipient) passes the frame to the next downstream node
- Node D recognises that it is the intended recipient. It therefore reads the frame and in one scenario subsequently modifies the frame. The frame is then re-released onto the ring and circulates back to the sending device (Node A)
- Node A receives the frame and recognises itself by the source address. This confirms to Node A that the frame was successfully received and copied by Node D
- Node A then releases the token back onto the ring where it becomes available to another device.

The above description provides a simplified overview of the token passing approach. In practice, various complications arise. For example:

- A mechanism is required so that when the LAN is powered on, a token is created. This may be done by a designated node or preferably by the first node that is booted
- We must guard against the possibility of a continually circulating frame. For example, considering the above description what would happen if Node D had been shut down?

One significant advantage of the token passing approach is the ease with which it is possible to accommodate transmission priorities. In the case of the CSMA/CD technique, this cannot be easily accomplished.

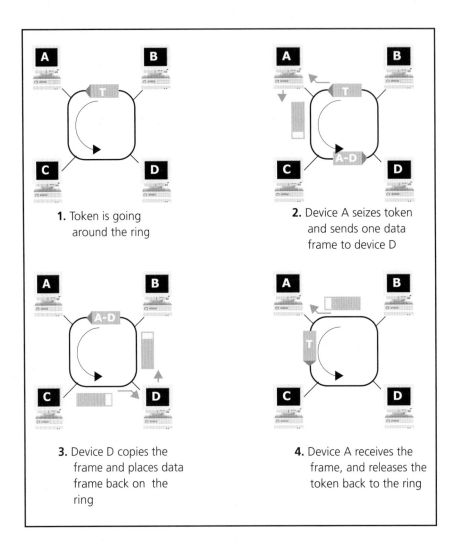

**1.** Token is going around the ring

**2.** Device A seizes token and sends one data frame to device D

**3.** Device D copies the frame and places data frame back on the ring

**4.** Device A receives the frame, and releases the token back to the ring

**Figure 10.21:** The 'token passing' approach ensures orderly network access

**The CSMA/CD and token passing approaches**

Consider the CSMA/CD and token passing techniques.

In each case identify one key weakness.

Activity 10.6

## 10.7 Summary

In this chapter we have introduced some of the key concepts that underpin the operation of the modern local area network. We have considered the advantages and disadvantages associated with the use of various types of transmission media – specifically, twisted pair cable, coaxial cable, and fibre optic cable. In terms of the latter, it is important to remember that this medium offers great superiority in terms of noise immunity and transmission bandwidth. Unfortunately, the large-scale deployment of fibre optic cable has occurred relatively slowly. This is because a great deal of previous investment has been made in laying down metallic cabling, and the move to replace this with optical fibre is a very expensive undertaking.

We have also reviewed the CSMA/CD protocol via which network devices contend for access to the transmission medium, and have contrasted this with the token passing technique. As indicated, token passing was most commonly associated with a ring topology. However, it is also possible to implement the token passing paradigm using alternative topologies.

## 10.8 Review questions

**Question 10.1** What is the meaning of the abbreviation CSMA/CD?

**Question 10.2** Distinguish between UTP and STP.

**Question 10.3** What do you understand by '10base5'?

**Question 10.4** Why is there a minimum length for an Ethernet frame?

**Question 10.5** In the case that the payload carried by an Ethernet frame is very small, how does the protocol ensure that the frame length is sufficient (i.e. is equal to the minimum length specification)?

**Question 10.6** In the case of the IEEE 802.3 standard, the DLL that is employed in the OSI reference model is divided into two sub-layers. Name these two layers.

**Question 10.7** In the case of an Ethernet bus topology, what purpose is served by the terminators that are connected to either end of the bus?

**Question 10.8** State two major advantages that are associated with fibre optic cable as compared to cabling based on metallic conductors.

**Question 10.9** Distinguish between 'Pure' and 'Slotted' Aloha.

**Question 10.10** In the case of a 'token passing' protocol, when is a node able to transmit a frame?

## 10.9 Feedback on activities

### Activity 10.1: Waveform characteristics

The amplitude is 3 volts and the peak-to-peak amplitude is 6 volts. The frequency is 1/T where T is the time for 1 cycle. In this case T=4 and therefore the frequency is 1/4 =0.25Hz.

### Activity 10.2: Frequency and wavelength

Speed= Frequency x Wavelength. Therefore:

$$Wavelength = \frac{Speed}{Frequency} = \frac{3x10^8}{10^8}$$

Thus, Wavelength= 3m.

### Activity 10.3: The use of time slots

#### *Advantages:*

All participants have the same opportunity to speak.

No single participant may dominate the discussion.

#### *Disadvantages:*

A participant may only need a few seconds to express a view – for the remainder of the time slot period no further discussion will take place (unless we cater for this possibility). As a result, time will be wasted.

A participant may have to wait a considerable time before their next time slot occurs. This time will depend on the designated time slot period and the number of participants.

### Activity 10.4: Slotted Aloha

#### *Advantage:*

In the case of Pure Aloha, collisions can occur at any point during the transmission process. Thus, for example a node may have broadcast 95% of a packet when another node begins transmitting – a part of the packets are then corrupted and both nodes must recommence transmission. In short, collisions are not limited to nodes that begin to transmit simultaneously – any transmission overlap causes a collision. This leads to the wastage of time and the problem is exacerbated as traffic densities increase. Slotted Aloha eliminates the possibility of partially overlapping transmissions – they will either totally overlap (due to simultaneous commencement of transmission) or will be collision free. This increases the rate of successful transmissions.

#### *Disadvantage:*

A common clock (or some form of clock synchronisation signal) must be distributed between nodes.

## Activity 10.5:  Node separation

The number of bits per frame equals 30x8=240.  Using Equation 10.4 we obtain:

$$\frac{240}{10^7} \geq \frac{2.D_{max}}{200x10^6}$$

Thus:

$$D_{max} \leq 2400m$$

## Activity 10.6:  The CSMA/CD and token passing approaches

In the case of the CSMA/CD approach, when a collision occurs, time is wasted.  This wasted time has two components – the time that has been spent in outputting the frames onto the LAN (prior to their collision), and the time for which nodes must 'back off' before re-sending.  As the level of traffic on the LAN increases, so to do the number of collisions, and thereby the amount of time wasted increases.  As collisions begin to occur with greater frequency, the performance of an Ethernet LAN rapidly falls.

In the case of the token passing approach, a node cannot transmit unless it has obtained the token.  Thus even in the case that there is no network traffic, a node cannot transmit until the token has circulated and been 'seized'.  In this way, time is wasted.  The amount of time lost in this way increases as we increase the size of the LAN or the number of nodes that are connected to it.  As traffic densities increases, the performance of a token–passing LAN tends to outstrip that of an equivalent Ethernet LAN.

# CHAPTER 11

# The Internet

## OVERVIEW

The Internet plays a vital part in today's computing activities. This enables machines located in practically any part of the world to communicate. In this chapter, we introduce some of the important concepts that underpin the operation of the Internet. Here, we introduce the Internet protocol, Internet addressing, address resolution, etc. Additionally, we briefly outline the operation of routers which are used to route Internet packets to their destination. As we will discuss, routers are able to adapt to ever-changing Internet conditions.

## Learning outcomes

On completion of this chapter you should be able to:

- Specify the nature of connection-oriented and connectionless transmission

- Outline the operation of bridges and routers

- Describe data encapsulation at different TCP/IP layers

- Discuss the Internet Procotol (IP) and the IP datagram format

- Identify traditional classes of IP address, the process of address resolution and the conversion of text-based Internet addresses into numerical IP addresses.

## 11.1 Introduction

In the previous two chapters we have generally assumed that communication takes place between devices (nodes) connected to a single homogeneous network, such as a LAN. In reality, communication exists between different networks, including LANs, MANs and WANs. These are interconnected to create a global network structure referred to as the Internet. This is made possible through the use of devices such as the bridges and routers that were briefly introduced in Chapter 10, which connect different segments of a network or interface between different networks.

Consider for a moment being seated before a computer that is connected to the Internet, via which we wish to transfer some sort of file to a friend who is also sitting in front of a computer at some distant location. We can achieve this task effortlessly, and for files that are relatively small the transfer will be effected almost immediately. In reality, this transmission is a complex process and relies on many different operations. Firstly, the file is broken into smaller units or chunks of data. To each of these chunks various information is appended, and it is this information that will be used to allow the chunk of data to traverse various networks on its voyage to the destination.

In this chapter, we review aspects of this voyage, and particularly the encapsulation process. Here we will see that each chunk of data must be encapsulated in such a way as to make it (as far as the voyage is concerned) independent of other chunks of data which constitute the original file. Interestingly, not all these chunks of data will necessarily traverse the same route on their way to the destination and, as we discuss, this can lead to them arriving 'out of order'.

In the next section we contrast 'connection-oriented' and 'connectionless' internetworking, and this paves the way for more detailed discussion in Section 11.3 concerning internetworking in general. Here we also briefly describe the functionality of two forms of 'protocol converter' – the bridge and router. In Section 11.4 we focus on aspects of the data encapsulation process. Section 11.5 provides discussion on the Internet Protocol (IP), and here we consider the IP datagram format. Section 11.6 presents an introduction to Internet addressing issues and the traditional classes of network are outlined. We also briefly consider the use of 'subnets'. The operation of the 'address resolution protocol' is introduced in Section 11.7, and finally in Section 11.8 we consider the 'domain name system' that enables Internet addresses represented in text to be automatically converted into a numerical form.

## 11.2 Connection-oriented and connectionless internetworking

In 'internetworking', two main methods are used for establishing a link between devices and for transporting data. These are referred to as 'connection-oriented' and 'connectionless' schemes. In a connection-oriented network, two nodes follow a set of rules to establish a formal connection so enabling data transfer. When data transmission is completed, a formal termination of the connection occurs. On the other hand, in connectionless networking there is no formal establishment or termination of the network connection.

### Connection-oriented transport

This mode may be readily understood by analogy to the telephone system. To make a telephone call we dial a number; this establishes the connection. When the call is answered, we talk (transfer data), and when finished we hang up – thus breaking the connection.

In network communications, connection-oriented transport (e.g. TCP) follows the following sequence (this is simplified for clarity):

- A device (Node A) that wants to establish a connection sends a request to the destination device. This is done by transmitting a connection request data packet to the intended receiver (Node B)
- The intended receiver (Node B) then accepts the connection request packet and conveys its intention to establish the connection by returning a confirmation data packet. A connection is then established
- Now the two devices are ready to transfer and receive data
- The connection is maintained throughout the transmission session (in principle)
- When data transmission is completed, a disconnection request packet is sent
- The receiving computer sends confirmation of disconnection
- This leads to a disconnection.

### Note

In practice, the establishment of a connection is somewhat more complex. In the scenario outlined above, the connection request sent from Node A to Node B may be delayed for some reason. This may lead Node A to believe the request has been lost, and therefore Node A may re-send a connection request and as a result a connection is established. However, the original connection request may subsequently arrive at Node B, leading to the establishment of a second connection. As a consequence, problems may ensue. To overcome this difficulty a 'three-way hand-shake' is used. Here, Node A makes a connection request, Node B acknowledges this request, and Node A acknowledges the acknowledgement. By employing sequence numbers within the 'transport protocol data units' that are used for the connection request and acknowledgements (recall that the transport layer is responsible for connection management), this three-way hand-shake ensures that multiple connections are not inadvertently created. A similar three-way hand-shake is used for the termination of a connection.

## *Connectionless transport*

This approach can be readily understood by analogy to the postal system. A letter (or parcel) contains a detailed destination address, and each letter is routed through the postal system independently of all other letters. Normally, we would expect that when two (or more) letters are sent to the same destination, the first that is mailed would be the first to arrive. As we know from experience, this sequence can be disrupted and the letters may arrive out of order (e.g. the last mailed may be the first to arrive).

In network communications, connectionless transportation allows applications to send messages to any destination at any time. This is achieved as follows:

- The data is encapsulated in a frame. The intended destination address is included (equivalent to placing a letter in an envelope and adding the destination address).
- Each message can be sent to a destination via a different route – in a similar fashion to the postal service. The route is not specified in advance.

Figure 11.1 illustrates these two styles of data transportation. In both diagrams, device A is sending messages F1, F2, F3 to device B. For the connection-oriented service (see Figure 11.1(a)), the three messages are sent as a stream across the same paths, i.e. via routers 1, 2 and 3 (a router is a network device that routes (directs) network traffic – we will discuss this device shortly.) In the connectionless mode (see Figure 11.1(b)) the messages are sent via different routes to the same destination (B) and, as indicated in the diagram, they may arrive out of order.

The connection-oriented mode offers 'quality of service' by generally exhibiting greater reliability than the connectionless scheme. The acknowledgement (by the receiving device) of the receipt of each message enhances reliability. This does introduce some delay (similar to waiting for a response when using the telephone), but is desirable in some applications.

The connectionless approach tends to be less reliable as there is no acknowledgement of receipt of each frame by the destination node – the message has a high probability of arrival, but this is not guaranteed. A message sent via a connectionless mode is referred to as a 'datagram'. This approach is said to operate on a 'best efforts' basis.

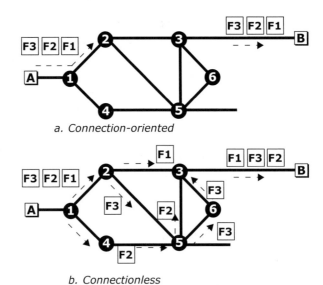

*a. Connection-oriented*

*b. Connectionless*

**Figure 11.1:** In (a) we illustrate the connection-oriented approach and in (b) connectionless transmission. Note: the numbered circles indicate network routers which are responsible for routing traffic through the network.

## 11.3 Internetworking

Until the early 1980s, typical computer communications took place across limited geographical areas or were achieved by dedicated connections. With the huge expansion in the extent and diversity of computer applications, coupled with the rapid increase in the number of smaller networks, the question that arose was how to bring together different networks and make them appear to work as a single cohesive entity. This was a particularly challenging issue since networks connected devices employing different operating systems, employed different transmission media and protocols, and were located in different countries/continents. Ultimately, this led to the emergence of the Internet, which is formed from the interconnection of independent physical networks, such as LANs, and WANs. Network devices known as 'routers' play a pivotal role in Internet operations. These are special-purpose computer systems that connect networks and support data transfer.

## *Virtual networks*

The Internet appears to be a single seamless communication system; i.e. devices appear to communicate as if they are attached to a single physical network. This illusion of a single homogeneous communication system is referred to as a 'virtual network'. It is virtual in the sense that the system is comprised of different physical networks that are not necessarily located in close proximity, yet neither the user nor the application programs are mindful of the nature of physical networks involved, or of the routers that connect them. In fact, the Internet protocol software masks from the higher layers of the protocol stack the physical nature of the connected networks. In such a virtual environment each device or router must run software, which allows application programs to exchange messages. The TCP/IP suite of protocols defines how transmissions are exchanged across the Internet. The virtual network is implemented based on a connectionless scheme of operation.

## *The Internet from a TCP/IP perspective*

As previously discussed (see Section 9.8), the TCP/IP transport layer defines two specific protocols. These are the Transmission Control Protocol (TCP), and the User Datagram Protocol (UDP). The Internet layer of the TCP/IP model (which corresponds to the network layer within the OSI model) describes the Internet Protocol. Figure 11.2(a) shows a simple Internet layout where different physical networks are connected by routing devices:

- A, B, C and D represent nodes that wish to communicate
- 1, 2, 3 and 4 are routers that pass packets between networks such as LANs
- I, II, III represent physical networks (e.g. LANs).

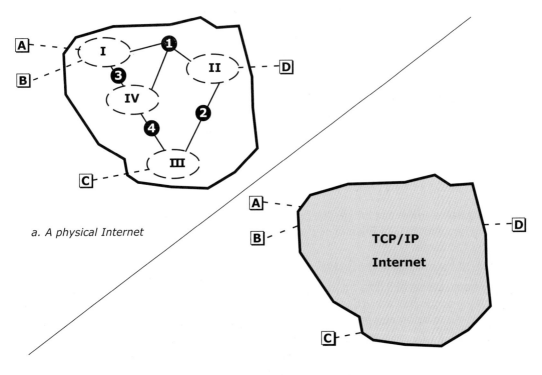

a. A physical Internet

b. A virtual Internet

**Figure 11.2:** (a) A physical, and (b) a virtual Internet

Through the use of TCP/IP, this Internet takes on a somewhat different appearance; see Figure 11.2(b). Here:

- All interconnected physical networks are seen as one large network – referred to as a 'cloud'
- All devices are considered to be connected to this larger 'virtual' network rather than to their individual physical networks.

Two devices (protocol converters) known as the 'bridge' and 'router' play a crucial role in enabling the seamless interconnection of networks. These are briefly introduced below:

## Bridges

Suppose that we wish to transfer a frame from one network to another. These two networks may employ frames that have different formats. In this situation we would employ a device known as a 'bridge'. This is a computer hardware product (a 'protocol converter') that is able to operate up to the second layer of the OSI protocol stack (the data link layer). Thus the bridge accepts and can reconstitute frames so enabling, for example, the interconnection of Ethernet and token passing networks. The operation of a bridge is summarised in Figure 11.3.

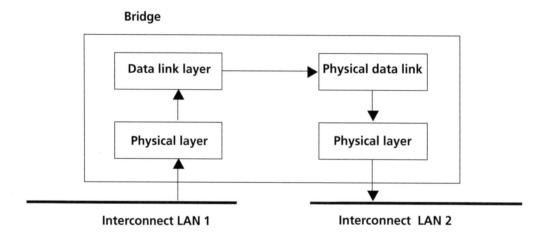

**Figure 11.3:** The 'bridge' – a protocol converter able to operate at the second layer level of the OSI model

A bridge is able to perform various tasks. For example:

- When a frame arrives at a bridge, the bridge examines the destination address. If this address lies on the 'other side' of the bridge, the bridge buffers the frame. Otherwise, the bridge ignores the frame
- Having buffered a frame, the bridge performs error checking
- If the frame format and data transfer characteristics (such as bit-rate) of the network from which the bridge has received the frame is the same as that used by the network onto which the frame is to be output, then the bridge simply outputs the frame
- If the data transfer characteristics of the two networks differ, then the bridge will make the necessary adjustments. Consider the case of a frame received from an Ethernet LAN that is to be output onto a lower-speed Ethernet LAN. The bridge must output the frame at the appropriate rate. Also the extent of the buffer in the bridge must be sufficient to ensure that the bridge does not become 'swamped' by incoming frames (this problem is exacerbated by

 the possibility of collisions that may occur on the LAN to which the bridge is outputting frames)

- If the two networks use different frame formats, the bridge must reconstitute the frame prior to outputting it

- A bridge not only forwards frames intended for nodes that reside on the network to which the bridge is directly connected, but also frames intended for nodes on other more distant LANs. For example, consider the situation illustrated in Figure 11.4. Suppose that a node connected to LAN 1 transmits a frame intended for a node that exists on LAN 3. This frame will be forwarded by Bridge 1 as this bridge 'knows' that it provides a path (route) from LAN 1 to LAN 3. When this frame reaches Bridge 2, it will again be forwarded and so reach LAN 3 and hence its ultimate destination.

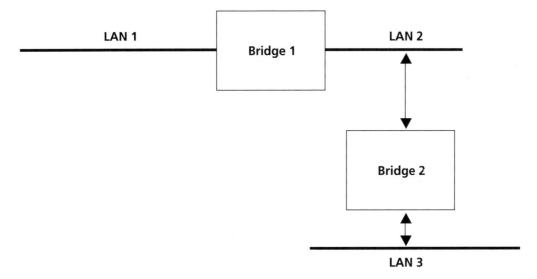

**Figure 11.4:** Bridge 1 will forward a frame from LAN 1 to LAN 2, even though the frame's ultimate destination is LAN 3

### Bridges

Suppose that due to an expansion in the number of nodes connected to an Ethernet LAN, network traffic increases to such an extent that performance begins to be compromised (i.e. due to the large number of collisions which are continually occurring).

Briefly explain how you could address this problem.

### Bridges and repeaters

For the question posed in Activity 11.1, explain why a repeater could not have been employed.

## *The router*

This is a network device that operates up to Layer 3 of the OSI model (i.e. up to the OSI network layer/ the TCP/IP Internet layer). This provides the router (also referred to as a 'gateway') with greater powers than those supported by the bridge (which only operates on the lower two layers of the OSI model). The operation of the router is depicted in Figure 11.5. A router is able to interconnect different types of network and as its name implies is responsible for 'routing' packets to their destination. In fact, by maintaining up-to-date (dynamic) 'routing tables', a router is able to take into account ever-changing network conditions (such as variations in traffic density) and so direct packets in an optimal (least cost) way. When a router receives a packet, it determines the packet's destination address and uses information contained within its routing table to find the next router to which the packet should be forwarded. The entries contained in a routing table can be set by an operator (fixed) or are determined dynamically by routers using 'routing algorithms' (such as the 'distance vector' approach which determines routing information on the basis of the number of router 'hops' that a packet will make when travelling between two locations). So as to maintain up-to-date (i.e. non-stale) routing information, routers exchange routing table entries frequently (e.g. in the case of RIP (Routing Information Protocol) a router will exchange routing information with its neighbours every thirty seconds).

**Repeaters**

The maximum number of repeaters that can (should) be employed on an Ethernet LAN is four.

Explain why you believe there is an upper limit on the number of repeaters than can be used.

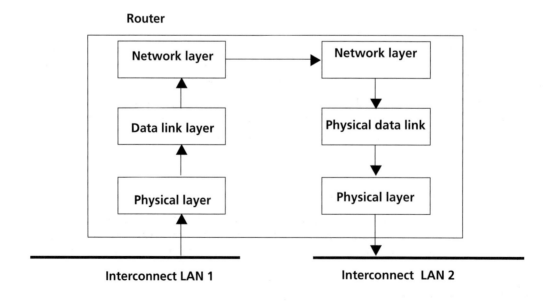

**Figure 11.5:** The 'router' – a protocol converter able to operate up to the third layer level (network) of the OSI model

## 11.4 Data encapsulation

The transmission of data across networks is analogous to sending an item by post. When we wish to mail an object, it cannot generally be sent in its 'raw' state – it has to be packaged in a parcel (or envelope) that adheres to some pre-agreed standards and specifications, such as size, packaging material and provides the addresses of both sender and recipient. Similarly, in the case of networking, data needs to be packaged – a range of vital information must be appended (e.g. the source and destination addresses). This process is referred to as 'encapsulation' and is attained by protocol software. These protocols are implemented as data proceeds from one layer to the next within the OSI or TCP/IP stack. Figure 11.6 illustrates the encapsulation of data units at the different layers of the TCP/IP protocol stack.

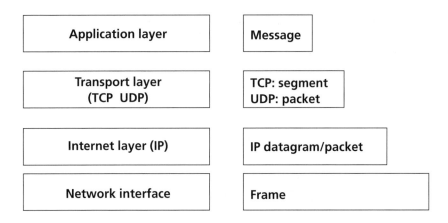

**Figure 11.6:** Data encapsulation in TCP/IP

When the IP layer receives a data block from the upper layer, it adds a 'header'. This specifies global address information including network identifier and end system identifier. We will refer to the data and associated header information as an 'IP datagram' or 'packet'.

**Note:** Confusion can arise from the use of the terms 'IP datagram' and 'packet'. For the purposes of this book, when referring to a TCP/IP Internet we will employ the former term to indicate the basic unit that is formed by the Internet layer. In the case that discussion is framed in the context of the OSI model, we generally use the term 'packet'.

This datagram is further encapsulated by the LAN protocols and is subsequently passed to a router. Datagrams are transmitted separately and may arrive out of sequence (in an order which differs from the order in which they were transmitted).

## 11.5 Internet Protocol (IP)

The objective of internetworking is to provide a system in which a program running on a networked computer can send data to a program running on another computer through the transportation of datagrams/packets. The IP is the backbone protocol for internetworking.

### *IP characteristics*

As indicated above, a packet sent across a TCP/IP Internet is referred to as an 'IP datagram' or simply as a 'datagram'. The IP treats each datagram independently. These datagrams are separated from each other and may travel through different routes and so arrive in a sequence that is different to the order in which they were launched. Each datagram must contain complete addressing and control information. Furthermore, IP is an unreliable, connectionless datagram protocol that provides a 'best-efforts' delivery service – similar to the postal service! In a best-efforts environment, IP relies on the underlying layers, as it does not include:

- Error checking
- A provision to determine if packets reach their destination, or take corrective action if they do not
- A means for verifying if packets were delayed or delivered out of order or out of sequence
- Ways of knowing whether data were corrupted in transit, datagrams lost or duplicated
- An alert to the receiving device of an incoming transmission.

IP is paired with other protocols, such as TCP, for reliable delivery of packets.

**Basic characteristics of IP**

From the list provided below, identify the word(s) that you consider most appropriate for each of the following statements. Each may be used once only, more than once, or not at all.

1. IP data packets are transmitted _____ of each other.

2. Packets that are transmitted by TCP/IP across the Internet are referred to as

_____

3. IP provides _____ quality service.

4. IP provides _____ communication.

5. Datagrams transmitted by a router can be _____ .

6. IP does not send back any _____ to confirm the packet has reached the destination.

7. Reliable delivery of IP can be ensured by coupling it with the _____ protocol.

**List of keywords**

| | |
|---|---|
| Error checking | Independently |
| TCP | Sequence |
| Datagrams | Lost |
| Best efforts | Connectionless |
| Duplicated | Acknowledgement |

## IP datagram format

The description presented below relates to version 4 of the IP (usually referred to as simply IPv4). IPv4 packets comprise two parts; the IP header that carries information essential for routing and delivery, and a variable-length data field. The general format of the header is illustrated in Figure 11.7.

- **Version - 4 bits:** The version number indicates the format of the Internet header (e.g. IPv4 in contrast to IPv6)

- **Header length - 4 bits:** The length of the Internet header in multiples of 32-bit words. The header length is variable and therefore it is necessary to indicate the beginning of the data

- **Type of service - 8 bits:** The type of service provides an indication of the quality of service required – such as priority, level of throughput, reliability and tolerated delay when transmitting a datagram through a particular network. The major choice is a three-way trade-off between low-delay, high-reliability, and high-throughput

- **Total length - 16 bits:** Defines the length of the datagram, measured as a multiple of 8 bits, and includes both the header and data. This field allows the length of a datagram to be up to 65,535 bytes

- **Identification - 16 bits**: An identifying value assigned by the transmitting computer to assist in assembling the fragments of a datagram when passing through different networks. All fragments of the same datagram have the same identification number

- **Flags - 3 bits** (only two used): One bit is used to tell routers that a datagram should not be fragmented. One bit is used to assist in the reassembly of fragments

- **Fragment offset - 13 bits**: This indicates the location of a fragment within the original datagram. The fragment offset is measured in units of 8 bytes

- **Time to live - 8 bits:** This defines the maximum time a datagram is allowed to remain in the Internet system before being discarded. The initial value is set by the transmitting computer and each router decrements the value. If this field contains the value zero, then the datagram must be destroyed. The intention is to prevent undeliverable datagrams from circulating indefinitely around the Internet, and to constrain the maximum datagram lifetime.

- **Protocol - 8 bits:** Indicates which upper-layer protocol data are encapsulated in the datagram (e.g. in the case of a TCP segment the value is 6 and in the case of UDP it is set to 17, etc.).

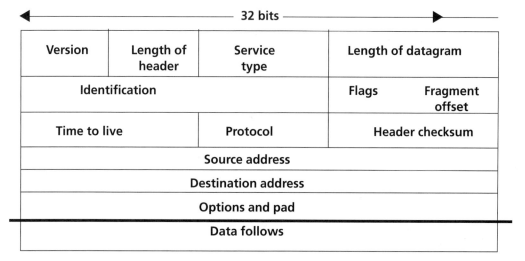

**Figure 11.7:** The format of the header employed in an IPv4 datagram

- **Header checksum - 16 bits:** This is used to detect error in the header that may occur during transmission. Since some header fields change during the transit of a datagram (e.g. time to live), it is necessary for each router to recalculate the checksum
- **Source address - 32 bits:** This identifies the original source of the datagram
- **Destination address - 32 bits:** This identifies the final destination of the datagram
- **Options - variable length:** This can carry additional fields to control routing, timing and datagram management
- **Padding - variable length:** Padding bits are used to ensure that the Internet header ends on a 32-bit boundary (i.e. the length is a multiple of 32 bits).

## 11.6 Internet addressing

In order to transfer IP datagrams from one networked device to another and enable them to successfully reach their ultimate destination, the IP has to provide an addressing scheme that contains the addresses of the *host* and of the *network* where the host is located. An IP address is a 32-bit number (here we assume the use of IPv4) written as four bytes. For our convenience, each byte is generally expressed in decimal form with decimal points separating each 8-bit grouping. This numbering system is referred to as the dotted-decimal notation. It is used for simplicity and is easy to remember in comparison to the binary format. The IP dotted-decimal format is illustrated in Figure 11.6.

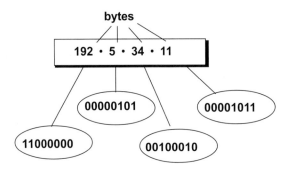

**Figure 11.8:** An IP address is expressed in dotted-decimal format

As we have discussed, an IP datagram contains the IP address of the sending device (i.e. source) and that of the receiving device (i.e. destination). These 32-bit IP addresses are divided into two main parts called the 'prefix' and 'suffix', as shown in Figure 11.9.

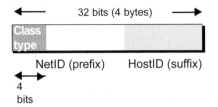

*An Internet address defines a host connection to a network; it is made up of four bytes (octets)*

**Figure 11.9:** IP address division

The address prefix defines the physical network to which the intended recipient is connected, while the address suffix identifies a particular device on that network. Both prefixes and suffixes are unique values and are respectively referred to as the 'network identification number' (NetID) and 'host identification number' (HostID). Globally unique addresses permit IP networks anywhere in the world to communicate with each other. The division between a network and the destined host residing on it represents a two-level hierarchy that makes transmitting a packet and routing it to its final destination more effective in that:

- When two computers are attached to different physical networks, their IP addresses have different prefixes
- When two computers are connected to the same physical network, their IP addresses have different suffixes.

## The IP address classes

In the original Internet scheme developed in the 1970s, designers had to determine how to divide the 32-bit IP address between prefix and suffix (clearly, increasing the number of bits devoted to one part means reducing the number of bits associated with the other). Division must ensure that:

- The **prefix** contains enough bits to permit a unique network number to be allocated to each individual physical network on the Internet
- The **suffix** ought to have sufficient bits to allow each host to be assigned a unique host number.

Traditionally, five different classes of IP address are used to accommodate the mixture of different-size physical networks that are encountered in the Internet. (In fact, as will be discussed shortly, only three classes are specifically used for this purpose.) This 'classful IP addressing system' enables a different number of bits within the IP address to be assigned to the NetID and HostID identifiers; see Figure 11.10. The first bits of the address are used to indicate the class of network referenced by the IP address. This in turn defines how the remainder of the IP address is divided into NetID (prefix) and HostID (suffix).

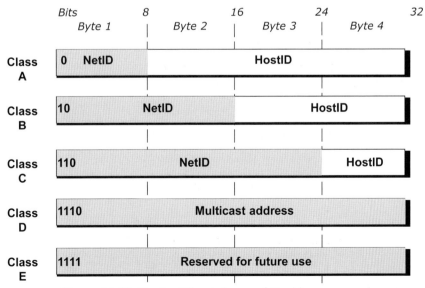

**Figure 11.10:** The traditional classes of IP address

Thus, for example, in the case of a Class A network, the left-most bit of the IP address is set to zero. The following seven bits are used for the NetID and the remaining 24 bits provide the HostID identifier. This enables 128 Class A networks to be defined – each containing up to 16,777,216 hosts. Clearly, not many organisations are likely to require a Class A network!

**Activity 11.5**

**The Class B and C networks**

Determine the number of Class B and C networks that may be defined (and the number of hosts that may exist on these two classes of network) using the 'classful addressing scheme' illustrated in Figure 11.10.

IP address class information is summarised in Figure 11.11. This 'classful addressing' scheme fails to take into account the rapid expansion of the Internet and does not readily match the requirements of today's organisations. For example, a Class B network accommodates more than 64,000 hosts – there are relatively few organisations with such extensive needs. On the other hand, a Class C network supports only 256 hosts – a number exceeded by many organisations. In short there is a great step in size between the Class B and C networks, and with the scheme introduced above many organisations must opt for a Class B network, even though they may be only employing a few hundred hosts. This leads to the wastage of addresses (called 'address depletion'), and other approaches have therefore been adopted. For example, IPv6 allows both source and destination addresses to be represented by 128 bits. (The assignment of network addresses is managed by the Internet Corporation for Assigned Names and Numbers (ICANN). This work had previously been undertaken by the Internet Assigned Numbers Authority (IANA). See, for example, **www.icann.org**). A process called 'subnetting' provides an alternative solution and is briefly outlined later.

**Activity 11.6**

**IP address interpretation**

Consider the IP address: 130.4.0.0.

Determine the Class, NetID and HostID.

**Class A:** 0NNNNNNN • HHHHHHHH • HHHHHHHH • HHHHHHHH

- First bit 0; 7 network bits; 24 host bits
- First byte (octet) range: 0 - 127
- $2^7 - 2 = 126$ networks could be present (0 and 127 are reserved)
- $2^{24} = 16,777,214$ hosts for each network

**Class B:** 10NNNNNN • NNNNNNNN • HHHHHHHH • HHHHHHHH

- First two bits 10; 14 network bits; 16 host bits
- First octet (byte) range: 128 - 191
- $2^{14} = 16,384$ networks could be present
- $2^{16} = 65,536$ hosts for each network

**Class C:** 110NNNNN • NNNNNNNN • NNNNNNNN • HHHHHHHH

- First three bits 110; 21 network bits; 8 host bits
- First octet (byte) range: 192 - 223
- $2^{21} = 2,097,152$ networks could be present
- $2^8 = 256$ hosts for each network

**Class D:** 1110MMMM • MMMMMMMM • MMMMMMMM • MMMMMMMM

- First four bits 1110; 28 multicast address bits
- First octet (byte) range: 224 - 239
- Class Ds are multicast addresses

**Class E:** 1111RRRR • RRRRRRRR • RRRRRRRR • RRRRRRRR

- First four bits 1111; 28 reserved address bits
- First octet (byte) range: 240 - 255
- Reserved for future use

| KEY |
| --- |
| **N** Network |
| **H** Host |
| **M** Multicast |
| **R** Reserved |

**Figure 11.11:** Summary of IP address classes

## *Subnetting: the rationale*

Here, for example, a Class B network (comprising 65,536 host addresses) is divided into, say 100-200 smaller networks each with around 200-300 host addresses. These smaller networks are known as 'subnets', and the adopted standard (RFC 950) became known as 'subnetting':

- Subnetting splits the 'host' field into 'subnet' and 'host' fields, creating a three-part address as shown in Figure 11.12
- The network field remains unchanged, and is determined through 'classful addressing'
- The boundary between the subnet and host fields can fall between any two bits, and is decided by using a 'subnet mask' – allocated by a network operator.

Due to the flexibility of this approach, subnetting rapidly emerged as the generally acknowledged method of managing the 'classful address space'.

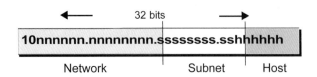

**Figure 11.12:** Subdividing the IP address

In Figure 11.13 we illustrate a Class B network that is divided into three smaller subnetworks. The external Internet is unaware of the internal division of the original network into a number of subnets; the site IP address (141.14.0.0) remains the same.

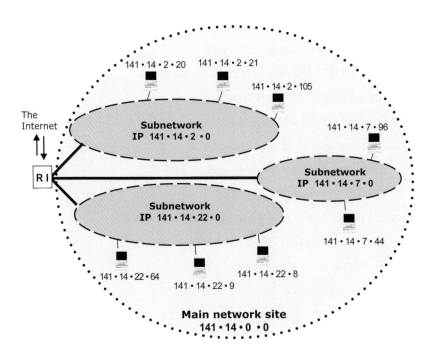

**Figure 11.13:** A Class B network that is divided into three subnets

Let us consider how this operates. A packet destined for host 141.14.2.21 reaches the router R1, see Figure 11.13. Although the main network site, 141.14.0.0 is unaltered, the router knows that:

- The network is now physically divided into three subnets 141.14.2.0, 141.14.22.0 and 141.14.7.0

- The last two octets in the IP address now define a 'SubNetID' and a 'HostID' (instead of the original division of 'NetID' and 'HostID')

- Consequently, 2.21 is interpreted by the router as SubNetID 2 and HostID 21.

The addition of subnetworks creates an intermediate or 3-level hierarchy – NetID, SubNetID and HostID – where:

- **NetID forms the first level**, i.e. the main network site
- **SubNetID is the second level**, i.e. the physical subnetwork
- **HostID is the third level** – pointing to the connection of a particular host to a subnetwork.

In the case of this three-level hierarchy, the routing of an IP datagram, involves three steps:

- **Delivery to the site**
- **Delivery to the subnetwork**
- **Delivery to the host.**

### IP addressing with subnets

Figure 11.14 shows a network site whose IP address is 141.106.0.0. From this:

- Verify the IP class by examining the first octet (byte) in the address

- Using the IP Class type, decide how to split the IP address into the NetID and HostID fields (i.e. how many octets (bytes) should be assigned to each).

The network is to be divided into three subnets (as illustrated in Figure 11.14), with the original HostID subdivided into SubNetID and HostID. In this case:

- Assign an IP address for each subnet

- Indicate which part is reserved for the SubNetID and which one for the HostID.

Assuming that each subnet has two devices (as illustrated in Figure 11.14):

- From the IP address of each subnet, assign an IP address for each device

- Indicate which part of the address provides the device number.

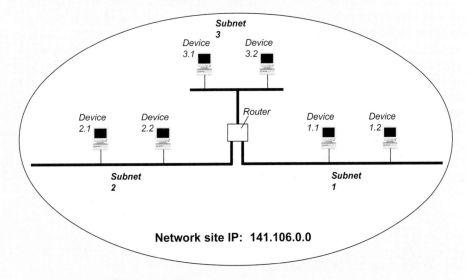

**Figure 11.14:** A network site comprising three subnets

## 11.7 Address resolution

As we have discussed, IP addresses enable datagrams to be routed across the Internet and are used by routers to determine the direction in which each datagram should be forwarded. Destination nodes are commonly connected to LANs which in turn are connected by routers to other networks (see Figure 11.15). A problem arises when we consider the role played by the IP address in enabling a datagram that has arrived at the router indicated in this illustration to reach a particular node on the LAN. After all, these nodes are connected to the LAN by Ethernet cards which know nothing about 32-bit IP addresses (recall, an Ethernet card uses a 48-bit Ethernet address).

The router must translate the IP destination address into an equivalent MAC address. This translation is referred to as 'address resolution'. Address resolution is network specific; i.e. a device can resolve the address of another device only if the two are connected to the same network. This operates within the IP layer of TCP/IP model. The main function of this protocol is to associate the logical IP address with the physical MAC address.

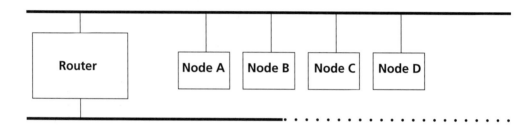

**Figure 11.15:** An Ethernet LAN that is connected to other networks via a router

### *The address resolution protocol mechanism*

To ensure standardisation of the address resolution technique, the TCP/IP protocol suite includes an address resolution protocol (ARP). Devices on the same network, such as a LAN, maintain an ARP table that contains the IP and MAC addresses of all other devices on the network. This is illustrated in Figure 11.16. The table is usually cached in RAM. If the destination MAC address cannot be located by the source Internet Protocol (due to, for example, adding a node without updating the ARP table on the network), then the new MAC address can be obtained from the destination via its IP address. ARP works by broadcasting a packet (as illustrated in Figure 11.17) to all nodes attached to a LAN (for example). The packet contains the IP address of the destination. All nodes read this packet and check their own IP address against the one that has been broadcast. The node whose IP address matches the one that has been transmitted responds by adding its MAC address to an ARP reply frame and sends it back to the source (see Figure 11.18). The source Internet Protocol will then combine the IP address with the MAC address and use them to encapsulate the data. The data packet is then sent out over the network to be picked up by the destination.

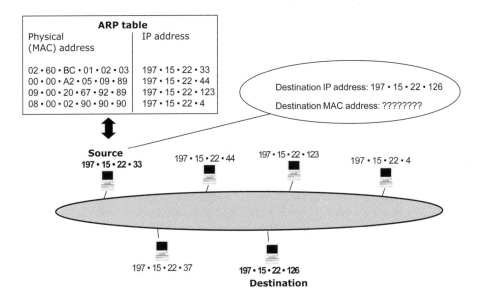

**Figure 11.16:** ARP frame broadcasting

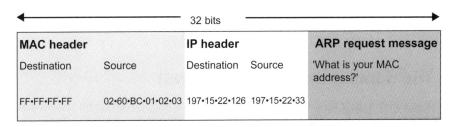

**Figure 11.17:** An ARP request frame

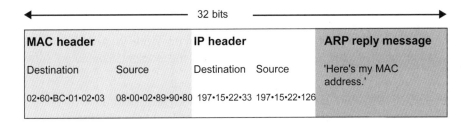

**Figure 11.18:** An ARP response frame

In summary – and using the configuration illustrated in Figure 11.15: suppose that an incoming datagram arrives at the router and is ultimately intended for Node C.

- The router will examine its ARP cache to see if it has an entry for this IP address. If the entry exists, the router places the datagram into an Ethernet frame, loads the destination address (MAC address for Node C) into the frame and injects the frame onto the LAN

- If the entry doesn't exist, then the router broadcasts an ARP request frame onto the LAN. Within this frame is the IP address whose MAC address is unknown

- All nodes examine the IP address that is carried by the frame (payload). The node whose IP address matches the one indicated in the ARP request frame responds and provides its MAC address

- The router updates its ARP cache and is now able to create a frame to carry the datagram that it previously received to Node C.

### *Reverse address resolution protocol (RARP)*

As discussed above, ARP is a protocol able to find out which MAC address corresponds to a given IP address. However, in some situations we need to do the converse – given the MAC address, what is the corresponding IP address of a networked device? This situation may occur in the case of a diskless workstation (i.e. networked computers which have no secondary storage facilities (hard disk)). When first booted (connected to the network and powered on), such a machine must:

- Obtain its copy of the operating system from a remote file server
- Know its IP address before it can transmit data to another device.

The reverse address resolution protocol (RARP) is a TCP/IP protocol that allows a workstation to broadcast using its MAC address, and expects a server to respond, informing it of its designated IP address.

## 11.8 The domain name system (DNS)

The naming scheme used on the Internet is referred to as the domain name system (DNS). It is a TCP/IP application service that converts user-friendly names to IP addresses. The name of a device on the Internet is structured to consist of a sequence of alphanumeric segments separated by full-stops. An example is the Middlesex University Web page, **www.mdx.ac.uk** - the domain name is mdx.ac.uk. This format is certainly easier to remember than the dotted-decimal address: 158.94.184.32!

With the use of this system, Internet users do not need to remember and enter an IP address in its 32-bit format. When e-mailing or specifying a site on the World Wide Web (WWW), a user enters a string identifying the recipient and the name of the recipient's computer. Software is used to:

- Allow entry of user-convenient symbols, e.g. ASCII characters
- Convert these ASCII characters to numerical (i.e. binary) network addresses.

Domain names are said to be hierarchical with different parts pointing to a particular location: one field indicating the address of the mailbox on the local site, while the other points to the domain name of the destination device. For example, when examining the e-mail address of Joe Smith at Middlesex University (see Figure 11.19), the most significant part of the name appears on the right {mdx.ac.uk}, while the left-most {joe1} identifies the name of a particular device. The process of translating domain names into IP addresses is handled by servers located at sites across the Internet and which operate a distributed database known as the 'Domain Name System'.

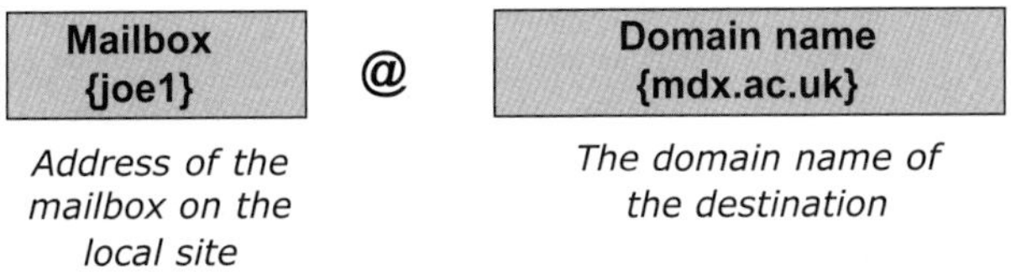

| Mailbox {joe1} | @ | Domain name {mdx.ac.uk} |
|---|---|---|

Address of the
mailbox on the
local site

The domain name of
the destination

**Figure 11.19:** The domain names hierarchy

In brief, this database contains Internet addresses (in text form) together with their corresponding numerical IP addresses. Servers holding this information are distributed across the Internet. When a machine needs to convert a text address into its numerical representation, it contacts a local name server. In the case that the server has the required information, then the enquiry need go no further. On the other hand, if the server does not have the required entry, other servers must be contacted. The choice of server is determined by entries within the Internet address hierarchy – for example, text addresses that end with '.edu', '.gov' and '.com' are handled by different servers. Thus, in the case that the local server is not able to supply the IP address, it will use information contained within the text address to determine the location of a server that may be able to perform the conversion.

## 11.9 Summary

In this chapter, we have discussed some of the basic ideas relating to the nature of internetworking and the techniques used for the transmission and delivery of data between networked devices. Irrespective of the location or proximity of devices, the process is achieved via different methods of connection and is implemented by a suite of protocols.

Two protocol architectures provide the foundation for standardised global communication – the OSI reference model and TCP/IP. The latter is the most widely used backbone for interoperable protocol architectures, while the OSI model has largely emerged as the template for designing and classifying network communication functions.

The Internet can be visualised as the interconnection of various networks via devices, such as bridges and routers. The resultant network gives the perception of a single seamless physical communication system, while in reality the different networks are linked by software. For this reason the Internet is often referred to as a 'virtual network'.

Before data can be transferred between networked devices, they need to be assembled in such a way as to enable the devices to successfully route them to their designated destination. This process of data packaging is referred to as 'encapsulation'. Here, each layer in the protocol hierarchy adds its own control information in the form of bits. During its passage across the Internet, devices such as routers extract the information from the datagram needed to convey it to its final destination.

We now take global Internet access for granted. Seldom do we pause and consider the considerable complexities associated with the almost instantaneous transmission of data, voice and video images from and to almost any part of the Earth's surface. In this chapter, we have briefly alluded to some of the complexities.

## 11.10 Review questions

**Question 11.1** Briefly explain the following:

a) What are the two main techniques used to transmit data between networked devices?

b) What protocol is usually used in connection-oriented data transmission across the Internet? Give an analogous example.

c) What protocol is normally used in connectionless data transmission across the Internet? Give an analogous example.

d) What is meant by 'quality of service' in data communications? Which technique offers better quality of service: connection-oriented or connectionless transmission?

e) What name is given to a message sent via a connectionless transmission?

**Question 11.2** Indicate if the following statements are true (T) or False (F)

1. Connection-oriented transmission is performed in three stages. (T/F)

2. Connection-oriented transmission does not need to establish and terminate a connection formally. (T/F)

3. Connection-oriented transmission is not a very reliable service. (T/F

4. Connectionless transmission is more flexible than connection-oriented. (T/F)

5. The unit of data packets that are transmitted in connectionless transmission system is called a datagram. (T/F)

6. Connectionless service requires smaller overheads than does connection-oriented service. (T/F)

**Question 11.3** Briefly answer the following:

a) To what does the term 'Internet' refer?

b) What is a router and what is its function?

c) What does the term 'virtual network' imply?

**Question 11.4** Indicate if the following statements are true (T) or False (F)

1. Internetworking basically works on similar types of network architecture. (T/F)

2. Internetworking establishes a connectionless type of data communication. (T/F)

3. To connect two LANs that are physically remote, only one router is needed. (T/F)

4. The same Internet Protocols are required to be implemented in both sender and receiver routers. (T/F)

**P** **Question 11.5**

a. What is meant by data encapsulation?

b. Make a sketch of how data units are encapsulated in TCP/IP, naming the data unit at each layer.

**P** **Question 11.6** Briefly explain each of the following:

a) What is a data packet communicated via a TCP/IP called, and what does it contain?

b) What is a best-efforts data transmission service in a TCP/IP network?

c) What does a port number refer to in TCP/IP communication?

d) How many main parts does an IP packet consist of? Name these and state the functions of each.

**P** **Question 11.7**

1. IP provides _____ service.

   a. connection-oriented       b. connectionless

   c. peer-to-peer               d. none of the above.

2. A router implements the _____ protocol

   a. TCP                        b. UDP

   c. IP                         d. none of the above.

3. The size of a datagram is decided by

   a. TCP                        b. IP

   c. UDP                        d. none of the above.

4. The ____ parameter decides the priority of a service

   a. data length       b. type of service

   c. flag                       d. None of the above.

5. An IP datagram consists of _____ parts.

   a. three                      b. two

   c. single                     d. none of the above.

6. The header of an IP datagram is _____ long.

a. 20-60 bytes                    b. 2-6 bytes

c. 5-15 bytes                     d. none of the above.

7. The flag of an IP datagram determines whether it is a _____ datagram.

a. fragmented                     b. out-of-sequence

c. erroneous                      d. none of the above.

### Question 11.8

1. An IPv4 address consists of _____ bits.

a. 16                             b. 24

c. 32                             d. none of the above.

2. The_____ holds information about the HostID in an IP address.

a. suffix                         b. prefix

c. class                          d. none of the above.

3. The _____ holds information about the NetID in an IP address.

a. suffix                         b. prefix

c. class                          d. none of the above.

### Question 11.9

Briefly answer the following:

a) Why is the IP addressing scheme referred to as hierarchical?

b) What does a dotted-decimal notation represent in IP addressing?

c) What are the two main parts of an IP address called, and what do they represent?

## 11.11 Feedback on activities

### Activity 11.1: Bridges

One simple and effective approach would be to physically split the LAN into two parts (see Figure 11.20). These would then be reconnected using a bridge. The bridge is selective in its forwarding of transmissions and so a transmission from Node A that is intended for

Node B will not appear on LAN 2. Similarly, for example, a transmission from Node C that is intended for Node D will not appear on LAN 1. Thus the traffic on the two individual LAN segments is reduced. One disadvantage of this approach is the delay introduced by the bridge (which buffers each frame) that is to be passed between LAN 1 and LAN 2.

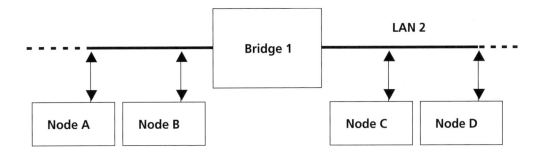

**Figure 11.20:** The use of a bridge to interconnect two LAN segments. The bridge is selective in its forwarding of transmissions.

### Activity 11.2: Bridges and repeaters

A repeater simply reconstitutes signals. It is not able to examine the information contained within frames. As a result, any signal that is applied to the repeater is transferred by the repeater. Hence, the repeater cannot be used for the selective forwarding of network traffic. If a LAN was split into two parts, and these two parts were connected by a repeater, there would be no change in the traffic level on either of the LAN segments.

### Activity 11.3: Repeaters

As we have seen, Repeaters reconstitute signals. This process occupies a finite time and as a consequence, a Repeater introduces a slight delay into signal transmission. This adds to the propagation delay of signals within the transmission media. As discussed in the previous chapter, when implementing the CSMA/CD protocol it is important to ensure that a node that is transmitting a frame is made aware that a collision has occurred prior to its having completed the injection of the frame onto the LAN. If too many Repeaters are used this can introduce an unacceptable worst-case delay into a sending node being notified of a collision (i.e. if the report of the collision has to pass through too many Repeaters, then the sending node may have finished frame injection onto the LAN before it gets to hear of the collision that has taken place).

### Activity 11.4: Basic characteristics of IP

| | | | | |
|---|---|---|---|---|
| Error checking | - | Independently | Q1 |
| TCP | Q7 | Sequence | - |
| Datagrams | Q2 | Lost | Q5 |
| Best efforts | Q3 | Connectionless | Q4 |
| Duplicated | - | Acknowledgement | Q6 |

### Activity 11.5: The Class B and C networks

**Class B:** NetID – 14 bits. This gives 16,384 networks.

HostID – 16 bits. This gives 65,536 hosts.

**Class C:** NetID – 21 bits. This gives 2,097,152 networks.

HostID – 8 bits. This gives 256 hosts.

### Activity 11.6: IP address interpretation

130 is equal to 10000010. Therefore a Class B network (indicated by the leading 10).

4 is equal to 00000100

0 is equal to 00000000

0 is equal to 00000000

Put the binary numbers in a block diagram showing NetID and HostID. Here the last two octets represent the HostID.

### Activity 11.7: IP address with subnet

For a hint on how to tackle this task, refer to Figure 11.13 and the associated text.

# CHAPTER 12

# Routers, satellites and security

## OVERVIEW

The transmission of data between geographically remote computers can be achieved by use of, for example, trans-oceanic undersea cables, or through the use of satellites. We begin this chapter by looking at geostationary and low-earth-orbit satellite systems. Additionally, we consider issues that relate to the secure transfer of data between source and destination computers. Here we introduce symmetric and public key encryption techniques.

| Learning outcomes | On completion of this chapter you should be able to: |
| --- | --- |

- Outline basic concepts in relation to the functionality of routers

- Discuss IRP and ERP techniques

- Describe geostationary (geosynchronous) satellite systems

- Describe the low-earth-orbit (LEO) satellite technique

- Discuss basic concepts relating to cryptography

- Distinguish between public key and symmetric key cryptography.

## 12.1 Introduction

In this final chapter we discuss several topics relating to networking and computer communications. We begin by extending previous discussion in relation to the operation of routers and briefly describe the use of interior and exterior router protocols (IRPs and ERPs). In Section 12.3 we turn our attention to satellite communications and begin by considering the use of geostationary (geosynchronous) satellites. These rotate with a period of 24 hours and so by positioning these satellites in an 'equatorial orbit', they remain (relative to the Earth) in a fixed position in the sky. Subsequently, we consider an alternative approach in which a number of satellites are located in a 'low-earth-orbit' and therefore complete each orbit in less than 24 hours.

In Section 12.4, we briefly introduce cryptography techniques that are used in order to ensure that (in principle at least) transmissions between computer systems cannot be understood by unauthorised third parties. Here, we describe the 'Caesar cypher' and 'symmetric key' cryptography techniques. Finally, in Section 12.5 we briefly outline the powerful 'public key' encryption approach.

## 12.2 Routers in networks

As discussed in Chapter 11, routers are devices connecting two or more networks. When routers receive data packets, routing decisions to steer the packets to their final destination have to be made based on network protocol information and on a knowledge of the topology and ever-changing traffic conditions. Such information is contained in routing tables that can be updated either manually or automatically. Additionally, routers maintain ARP (address resolution protocol) tables so as to match MAC to IP addresses for all the networks to which they are attached.

In Figure 12.1 we illustrate two routers that connect two LANs via a WAN 'cloud' and indicate the manner in which data packets are transmitted between devices that are located on different networks. Suppose that Node A on LAN 1 has a IP datagram which is to be transmitted to Node B on LAN 2:

- This includes the IP address of Node B
- The IP software in Node A recognises that Node B is on a different network
- The datagram is therefore sent to Router X:
    - the IP passes the datagram down to the LLC sublayer with instructions to send to Router X
    - the LLC passes these instructions down to the MAC sublayer
    - the MAC sublayer adds the MAC address of Router X
- It is then transmitted through LAN 1 and includes:
    - data from the layers above TCP
    - the TCP header, IP header, LLC header and MAC header and trailer
- It reaches Router X:
    - this removes the MAC and LLC fields and analyses the IP field to determine the final destination of data

- As Node B resides on a different network that is reached via Router Y, Router X has to make a decision as how to deliver the packet:
  - it constructs a new datagram by appending the address of Router Y to the original IP data unit
  - it appends the MAC address of Router Y and then sends it to Router Y
- Once it arrives at Router (Y):
  - the header is removed and the router establishes that the datagram is destined for Node B, which resides on LAN 2
  - as LAN 2 is directly connected to Router Y, the latter constructs a packet that contains the MAC and IP addresses of Node B and sends it over LAN 2. When it finally arrives at device B, both MAC and IP fields are removed.

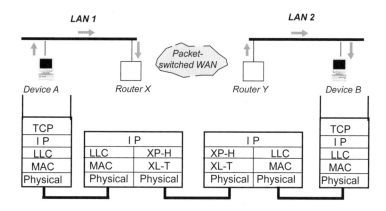

**Figure 12.1:** Router operation. Note XP-H and XL-T denote encapsulation for transmission across the interconnecting network (X.25). Details of this process need not concern us here.

## 12.2 The process of routing

As we have seen, routers are responsible for steering packets across various networks, and so to their final destination. A router makes routing decisions based on a knowledge of the topologies and conditions of the networks. This is achieved by examining incoming packets and making path selections based on information stored in the router's routing table.

In simple networks, a fixed routing scheme (i.e. static) is often appropriate. However, for more complex networks, dynamic routing tables are needed. This enables:

- Avoidance of failed sections of networks
- Avoidance of network segments that are congested with traffic.

Dynamic routing requires the exchange of routing information via the use of special-purpose protocols. These protocols are used to exchange routing tables and share routing information regularly. The information includes:

- Information concerning which networks can be accessed by which routes
- Information on the transmission delays associated with different routes.

Routing protocols enable routers to internally create a map of the accessibility of the Internet. These maps become part of each router's routing table. The two main routing protocols are the interior router protocol (IRP)/interior gateway protocol (IGP), and the exterior router protocol (ERP)/exterior gateway protocol (EGP). The main goals of routing protocols are:

- To dynamically store in the routing table the routes to all subnets in the network
- To determine the best possible (least cost) path (in principle)
- To exclude any invalid route from a routing table
- To replace any lost routes with a possible best route.

## *IRPs/IGPs*

These are used to exchange routing information within an autonomous network system (see Figure 12.2), e.g. within a single network that is divided into subnets.

An autonomous network system is signified by the following:

- It consists of a number of routers exchanging routing information through the application of a shared routing protocol
- The routers and networks are managed by a single organisation
- There exists a path between any two pairs of nodes – except at times of failure.

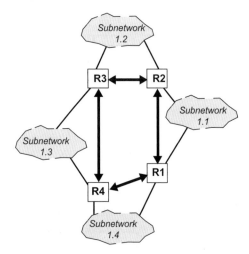

**Figure 12.2:** Routing in an autonomous network system

IRPs construct quite detailed maps of the interconnection of routers within the autonomous network. This is essential for verifying the optimum cost-effective path from a particular router to any network within the system.

### Routing information protocol (RIP)

One of the most common IRPs is the routing information protocol (RIP). This protocol is used to move routing information between routers that are located on the same network, and allows the routers to update their routing tables at programmable frequencies – typically, every thirty seconds. The mechanism by which routers decide what path will be used to send data is based on a concept referred to as the 'distance-vector' technique.

It accomplishes a number of tasks – for example:

- To indicate directly connected routers
- To indicate routing updates
- To learn about new route updates
- To provide topology information
- To provide information about route performance.

RIP simplifies the routing process and calculates the distance travelled by data packets to a destination device by assuming that:

- Whenever data passes through a router it is said to have travelled 'one hop'
- A path with a 'hop count' of three indicates that data would have to pass through three routers before it reaches its final destination.  This is illustrated in Figure 12.3 – for a transmission from Subnet 1 to Subnet 8.

RIP creates a table that includes at least three columns, which indicate the network ID, cost and next hop.  The network ID determines the final destination, the cost determines the number of hops that are required to reach to the destination and next hop indicates the next router.

## Open shortest path first (OSPF)

This represents another router internal protocol (RIP).  It is used in determining the optimum cost-effective path to a destination located in an autonomous network system by means of several criteria:

- **Route speed**
- **Reliability**
- **Traffic conditions**
- **Security.**

Each router maintains descriptions of the state of local links and transmits updated information regularly to other routers within the system.  A database is created for each router, which includes information about a router's neighbouring routers.

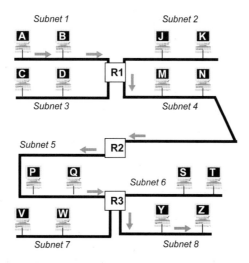

**Figure 12.3:** The use of RIP

### *ERPs/EGPs*

This is used to exchange routing information between routers in different autonomous network systems, as illustrated in Figure 12.4. ERP supports the exchange of a summary of information on reachability between separate autonomous systems. The limited nature of information involved makes ERPs simpler than IRPs. The protocol allows the multiple routers situated in different autonomous systems to cooperate with each other for the sake of exchanging routing information. The protocol sends a message to determine neighbour reachability and network reachability. When two routers are situated in two different autonomous systems the protocol 'acquires' the neighbour in order to send information. This is achieved by sending a request to the neighbouring router. The neighbour can accept or refuse the request depending on its own network traffic or congestion. Once this neighbour acquisition is accomplished then the neighbour reachability phase knows the relationship between two autonomous network systems. The network reachability phase supplies the network address to access the particular network. This is accomplished by the routers that maintain a database of all routes to a network. Databases are updated regularly by the routers.

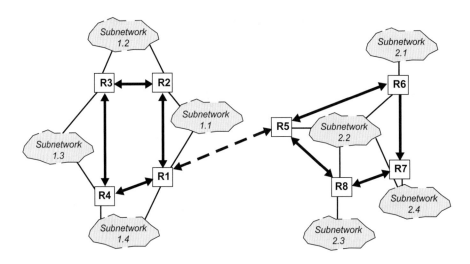

**R1 ... 8: Routers**

**Figure 12.4:** Routing between autonomous network systems

**Routing**

Briefly answer each of the following:

a) Why is a dynamic routing required in a complex network?

b) What are routing protocols?

c) What is the main difference between IRPs and ERPs?

d) What does an RIP do?

e) What concept do routers use in selecting a path for sending data?

*Activity 12.1*

# 12.3 Satellite communications

The first communications satellite was named Telstar and was launched in 1962. This was a 'geostationary' ('geosynchronous') satellite – meaning that its period of rotation was 24 hours. Thus Telstar rotated at the same rate as the Earth and so maintained a fixed location in the sky (which was over the mid-Atlantic). Consequently, Telstar was used to relay signals between the US and Europe.

A communications satellite is able to relay signals – see Figure 12.5. The signal transmitted from the Earth's surface is called the 'uplink' signal and the signal transmitted from the satellite back to the Earth's surface is the 'downlink' signal. So as to avoid cross-interference, the uplink and downlink signals are transmitted at different frequencies.

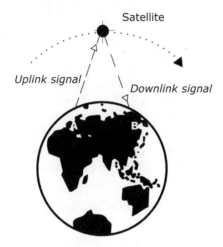

**Figure 12.5:** Signals relayed by a satellite

Satellites follow paths (tracks) indicated by Kepler's Laws and Newtonian Mechanics. The gravitational force of attraction (F) between two objects (in this case the Earth (of mass $M_e$) and a satellite (of mass $M_s$)) is given by Kepler's Law:

$$F = \frac{GM_e M_s}{r^2}$$

**Equation 12.1**

where r represents the distance between the centre of the Earth and the satellite and G is the 'Universal Gravitational Constant' ~ $6.7 \times 10^{-11}$N.m².Kg⁻². This provides the force that is needed to ensure that the satellite moves in a circular (or elliptical) path. For the simpler case of a circular orbit (i.e. ignoring the elliptical orbit), we can write:

$$F = \frac{GM_e M_s}{r^2} = M_s \omega^2 r$$

**Equation 12.2**

... where the right-hand term represents the centripetal force for circular motion and $\omega$ is the angular velocity ($\omega = 2\pi/T$ (T is the period of rotation)). Rearranging this expression yields:

$$r = \left( \frac{GM_e T^2}{4\pi^2} \right)^{1/3}$$

**Equation 12.3**

### The geostationary orbit

Using Equation 12.3 and the following data, calculate the approximate altitude above the Earth's surface of a satellite which follows a circular geostationary orbit.

$G \sim 6.7 \times 10^{-11} N.m^2.Kg^{-2}$

Mass of the Earth $\sim 6 \times 10^{24}$ Kg

Radius of the Earth $\sim 6.4 \times 10^6$ m

- Note: Inspection of Equation 12.3 indicates that the radius of orbit is linked to the period of orbit. Thus all satellites (in circular motion) that orbit the Earth with a period of 24 hours are at the same altitude. This point is commonly overlooked by students. If we increase or decrease the radius of orbit, then the period will change. For ease of calculation, the values given in Activity 12.2 are approximated. Using more exact values gives, for a geostationary satellite, a height of orbit (over the Equator) of 35,700km.

Geostationary satellites are important because they remain at a fixed point in the sky. (If you access satellite TV, you adjust your satellite dish to point to a particular satellite. Subsequently, since the position of the satellite is fixed you need not reposition the satellite dish.) Various strengths and weaknesses of the geostationary approach are summarised below:

- High launch costs – a considerable amount of energy is required to place a satellite into a geostationary orbit

- All satellites operate in extremely harsh conditions. As a consequence, they must employ highly rugged technologies. Repair costs are very high and so too are the costs associated with implementing hardware upgrades

- Signals broadcast from satellites can be easily intercepted and this can lead to security problems

- Geostationary satellites are in a high-earth-orbit and are therefore able to receive and transmit signals from and to a large area of the Earth's surface. This area is referred to as the satellite's 'footprint'. In principle a single geostationary satellite can communicate with nearly 1/3 of the Earth's surface. In practice, the footprint is somewhat more limited

- As with all radio/microwave transmission links, signals are subjected to interference from a variety of sources

- There is a significant propagation delay associated with the relaying of signals via a geostationary satellite. These are caused by the transmission time to and from the satellite.

### Satellite propagation delay

Estimate the minimum propagation delay associated with a signal that is relayed by a satellite in geostationary orbit. (You may assume that the signal travels at the speed of light ($\sim 3 \times 10^8 m.s^{-1}$) and that the satellite relays the signal instantaneously.)

Activity 12.4

### Altitude of a geostationary satellite

So as to gain a better appreciation of the height of a geostationary satellite above the surface of the Earth, draw a scale drawing showing the Earth (as a circle of appropriate radius) and a circular satellite track. Indicate on your diagram the approximate extent of the satellites 'footprint'.

As their name implies, low-earth-orbit (LEO) satellites circle the Earth at a relatively low height and can be put into orbit more cheaply than the geostationary satellites referred to earlier. Additionally, access to the LEO satellites for maintenance and/or retrieval is also simplified. Such satellites do not maintain a fixed position in the sky but as with the Moon (which is a high orbit satellite) rise, pass across the sky and sink below the horizon. Inspection of Equation 12.3 indicates that if we reduce the *radius* of a satellite's orbit then there must also be a reduction in its *period* of satellite rotation. In fact the velocity of an LEO satellite is greater than that of a geostationary satellite (this is perhaps somewhat non-intuitive).

Ground stations must track LEO satellites – the satellite dish moving so as to follow the position of the satellite. Because of the motion of the satellite, a single ground station is able to communicate with an LEO satellite for a limited period of time during each of its orbits. Effective use of an LEO satellite may therefore require the use of a number of ground stations distributed along its orbital track.

In the 1990s, a consortium led by Motorola conceived and pioneered an LEO global communications network known as the 'Iridium Project'. Initially, some 77 satellites were to be launched (in circular Polar orbits) – however, the number was subsequently reduced to 66. (Iridium is the 77th element in the Periodic Table – hence the use of this name for the original project.) The objective was to enable global communications by means of hand-held devices that would enable users to establish bi-directional communications with an LEO satellite (the number, positioning and orbits of the satellites ensures that there is always at least one satellite in 'line of site' with a user – disregarding mountainous areas, etc.). Communications are then relayed (routed) between LEO satellites until they arrive at a satellite which is in a suitable location to establish the downlink transmission. Unfortunately, the original Iridium project was ill-fated and went into bankruptcy in 1999. However, the service recommenced in 2001. Globalstar and Teledesic provide two other examples of projects involving the use of LEO satellites for global networking.

Activity 12.5

### Iridium satellites

Iridium satellites are located at an altitude of 750km. So as to most readily compare this orbit with that used by geostationary satellites, illustrate the track of an Iridium satellite on the scaled diagram that you produced for Activity 12.4.

## 12.4 Cryptography

Here, and in the next section, we focus upon security issues in relation to the transmission of data across a network. Since we assume that any physical medium, such as cable, radio transmission, cannot be fully protected, cryptography techniques are used to ensure that transmitted data is meaningless to all but the intended recipient.

The term 'plain text' is used when referring to a message that is to be transmitted. Encryption is used to generate the secret message (called the 'cipher text') and decryption returns the cipher text to plain text – see Figure 12.6.

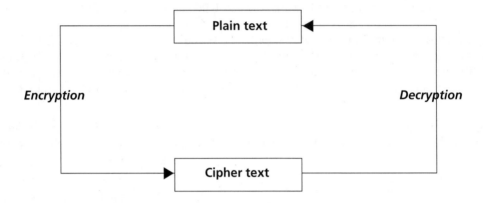

**Figure 12.6:** The processes of encryption and decryption

One of the oldest approaches to cryptography is know as the Caesar cipher – also known as the mono-alphabetic cipher. This is said to have been used by Julius Caesar – some two thousand years ago! The method provides only rudimentary security and is readily understood by means of a simple example.

Suppose that Caesar wished to encrypt the phrase: 'Let the invasion of Britain begin!'

He may chose to use an encryption key of, say 2, – meaning that each letter in the plain text is replaced with a letter appearing two places further along in the alphabet. In this way, 'a' becomes 'c', 'b' becomes 'd', etc. At the end of the alphabet, 'y' would become 'a' and 'z' becomes 'b' – i.e. 'wrap around' is used. The plain text and cipher text are given in Figure 12.7.

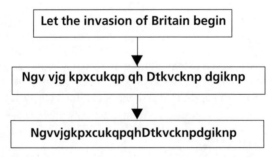

**Figure 12.7:** The use of the Caesar cipher with an encryption key of two. In the lower box, the cipher text is further complicated by the removal of spaces – additionally, spaces could be inserted at random intervals

### The decryption process using the Caesar cipher

Decrypt the two following messages (which have been encrypted using the Caesar cipher). Note the key used for each message is different. Hint: the value of the encryption key is less than 5.

Wklv lv wkh odvw fkdswhu

Gv vx dtwvg

### The Caesar cipher

Identify two weaknesses associated with the Caesar cipher.

The Caesar cipher provides us with an elementary example of the 'symmetric key' encryption approach. Here, the same key is used for both the encryption and decryption processes. Thus, in the case of computer communications, the symmetric key approach necessitates both the transmitting and receiving nodes having access to the key. Secure key distribution denotes an essential weakness. In, for example, World War II, codebooks were distributed to allow the encryption and decryption of messages. However, if one of these codebooks fell into the hands of the enemy, they would then be able to decrypt coded communications. The use of a key that can have an enormous range of values and which can be protected is an essential part of today's computer communications. In the next section, we briefly examine a process called 'public key' encryption. This circumvents the need for distribution of the decryption key.

## 12.5 Public key encryption

So as to most readily understand this technique, let's consider a simple example in which a secure (secret) message is to be sent between two computers (i.e. from Node A to Node B). Node A will begin by transmitting a message to Node B indicating the wish to make an encrypted transmission. Node B will process the request by generating some numbers, and undertaking some computation on these numbers. As a result of this computational process, two sets of numbers are produced. One of these sets of numbers will then be transmitted to Node A – this is called the 'public key', and will be used by Node A for the encryption process. Notice that since these numbers have been transmitted across the network, we cannot be sure that others using the network do not in some way gain access to them. One merit of this technique is that we don't care. Let anybody see the public key numbers – it doesn't make any difference! The other set of numbers are referred to as the 'private key', and these numbers will stay on Node B – they are retained so that nobody else can gain access to them.

Going back to the original scenario – Node A wishes to send a secret message to Node B. Once Node A has indicated that it wishes to make an encrypted transmission, Node B generates a private and a public key. The public key is sent to Node A, and is then used by the encryption algorithm housed on Node A to encrypt the message. Once encrypted, the message is sent across the network as cipher text to Node B.

Node B uses the private key (which nobody has seen) to undertake the decryption process. Thus, the public key is used for encryption by Node A, and the private key is used for decryption by the recipient – Node B. The private key has never been transmitted across the network, and so nobody other than Node B is able (in principle) to undertake the decryption process. It's interesting to note that both the public key and the algorithm that Node A uses for message encryption can be known by anybody. This raises one potential problem – authentification. If anybody else has intercepted the public key, they could pretend to be Node A and so send a false message. However, techniques have been developed to deal with this problem.

The public key technique is summarised in Figure 12.8.

---

**Node A indicates to Node B that it wishes to make a secure transmission using the 'public key' technique.**

**Node B generates two sets of numbers – we will call these Set $\alpha$ and Set $\beta$. Set $\alpha$ will correspond to the 'public key' and Set $\beta$ to the 'private key'.**

**The 'public key' (number set $\alpha$) is transmitted to Node A.**

**Node A uses these numbers as an input to the encryption algorithm and encrypts the message.**

**The encrypted message is sent to Node B.**

**The encrypted message is sent to Node B.**

**Node B uses the 'private key' (number set $\beta$) to decrypt the message.**

---

**Figure 12.8:** The public key technique. In this example, Node A wishes to make a secure (secret) transmission to Node B.

For our current purposes, it is not necessary to understand the mathematics used in the generation of the two sets of numbers. (For those interested in looking into this process an excellent account is provided in: *Computer Networking: A Top-Down Approach Featuring the Internet* (3rd Edition) by James F Kurose and Keith W Ross.) However, it is instructive to briefly mention two issues that underpin the encryption/decryption processes.

Firstly, a mathematical function and its inverse are often not equally complex. Take, for example, the determination of the prime factors of a number (for example, the prime factors of 6 are 3 and 2). When we are dealing with large numbers, the determination of prime factors is a difficult undertaking (as it is computationally expensive). On the other hand, once we have found the prime factors of a number it is very easy to verify via multiplication that we have obtained the correct result. In short, factoring a number and identifying that the factors are correct represent two processes that are not equal in computational complexity.

### Activity 12.8

### Prime factors

As indicated above, the determination of the prime factors of a number becomes ever-more difficult as the size of the number increases. However, once we have obtained the prime factors, the process of verifying their validity is trivial. By way of a simple example, determine the prime factors of 210 and verify the answer that you have obtained.

A second, technique used in the encryption process makes use of 'mod' arithmetic. For example, $x$ *mod* $y$ is the integer *remainder* when $x$ is divided by $y$. Thus, 7 mod 3 = 1, 8 mod 3 = 2. When we carry out a division process on a calculator, the calculator shows the fractional remainder expressed as a decimal value. However, in the case of the mathematical expression 'mod', we are interested in the remainder being expressed as an integer. As a further example: consider 100 mod 24. We know that there are four 24s in a 100, leaving a remainder of 4. This remainder of 4 is the result of the mod operation. When a secure message is transmitted between two computers, the transmission comprises integer remainders resulting from 'mod' operations. However, many combinations of nominator and denominator can give rise to the same integer remainder. For example, 100 mod 24 is 4 – but 18 mod 7 *also* equals 4. Therefore, when we try to find the original message from the information that is transmitted across the network, each transmitted value can map on to a great range of possible plain text letters. Given the very large numbers that are used in the encryption process, if we don't have access to the private key, determination of the message content is extremely difficult.

The public key encryption/decryption processes require significant computation and although this approach gives great security, it may not be appropriate when large amounts of data are involved (especially in the case of real-time applications). On the other hand, although the symmetric key encryption technique that we have previously considered is relatively computationally inexpensive, it suffers from the weakness of secure key distribution – how do we distribute keys in such a way that unauthorised parties cannot gain access to them? One approach is to employ the public key technique for the distribution of the keys used for symmetric key cryptography. In this way:

- By employing public key encryption techniques for key encryption, we ensure that the keys are distributed in a secure manner
- We employ symmetric key techniques for file (message) encryption. Consequently, we avoid the computational overheads associated with the application of public key encryption/ decryption to large volumes of data.

## 12.6 Summary

In this final chapter, we have considered several topics that relate to computer communications. Discussion opened with a brief description of the operation of routers for the transfer of messages between computers. Here, we discussed a router's ability to make decisions upon the direction in which individual datagrams should be forwarded. Such decisions are based on the most cost-effective route to a destination and this can take into account continuously changing traffic densities (network congestion) and the failure of network segments.

Brief discussion has been presented upon the use of satellite communication techniques and we have distinguished between geostationary (geosynchronous) satellites (which co-rotate with the Earth and so maintain a fixed position in the sky) and low-earth-orbit satellites whose position in the sky (relative to the Earth) continually changes. Although there are sound advantages associated with the use of geostationary satellites there are also a number of difficulties. These include high launch costs, the difficulty of repair and the transmission latency that results from the large distance over which transmissions must travel. This latency can be particularly problematic in, for example, real-time applications (e.g. the carrying out of remote surgery or the remote control of robotic systems).

Finally, we have outlined several issues relating to cryptography and have considered two general techniques – symmetric key and public key encryption. As discussed, the former relies on the distribution of keys between communicating entities and this must be accomplished in such a way that they cannot be intercepted by unauthorised parties. In contrast, in the case of the public key encryption technique, the key used to decrypt a message is never transmitted and therefore is (in principle) secure. However, it is important to remember that no technique is one hundred per cent secure – secure message transmission can never be guaranteed!

## 12.7 Review questions

**Question 12.1** Choose the correct answer from the list:

1. In _____ routing, decisions are made 'instantly' regarding the possible paths.

  a. static                        b. dynamic

  c. hybrid                      d. none of the above.

2. IRPs are used to exchange routing information within a(n) _____ system.

  a. autonomous network          b. different network

  c. heterogenous network         d. none of the above.

3. In an autonomous network system networks are managed by _____ organisation(s)

  a. multiple                    b. single

  c. different types of            d. none of the above.

4. IRP defines _____ paths.

  a. longest                              b. cost-effective

  c. shortest                             d. none of the above.

5. The mechanism of IRP is based on the _____ concept.

  a. shortest-path                        b. longest-path

  c. distance-vector                      d. none of the above.

6. IRP counts the number of _____ that must be made.

  a. hops                                 b. network paths

  c. subnets                              d. none of the above.

7. An IRP table consists of at least _____ column(s).

  a. one                                  b. two

  c. three                                d. none of the above.

8. Shortest path first protocol is based on the_____ concept.

  a. distance-vector                      b. longest path

  c. tree structure                       d. none of the above.

9. Shortest path first calculates the _____ to reach a destination.

  a. number of routers                    b. cumulative cost

  c. number of network paths              d. none of the above.

**Question 12.2** State two strengths and two weaknesses associated with the geostationary satellite technique.

**Question 12.3** State two strengths and two weaknesses associated with the low-earth-orbit satellite technique.

**Question 12.4** Using the Caesar cipher, encrypt the words 'Hello World'. You should use a key of 1.

**Question 12.5** What is meant by the term 'plain text'?

**Question 12.6** State two essential weaknesses associated with the Caesar cipher.

**Question 12.7** State one weakness associated with symmetric key encryption. How may this be overcome?

**Question 12.8** What is the process of 'authentification'?

**Question 12.9** State one major strength of public key encryption.

## 12.9 Feedback on activities

### Activity 12.1: Routing

a) To avoid non-operational sections of networks and those with high traffic congestion.

b) Special-purpose protocols that are used to exchange routing tables and share routing information.

c) IRPs are used within a particular network system while ERPs are used between different network systems.

d) It is used in moving routing information between routers that are located on the same network.

e) They use the distance-vector concept. This calculates the distance travelled by data to reach its destination by counting the number of routers in a transmission path.

### Activity 12.2: The geostationary orbit

Using Equation 12.3, we obtain $42.4 \times 10^6$m (remember to convert T into seconds (i.e. T=24x60x60)). So as to obtain the approximate height above the Earth's surface we now subtract the radius of the Earth. This gives a height of ~ 36,000km (approximately 22,300 miles above the Earth's surface).

### Activity 12.3: Satellite propagation delay

The minimum delay would occur when the signal travels the shortest distance – i.e. up to and down from a satellite that is directly overhead. From previous discussion this distance is ~35,700km (i.e. $35.7 \times 10^6$m). Using 'speed equals distance travelled divided by time taken', we obtain:

$$Time = \frac{35.7 x 10^6 x 2}{3 x 10^8}$$

The factor of two accounts for the signal travelling to and from the satellite. Thus the propagation time is ~ 0.2 seconds. In the case that we implement a communications link using such a satellite and that employs a two-way hand-shaking protocol, a transmission would not be acknowledged in less than 0.4 seconds after it had been transmitted.

**Activity 12.4:  Altitude of a geostationary satellite**

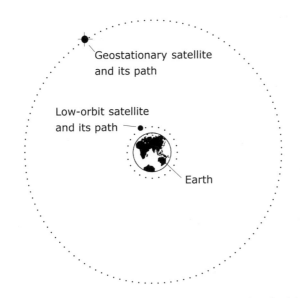

**Figure 12.9:** A scale drawing showing the height of orbit of a geostationary satellite relative to the radius of the Earth

**Activity 12.5:  Iridium satellites**

No feedback is necessary.

**Activity 12.6:  The decryption process using the Caesar cipher.**

First line: 'This is the last chapter'

Second line: 'Et tu brute'

**Activity 12.7:  The Caesar cipher**

The Caesar cipher is not a very secure way of transmitting secret messages.  One issue concerns the frequency of usage of characters in the alphabet when we write.  Some letters are used more frequently than others, and with this in mind the decryption process can be made somewhat easier.  (The most commonly used letters in the English language are e, t, o, a and n.)   Also, the Caesar cipher does not permit the usage of many different keys.  The key is the information that we employ during the encryption and decryption process.  In the case that we have an alphabet comprising 26 letters, then there are only 25 different keys.

**Activity 12.8:  Prime factors**

The prime factors of 210 are 2, 3, 5 and 7.

# Answers to review questions

# Chapter 1

## Question 1.1

A computer is able to store data/information, and execute a series of instructions in sequence by selection and by iteration.

## Question 1.2

This means that signals within a computer can only take on certain states. Since today's computers operate in binary, signals are only able to take on one of two states (zero and one).

## Question 1.3

The base 10 number 21 corresponds to the binary number 10101. The binary number 1001 corresponds to 9 in base 10. Note that the terms 'binary' and 'base 2' are interchangeable and have the same meaning. Similarly, the terms 'base 10' and 'decimal number base' have the same meaning.

## Question 1.4

Instructions are stored in the computer's memory and are represented as numerical codes.

## Question 1.5

(a) 16

(b) Two bytes represent 16 bits. These can take on 65,536 values.

## Question 1.6

The abbreviation CPU stands for central processing unit. The CPU in the modern computer takes the form of a silicon chip upon which, typically, millions of transistors are fabricated. The CPU is responsible for controlling the computer hardware, and for executing program instructions. It is, as the name implies, the central part of the computer. It is often simply referred to as the 'processor'.

## Question 1.7

11110

## Question 1.8

A general-purpose programmable machine is a machine that can be used to carry out a wide range of different tasks. It can be told to do a specific task by the means of a computer program.

# Chapter 2

### Question 2.1

The small circle indicates that the gate has an inverting function.  For example, the NAND gate has such a symbol and when both inputs are a logic high, the output is a logic low.  Conversely, when both inputs are a logic low, the output is a logic high.

### Question 2.2

The output from a NAND gate is a logic high when either or both inputs are a logic low – 'any low gives a high'.

### Question 2.3

When the input(s) applied to a logic gate is changed, it takes a finite time for the gate to respond and produce a new output.  The time that it takes for this to occur is referred to as the gate's 'propagation delay'.  Typical propagation delays for gates are of the order of a few nanoseconds.

### Question 2.4

In the case of combinational logic the logic states of a circuit's output are defined entirely by the combination of inputs applied to the circuit.  Thus, a certain combination of input values will always produce the same output from the circuit.  This contrasts with sequential logic circuits, in which the output is determined not only by the input values, but also by the circuit's previous state.

### Question 2.5

The RS bistable is an example of a sequential logic circuit.

### Question 2.6

Registers are used within a computer's processor and also within various integrated circuits found within computers.  They provide a means of storing strings of binary digits.  In terms of the registers located within the processor, they support the temporary storage of binary values.  These values may be used to control the operation of the processor or for arithmetic and logical operations.  Since the registers are located on the processor chip, they are able to operate at very high speed.  Typically, processors are equipped with small numbers of registers ranging from less than ten, through to some tens of registers.

### Question 2.7

The rising edge of a digital waveform occurs when the waveform changes state from a logic low to a logic high.  This contrasts with the falling edge of the waveform, which corresponds to the transition from a logic high to a logic low.

### Question 2.8

Writing out long strings of binary numbers is tedious and prone to error.  Furthermore, it is difficult to vocally express long strings of bits.  Whilst binary is the language of the machine, it is certainly not a friendly number base as far as the human is concerned.  However, we can easily represent binary numbers in higher number bases.  Traditionally, base 8 was commonly employed for this purpose (base 8 is also referred to as octal).  However hexadecimal (base 16) is now widely used.  In the case of base 16 we make use of our ten numeric symbols (0 through to 9), together with the letters A through to F.

# Chapter 3

### Question 3.1

The processor uses the address bus to indicate the address of a memory location to which it wishes to perform a read or write operation. Signal flow on the address bus is uni-directional. The data bus supports the transfer of instructions and data to and from memory (and other devices such as integrated circuits that support input and output). The data bus is bi-directional.

### Question 3.2

An assembler is a special program that is able to convert programs that are written in assembly language into machine code.

### Question 3.3

10 μs equals 10,000 nanoseconds.

### Question 3.4

The contents of an EPROM are erased by shining ultraviolet (UV) light through a transparent quartz window) this is located directly above the silicon chip). A quartz window is used (rather than conventional glass) as ordinary glass exhibits poor transmission characteristics to UV light.

### Question 3.5

The term 'op-code' refers to a machine code (or assembly language) instruction. It is an abbreviation for 'operation code' and dates back to the early days of computing. Some op-codes are 'self-contained' and others require additional information. This additional information is referred to as the operand. For example, consider an instruction that indicates that a certain numerical value is to be loaded into a register. Here, the op-code takes the form of the load instruction and the operand is the numerical value that is to be inserted into the register.

### Question 3.6

The program counter (PC) is a register within the processor that contains the address of the instruction that is currently being executed (i.e. the PC keeps track of program execution). If the contents of the PC are corrupted, the processor would fail in its execution of a program.

### Question 3.7

The examination of programs in execution reveals that if an instruction has been recently executed by the processor, then it is likely that it will be executed again in the near future. The transfer of groups of instructions from main memory to a local high-speed cache memory takes advantage of this principle. Improvements in performance are gained on a statistical basis.

### Question 3.8

*Advantage:* Each storage cell can be constructed using a single active component and capacitor.  This compares to the 4 to 6 active components used in the implementation of an SRAM cell.  This reduces the cost per unit of storage capacity.

*Disadvantage:* The charge stored in each SRAM cell gradually drains away and this results in a loss of cell content (i.e.  the cell gradually 'forgets' the bit value stored in it).  As a consequence, cells must be regularly 'refreshed'; this process restores the level of charge stored in each cell.  This requires additional circuitry and increases complexity.

### Question 3.9

This is generally used to indicate that the numerical value immediately following the $ symbol is to be interpreted as a hexadecimal (base 16) value.

### Question 3.10

Electrically Erasable Programmable Read Only Memory.

# Chapter 4

## Question 4.1

001100

## Question 4.2

This refers to the power to which a number is raised. For example, in the case of 43, the exponent is 3.

## Question 4.3

This results in a return to the original answer. For example, consider the binary number 10010. The 2s complement of this is 01110. Taking the 2s complement of this number gives 10010 – i.e. the original number.

## Question 4.4

By using the 2s complement approach to represent negative integers, it is possible to perform subtraction operations using the same hardware that is employed for addition. This simplifies hardware design.

## Question 4.5

The processor completes the execution of the current instruction. The contents of the processor's registers are saved in a designated area of memory (RAM). Control is passed to the interrupt service routine.

## Question 4.6

NMI: Non-maskable interrupt

## Question 4.7

Polling refers to the processor regularly reading the contents of one or more addresses to determine whether some event has occurred. For example, the pressing of a switch may modify the binary value stored at a particular location within the address space. The processor may continually read the contents of this address to determine whether the switch has been pressed.

## Question 4.8

A maskable interrupt may be disabled, whereas a non-maskable interrupt cannot be disabled. Hence the latter are generally used when dealing with particularly critical situations.

## Question 4.9

ASCII: American Standard Code for Information Exchange
EBCDIC: Extended Binary Coded Decimal Interchange Code.

## Question 4.10

Add the hexadecimal value 20: for example, 'A' is represented as 41 (hex) and 'a' as 61 (hex). The addition of the binary number 00100000 (20 (hex)) converts between these two symbol codes.

# Chapter 5

### Question 5.1

The spacing between the read/write heads and the surface of the disk is very close. The read/write head literally flies across the surface of the disk and is separated from it only by an extremely thin layer of air. Small particles of dust, smoke particles, and even fingerprints can disturb the transit of the head with respect to the disk. The presence of such material can cause catastrophic failure of the hard disk.

### Question 5.2

Normally, the hard disk provides the largest storage capacity and offers the highest read/write speed. The floppy disk provides the smallest storage capacity and supports the lowest read/write speed. It should be noted that for the CD-ROM, the read speed is greater than the write speed.

### Question 5.3

Increasing the rotational speed of a hard disk reduces the rotational latency. This is one of the time components that constitute the overall latency of the disk in response to read or write operations. It corresponds to the time that must elapse in order that a disk rotates so that the desired sector passes beneath the read/write head.

### Question 5.4

A hard disk comprises a set of platters. Each platter stores data along a series of concentric tracks. A set of read/write heads are arranged such that a separate head is used to read or write data to each surface of each platter. Thus in the case that a hard disk employs four platters, eight read/write heads would be used. The heads are driven by a common actuator such that they all lie at the same radial distance from the disk's axis of rotation and in this way each is able to simultaneously read or write to tracks of the same radius. A set of tracks that are of the same radius is referred to as a cylinder. Each cylinder is identified by a unique 'cylinder number'.

### Question 5.5

Data can be simultaneously written to or read from the surfaces of each platter. Therefore, read/write operations occur in parallel across a number of read/write heads. This increases the throughput and thereby the performance of this disk drive. For example, if we employ four platters, we would expect the drive to exhibit four times the performance that we would obtain from an equivalent disk that used a single platter.

### Question 5.6

Individual bits are not written to or read from a disk. In fact, groups of bits are stored or accessed. The smallest group of bits that can be written to or read from a disk is referred to as a 'block'. A block is also frequently referred to as a sector and typically comprises some hundreds of bytes.

### Question 5.7

This term refers to the cooperation that exists between a transmitter and receiver when passing data using the asynchronous communication technique. In brief, a group of data bits are transmitted and when these arrive at the receiving end of the data transfer link (and have been suitably dealt with), the receiver returns an acknowledgement signal. Upon receipt of this signal, the transmitter may send a further group of data bits. This type of protocol is referred to as 'hand-shaking'.

### Question 5.8

Parallel transmission: a group of bits are sent at the same time – each along a separate connection (e.g. wire). Serial transmission: a group of bits are sent one after another by using the same connection.

Since a parallel connection employs more wires (connections) than does the equivalent serial link, parallel interconnects are generally more expensive to implement. As a result, parallel data transfer links tend to be used for transmission over shorter distances.

### Question 5.9

In the case of synchronous transmission, both the transmitter and receiver employ a common clock for synchronisation (timing) purposes. In the case of asynchronous transmission, the transmitter and receiver employ separate clocks.

### Question 5.10

Consider two clock signals that are of the same frequency – as illustrated in Figure 5.15(a). In this illustration, the rising and falling edges of the signals occur at the same time – there is no phase shift. However, in Figure 5.15(b), although the signals are still identical in terms of frequency, their rising and falling edges are no longer coincident – one is shifted in phase relative to the other.

# Chapter 6

### Question 6.1

An analogue-to-digital converter (ADC) has a limited precision and is therefore only able to represent the input voltage with a finite range of output values. For example, a 12-bit ADC can represent the input voltage as one of 4,096 different values. Consequently, there is likely to be an error (or difference) between the actual voltage applied to the ADC and the binary representation of this voltage. This represents a source of error and is generally referred as 'quantisation error'. The quantisation error is actually the difference between the actual voltage applied to the ADC and the closest approximation that the ADC can make to this voltage.

### Question 6.2

The term 'batch processing' is used to describe a technique widely employed in the early days of computing. In this scenario, a computer user would submit a program on some form of storage media to a computer operator. The computer operator would run the program at some future time and return the results to the user. In later systems, the user would submit the program directly to the computer and execution would occur as and when time became available. The important point to note is that in this computing model, as far as the user is concerned there is no interaction with the computer during program execution. Today, interaction is an extremely important part of our interface with the computer.

### Question 6.3

The QWERTY keyboard layout is used widely in countries where English is the first language and indicates the order of six alphabetic keys on the keyboard. This layout was originally devised over a hundred years ago in connection with keyboards intended for use with mechanical typewriters. The keyboard layout was designed to reduce typing speeds by increasing the distance through which the fingers have to move when typing. In this way it was hoped to reduce the frequency with which mechanical typewriters jammed. Despite attempts that have been made to develop a better keyboard layout (which would actually increase typing speeds), this has been unsuccessful. There are a number of reasons for this, one of which is that there are too many people who are trained on the normal QWERTY keyboard and who are therefore reluctant to move to alternatives.

### Question 6.4

Movement of the mechanical mouse causes the rotation of a ball, which in turn rotates two wheels. These are arranged at right angles (orthogonal) to each other. As these wheels rotate, their movement is encoded electrically and transmitted to the computer. The non-mechanical mouse uses a special mouse-pad upon which vertical and horizontal lines are printed in two different colours. Optical sensors within the mouse are able to detect the passage of the mouse over these lines. As the mouse moves over the lines, signals are passed to the computer and in this way the computer is able to monitor the direction of mouse movement and the distance that it has travelled.

## Question 6.5

The name 'pixel' is an abbreviation for 'picture element' and is the fundamental 'element' from which images are generated on a computer display. A computer image is formed from a set of pixels that are illuminated (under computer control) in different colours and at different levels of brightness. Individual pixels may be seen by looking very closely at a computer monitor – a better view will be obtained if a magnifying glass is used.

## Question 6.6

The colour of each screen pixel is created by mixing together different amounts of the three primary colours (red, green and blue). Each electron beam is made responsible for the generation of one of these primary colours: thus, one electron beam generates shades of red; the next, shades of green; and the third, shades of blue. The three electron guns scan the screen together in a series of horizontal lines.

## Question 6.7

The shadow mask ensures that each of the three electron beams referred to in the previous review question can only excite a phosphor of a certain colour. This is achieved by defining the geometry by which the beams strike the phosphor dots that are printed onto the surface of the CRT screen.

## Question 6.8

n steps.

## Question 6.9

Periodic time equals the reciprocal of the frequency.
Thus periodic time = 1/20 = 0.05 seconds.

## Question 6.10

Using Ohm's Law: voltage = current x resistance. Thus voltage = 5x20 = 100 volts.

# Chapter 7

**Question 7.1**

[PC] ←[PC]+1

**Question 7.2**

The MBR interfaces the data bus with several sub-units within the CPU that deal with the processing of op-codes and operands.  Thus when data is to be written to memory, or when a read operation is performed, the MBR serves as a temporary buffer.

**Question 7.3**

The individual bits that comprise the CCR have different meanings and are set or reset according to the outcome of the last operation performed by the ALU.  When conditional branch operations are encountered (e.g. 'branch if zero' – meaning that the action taken depends on whether or not the outcome of the previous instruction that was executed was zero (or otherwise)), the CU will obtain this information from the CCR.

**Question 7.4**

This would result in a failure to return from the ISR – the return address (PC value) and the contents of the registers within the CPU prior to entry into the ISR would be lost.  Thus a return would not be possible.

**Question 7.5**

ALU←[Register X]

**Question 7.6**

A write operation.

**Question 7.7**

Yes – a full adder can be implemented using two half-adders and an OR gate.

**Question 7.8**

The contents of processor registers are saved on the stack.

**Question 7.9**

Last in, first out (LIFO).

**Question 7.10**

By placing the RTL statements on the same line and separating the statements by means of a ';'.

# Chapter 8

## Question 8.1

BIOS: Basic Input Output System.  This is the name given to a set of routines used to control the input and output of data.  One function of the BIOS is to perform the bootstrapping of the computer: loading key parts of the O/S from secondary storage into main memory.

## Question 8.2    For example:

File management

Provision of the user interface

Multi-tasking, etc.

## Question 8.3

Distributed systems can be defined as a collection of autonomous heterogeneous machines connected to each other and to the outside world via a network running distributed software, which may not be homogeneous.

## Question 8.4

It is possible – but not easy.  Reasoning: the O/S is simply a program so you could incorporate some of its functionality into your own program.  However, this would mean that your program is responsible for all activities.  For example, it must contain the routines that support communication with the user and/or peripheral hardware.

## Question 8.5

The term 'device driver' is applied to software that interfaces to peripheral hardware that is connected to the computer.  The device driver acts as the intermediary between the peripheral hardware and the operating system.  Some device drivers are supplied with the O/S whereas others are provided by the manufacturers of peripheral hardware products.

## Question 8.6

Within the context of a pre-emptive multi-tasking system, the timeslice determines the time period for which a process may occupy the CPU before being returned to the 'ready queue'. In terms of the model outlined in this chapter, a process may only occupy the CPU for multiple consecutive timeslices if either (a) no other processes are in the ready queue, or (b) none of the processes in the ready queue have a higher priority than the one that is currently active.  Note: in this latter case, precautions must be taken to ensure that lower-priority processes are not continually blocked from gaining CPU access.  For example, at the end of each timeslice, a 'priority flag' assigned to the process that is currently active can be decremented.  The new value is then compared to the priorities of all processes in the ready queue.  If any other process has a higher priority than that indicated by the 'priority flag' of the active process, then the active process is returned to the ready queue.

**Question 8.7**

(a) The accuracy of the computed value(s).

(b) The time in which the value(s) are delivered.

**Question 8.8**

(a) The number of users currently sharing a computer.

(b) The nature (type) of applications being run.

**Question 8.9**

All pages that are in main memory and which have been modified are returned to the hard disk.  When a page in main memory is modified, it is said to have been 'touched'.  Thus all 'touched' pages are returned to the disk.

**Question 8.10**   A process may change from an 'active' to a 'wait' state when, in order to continue execution, some form of input is required.  For example, this may be in the form of a user response to a question or data that needs to be fetched from the hard disk.

## Chapter 9

### Question 9.1

1   c. information        2   b. local       3 c. connected      4   c. medium

5   d. set of rules       6   b. medium      7 d. protocol

8   a. Delivery, accuracy and timeliness.

### Question 9.2

1   b. point-to-point      2   a. multipoint

3   a. multipoint          4   b. WAN

5   a. LAN

### Question 9.3

a)  When every device is connected to the other via a dedicated path.

b)  Local area network (LAN), metropolitan area network (MAN), wide area network (WAN).

c)  Circuit switching and packet switching.

### Question 9.4

1   a. to make devices compatible and interconnectable with each other

2   b. true              3   b. true

4   c. NATO              5   c. ANSI

### Question 9.5

a) A set of rules that govern the exchange of data between two devices

b) Syntax, semantics, timing.

### Question 9.6

a) Open system interconnections.  It is a model used for designing network architecture.

b) Seven layers: physical, data link, network, transport, session, presentation, and application.

c) Transmission Control Protocol/Internet Protocol.  It is a set of protocols that defines how transmission is exchanged across the Internet.

# Chapter 10

**Question 10.1** Carrier Sense, Multiple Access with Collision Detection.

**Question 10.2**

UTP: unshielded twisted pair;      STP: Shielded twisted pair

The shielding helps to increase noise immunity enabling, for example, an increase in the length of an interconnect.

**Question 10.3**

10Mbps operation

baseband

500m segment length

This specification applies to the 'Thicknet' Ethernet bus.

**Question 10.4** A node that is transmitting a frame must know that a collision has occurred prior to completing the launch of the frame onto the LAN.

**Question 10.5** The 'pad field' is employed.  This is used to ensure that the total payload (data+pad) is of a sufficient size.  In the case that only a small amount of data is to be transferred, additional pad bits are included.  In this way we ensure that the frame is not below the minimum specified length.

**Question 10.6**

The logical link control layer;      The medium access control layer.

**Question 10.7** The terminators prevent signals that reach the end of the bus from being reflected back along the bus.  Such reflections may cause the corruption of other signals travelling in the medium.

**Question 10.8**

Bandwidth;        Noise immunity.

**Question 10.9** In the case of Pure Aloha, transmissions can occur at any time – collisions may be total or only partial.

In the case of Slotted Aloha, transmissions can only begin at the commencement of a 'time slot'.  In this case, partial collisions are avoided.

**Question 10.10**

Only when it has 'seized' the token.  The use of a token prevents more than one node transmitting at any one time.

# Chapter 11

## Question 11.1

a) Connection-oriented and connectionless.

b) The Transmission Control Protocol (TCP). Using the telephone.

c) The user data protocol (UDP). Posting a letter or parcel.

d) Quality of service refers to how reliable the transmission and delivery of data is. Connection-oriented transmission offers a better quality of service than does connectionless transmission.

e) It is called a datagram.

## Question 11.2

| | | |
|---|---|---|
| 1. True | 2. False | 3. False |
| 4. True | 5. True | 6. True |

## Question 11.3

a) It refers to the interconnection of independent physical networks via routers and other network devices.

b) It is a special-purpose computer, used in connecting physical networks and moving data between them.

c) It is virtual because the networks are connected by Internet Protocol software and this provides a virtual connection between nodes.

## Question 11.4

| | |
|---|---|
| 1. False | 2. True |
| 3. False | 4. True |

## Question 11.5

a. It refers to placing data inside a frame that contains addresses information and various control fields necessary for the successful delivery of the data.

b. Refer to Figure 11.6.

## Question 11.6

a) It is called an IP datagram, and contains complete addressing and control information in addition to data.

b) It refers to a potentially unreliable data delivery service – delivery is not guaranteed. An example is the connectionless IP datagram protocol.

c) It is the address of an end point, specified by the sending device to enable a particular application to communicate with another one running on the recipient node.

d) An IP packets consist of two main parts, a header and a data field. A header carries information essential for routing and delivery, whereas the data field carries the actual data being transmitted.

## Question 11.7

1  b. connectionless

2  c. IP

3  b. IP

4  b. type of service

5  b. two

6  a. 20-60 bytes

7. a. fragmented

## Question 11.8

1  c. 32

2  b. prefix

3  a. suffix

## Question 11.9

a) Because it divides network addressing into different parts that give information about locations, similar to a telephone system.

b) This is a numbering system used to simplify the writing of IP addresses. The binary numbers are expressed in groups of 8 bits (bytes or octets) and are then written in their decimal equivalent form.

c) They are called **prefix** and **suffix**. A prefix identifies the physical network to which a device is connected, whereas a suffix identifies a particular device on that network.

# Chapter 12

## Question 12.1

1. In _____ routing, decisions are made 'instantly' regarding the possible paths.

   b. dynamic

2. IRPs are used to exchange routing information within a(n) _____ system.

   a. autonomous network

3. In an autonomous network system networks are managed by _____ organisation(s)

   b. single

4. IRP defines _____ paths

   b. cost-effective

5. The mechanism of IRP is based on the _____ concept

   c. distance-vector

6. IRP counts the number of _____ that must be made.

   a. hops

7. An IRP table consists of at least _____ column(s).

   c. three

8. Shortest path first protocol is based on the_____ concept.

   c. tree structure

9. Shortest path first calculates the _____ to reach a destination.

   b. cumulative cost

## Question 12.2

### Strengths:

Fixed location in the sky                    Large 'footprint'

### Weaknesses:

High launch costs                    Signal transmission latency

## Question 12.3

### *Strengths:*

Low signal transmission latency

Low launch costs (and relative ease of maintenance)

### *Weaknesses:*

Continually changing location in the sky.

Relatively small 'footprint'.

## Question 12.4

Ifmmp Xpsme

## Question 12.5

Plain text is the name given to text messages prior to their being encrypted.  The encrypted text is known as the 'cipher text'.

## Question 12.6

1. The limited number of keys available.

2. The cipher does not disguise the frequency of letter usage.  Code breaking is therefore facilitated by examining which letters most frequently occur in the cipher text and comparing this with the frequency with which letters occur in normal text.

## Question 12.7

The secure distribution of keys.  This may be overcome by employing public key encryption for the encryption of keys prior to their distribution.

## Question 12.8

This refers to ensuring that an encrypted message has been sent from a particular source.  In the case of public key encryption, efforts have to be made to ensure that messages have not been sent by a source that is representing itself as a different party.

## Question 12.9

The key that is used for the decryption of a message is never transmitted across a network (or otherwise distributed).